ORGANIZATIONAL EFFECTIVENESS
A Behavioral View

Goodyear Series in
Management and Organizations
Lyman W. Porter, Editor

Published:

Hall *Careers in Organizations*
Lawler / Rhode *Information and Control
in Organizations*
Schneider *Staffing Organizations*
Steers *Organizational Effectiveness:
A Behavioral View*

Forthcoming:

Beer *Organizational Development*
Campbell / Motowidlo *Leadership Theory,
Research, and Practice*
Dachler *Motivation in Organizations*
Duncan *Organizations and Their Environment*
Lewicki *Conflicts in Organizations*
Schollhammer *Comparative Business Management*
Stone / Braunstein *Research Methods in
Organizational Behavior*
Tosi *Organization and Management Theory*

ORGANIZATIONAL EFFECTIVENESS
A Behavioral View

RICHARD M. STEERS
University of Oregon

Goodyear Publishing Company, Inc.
Santa Monica, California

Library of Congress Cataloging in Publication Data

Steers, Richard M
    Organizational effectiveness.

    (Goodyear series in management and organizations)
    Includes indexes.
    1. Organization.   2.   Organizational behavior.
3. Management.   I. Title.
HD31.S6877   658.4   76-17203
ISBN 0-87620-655-0
ISBN 0-87620-639-9 pbk.

GOODYEAR SERIES IN MANAGEMENT AND ORGANIZATIONS

Y-6550-1 (Case)
Y-6399-3 (Paper)

Current printing (last digit):
10 9 8 7 6 5 4 3 2 1

Printed in the United States of America

*To My Parents
and Grandparents*

CONTENTS

FOREWORD

The Goodyear Series in Management and Organizations embodies concise and lively treatments of specific topics within the broad area indicated by the Series title. These books are for supplemental reading in basic management, organizational behavior, or personnel courses in which the instructor highlights particular topics in the larger course. However, the books, either alone or in combination, can also form the nucleus for specialized courses that follow introductory courses.

Each book stresses the *key issues* relevant to the given topic. Thus, each author, or set of authors, has made a particular effort to "highlight figure from ground"—that is, to keep the major issues in the foreground and the small explanatory details in the background. These books are, by design, relatively brief treatments of their topic areas, so the authors have had to be carefully *selective* in what they have chosen to retain and to omit. Because the authors were chosen for their expertise and their judgment, the Series provides valuable summary treatments of the subject areas.

In focusing on the major issues, the Series' authors present a balanced content coverage. They have also aimed at breadth by the unified presentation of different types of material: major conceptual or theoretical approaches, interesting and critical empirical findings, and applications to "real life" management and organizational problems. Each author deals with this body of material, but the combination varies according to the subject matter. Thus, each book is distinctive in the particular way in which a topic is addressed.

A final word is in order about the audience for this Series: Although the primary audience is the student, each book in the series concerns a topic of importance to the practicing manager. Managers and supervisors can rely on these books as authoritative summaries of the basic knowledge in each area covered by the Series.

The topics included in the Series to date have been chosen on the basis of their importance and relevance for those interested in management and organizations. As new appropriate topics emerge on the scene, additional books will be added. This is a dynamic Series both in content and direction.

Lyman W. Porter
Series Editor

PREFACE

In the literature on organizations, references to the notion of organizational effectiveness are often seen. Most writers allude to the concept as some sort of end state that managers strive to achieve. Unfortunately, however, the notion of organizational effectiveness is referred to in the literature far more than it is studied in any systematic way. Thus, if we accept the contention that effectiveness is a desirable trait for most organizations, questions are logically raised concerning how we assess the relative degree of organizational success and what managers can do to facilitate it. It is toward questions like these that this volume is addressed.

The approach taken here to the study of effectiveness is to integrate organization-wide factors, such as structure and technology, with individual factors, such as employee motivation, attachment, and performance. This is done in the belief that any dynamic model of organizational effectiveness must examine the processes by which individual effort and behavior influence subsequent organizational performance. Thus, a major focus of this book will be on human behavior in organizations and how such behavior relates to organizational goal attainment.

The first two chapters of the book attempt to provide a foundation by examining a general formulation of effectiveness and by reviewing the role of systems theory and the goal concept in such a formulation. Chapter 3 represents an in-depth analysis of various assessment techniques used to measure effectiveness in organizations, along with a consideration of several limitations on such techniques. Chapters 4 through 9 then examine sequentially several of the more important determinants of effectiveness. It is argued that four such categories of determinants can be identified: (1) organizational characteristics; (2) environmental characteristics; (3) employee characteristics; and (4) managerial policies and practices. In all, several hundred studies are reviewed here that relate in some fashion to the concept of organizational effectiveness. Finally, Chapter 10 attempts to summarize and integrate the various findings into a concise statement of the major processes involved in effectiveness. Throughout, an attempt will be made to relate theoretical and empirical materials with practical managerial applications.

In view of the scarcity of comprehensive, model-building investigations of organizational effectiveness, much of what we know on the topic is the result of piecing together a variety of disparate research findings. This approach has obvious limitations in terms of validating models of effectiveness. Thus, a major purpose of this volume is to stimulate renewed efforts to learn more about the nature and determinants of organizational effectiveness. If this book can stimulate such interest, the author will be more than satisfied.

The utility of a book is heavily influenced by the quality of inputs that an author receives from acknowledged scholars in the field. I feel particularly fortunate in having the advice and counsel of several prominent investigators in the area. In particular, I would like to express my sincere appreciation to the following individuals for reviewing and commenting on various portions of the manuscript: Tom Burns, Warren B. Brown, Robert Duncan, Amitai Etzioni, J. G. Hunt, James L. Koch, Paul R. Lawrence, Thomas A. Mahoney, James L. Price, Derek S. Pugh, and Eugene F. Stone. Moreover, a special intellectual debt of gratitude is due Peter J. Frost, Larry Greiner, Douglas T. Hall, Richard T. Mowday, Lyman W. Porter, and Daniel G. Spencer for reading the manuscript in its entirety and offering many useful suggestions for improvement.

Many of the research findings by the author reported in this volume were supported by grants from the Office of Naval Research and the National Institute of Mental Health. Appreciaton for such support is expressed here. Also, I am indebted to Rita Edwards, Christina Reese, and Dorothy Wynkoop for their valuable assistance in preparing the manuscript for publication. Finally, I wish to express my special thanks to my wife, Sheila, for her support, encouragement, and patience throughout the project.

Richard M. Steers

ORGANIZATIONAL EFFECTIVENESS
A Behavioral View

EFFECTIVENESS IN ORGANIZATIONAL SYSTEMS

It has often been suggested that the true test of good management is its ability to organize and utilize available resources to achieve and maintain an effective level of operations. The key word in this notion is *effective* because it is against the concept of effectiveness that managerial and organizational success are ultimately judged. Although many people would agree on the central role of management in achieving organizational effectiveness, it is much more difficult to specify what is meant by the concept itself. To an economist or financial analyst, organizational effectiveness is synonymous with profit or return on investment. To a production manager, effectiveness often means the quality or quantity of output of goods or services. To a research scientist, effectiveness may be defined in terms of the number of patents, inventions, or new products of an organization. And for a number of social scientists, effectiveness is often viewed in terms of the quality of working life. In short, the concept of organizational effectiveness means different things to different people, depending upon one's frame of reference.

Considering the diversity of opinions as to the nature and composition of organizational effectiveness, it is not surprising that there is so much disagreement concerning ways to improve it in ongoing organizations. It appears that a major reason for this lack of agreement stems from the rather limited views that exist concerning effectiveness. For instance, managers and organizational analysts often assume that there is only one appropriate evaluation criterion for effectiveness (for example, profit). Such is typically not the case, however. It is difficult to conceive of **1** an organization that would survive for long if it pursued a profit goal exclusively and ignored completely the needs and goals of its employees and of society at large. Moreover, there are many organizations (for example, police departments, welfare agencies) that are not intended to run at a profit. Thus, organizations often pursue multiple goals, and these goals may not be identical across organizations.

In addition, it has often been assumed that the evaluation criteria for effectiveness can be easily identified. Again, such is typically not the case. For example, although the primary goal of NASA was to put a man on the moon, the means by which this goal was to be attained were not so clear. Similarly, concensus has seldom been reached concerning the specific operational goals of a university or a state or federal government—or, for that matter, a major corporation. Instead, the evaluation of organizational effectiveness appears to be largely the result of who is doing the evaluation and what their specific orientations are. Given such problems, it appears appropriate to take a fresh look at the concept of organizational effectiveness, what we mean by it, and how organizations strive to attain it.

MAJOR AIMS OF BOOK

Organizations by their very nature tend to be complex entities that strive for the rational allocation of their resources for purposes of goal attainment. Although complete rationality is seldom if ever achieved, its pursuit remains a hallmark of contemporary management. The more rational an organization, it is generally believed, the greater the focused effort that is available for goal-directed activities. Moreover, the greater the progress that is made toward such goals, the more effective the organization. Effectiveness is therefore seen as the ultimate goal of most organizations—at least in theory. Unfortunately, this oversimplified view of organizational dynamics tends to ignore what is perhaps the most important aspect of the entire process: namely, an organization's *human* resources. In the study of organizational effectiveness, human resources and human behavior emerge as the primary focal point, and attempts to improve effectiveness must necessarily begin with an examination of such behavior at work.

When employee behavior in organizational settings is examined, several major problems, which threaten to impede attempts by management to improve effectiveness, become apparent. For instance, absenteeism and turnover have risen markedly in recent years, as have other forms of withdrawal. Output restriction continues to be the norm on many blue- and white-collar jobs. Moreover, worker alienation and job dissatisfaction persist as problems as employees have come to expect more and more from their jobs and management has been either unwilling or unable to deliver. Such problems are compounded by the current tendency toward larger organizations, in which individuals often experience a loss of personal identity and managers find it increasingly difficult to simultaneously satisfy employee needs and corporate objectives.

In view of these problems and in view of the fact that organizations are encountering greater difficulty in securing the scarce and valued resources necessary to meet both personal and organizational objectives, the need to understand the nature and process of organizational effectiveness is of paramount importance to modern managers. If organizations are to survive and compete successfully in turbulent and often hostile environments, greater attention must be focused on efforts to identify those variables that differentiate successful organizations from less successful ones. This book attempts to contribute toward this understanding of the nature of organizational effectiveness by pursuing two related objectives. First, the general concept of effectiveness will be examined, focusing on the meaning of the concept as well as on its relevant dimensions. Second, the issue of how organizational effectiveness is achieved—or at least pursued—will be explored.

In many ways, it may appear somewhat presumptuous to attempt a book on organizational effectiveness. After all, it can be argued, the entire study of behavior in organizations is ultimately aimed at improving effectiveness and efficiency in operations. Moreover, because of the multitude of contributing factors involved, it can be further argued that the topic is too broad and all-encompassing to be covered in one short volume. Although such criticisms may be well taken, it appears that the topic is of sufficient importance to justify attempts to summarize the more salient features of the concept and put them together in such a way so that they are useful to both managers and organizational analysts. Thus, although the ultimate goal here may be somewhat ambitious, the proposed means to that goal are much more modest. We simply wish to examine our current level of understanding on this important topic and to consider what conclusions and recommendations can be made concerning the "state of the art." In so doing, we will attempt to build upon several earlier works on the topic (Campbell, Bownas, Peterson, & Dunnette, 1974; Georgopoulos, 1975; Ghorpade, 1971; Mott, 1972; Price, 1968) and to extend such efforts by summarizing the results of several hundred studies that in some fashion relate to the issue of organizational effectiveness. It is thus hoped that our understanding of this topic can be advanced in meaningful ways that will set the stage for future efforts of a more comprehensive nature.   **3**

APPROACH TO THE STUDY OF EFFECTIVENESS:
A PROCESS MODEL

An examination of the available literature on organizational effectiveness reveals little agreement concerning the exact nature of the construct. Moreover, there are several problems with many of the existing approaches to effectiveness that serve to reduce their utility for purposes of organizational analysis. (These problems are discussed in detail in Chapter 3.) We are thus in need of a generalized approach to the topic that can be used in a wide variety of organizations and that overcomes to the extent possible many of the existing problems. Such an approach is proposed here.

Essentially, we will suggest a *process model* for understanding organizational effectiveness. Such a model is proposed in the belief that managers and organizational analysts can do more to facilitate effectiveness if they understand the major processes that influence it. Our process approach to understanding effectiveness consists of two related parts. First, we will examine three interrelated dimensions that are believed to be appropriate for an analysis of effectiveness. Following this discussion, we will present an analytical framework with which to organize the various related aspects of research on organizational performance and success. Together, such information should prove useful in facilitating an understanding of the dynamics of effectiveness in ongoing organizations.

Multidimensional Perspective

In view of the complexity of the topic, it appears most appropriate to use a multidimensional approach to the study and evaluation of effectiveness in organizations. A multidimensional approach is useful here in attempting to find some common ground among the many diverse views that exist on the subject. Essentially, it is suggested that effectiveness can best be examined by jointly considering three related concepts: (1) the notion of goal optimization; (2) a systems perspective; and (3) an emphasis on human behavior in organizational settings. This multidimensional approach has several advantages over earlier (and often more narrow) approaches, as we shall see. In particular, it has the advantage of increasing the comprehensiveness of analyses aimed at better understanding a highly complex subject. Let us examine each of the three dimensions separately.

Goal optimization. When we examine the various approaches to evaluating effectiveness, it appears that the majority rest ultimately on some measure of organizational goal attainment. Although a few models disclaim such a foundation and often employ unique terminology, they invariably return to the goal concept upon closer analysis (see Hall, 1972). The major advantage of the goal approach in evaluating effectiveness is that organizational success is measured against organizational intentions instead of against an investigator's value judgments (that is, what the organization "should" be doing). Because different organizations pursue widely divergent goals, it is only logical to recognize this uniqueness in objective evaluation attempts.

The use of goal approaches to the study of organizational effectiveness has often led to confusion in the past (Etzioni, 1960, 1975; Hall, 1972; Yuchtman & Seashore, 1967). This confusion has resulted largely because of the different meanings that have been attached to the goal concept. For instance, Yuchtman and Seashore employ the term to mean the "ultimate mission" of an organization. The approach to be taken here is somewhat different. Specifically, *effectiveness* is defined in terms of an organization's capacity to acquire and utilize its scarce and valued resources as expeditiously as possible in the pursuit of its operative and operational goals. In other words, instead of evaluating success in terms of the extent to which goal attainment has been maximized, we recognize a series of identifiable and irreducible constraints (for example, money, technology, personnel, and so on) that serve to inhibit goal maximization. When these constraints are recognized and accounted for, it is then possible to identify the resulting *optimized* goals (that is, an organization's desired goals as constrained or modified by available resources).

The use of a goal optimization approach differs from many earlier models in one important respect: It presumes that goal maximization is probably not possible and that, even if it were, it might be detrimental to organizational well-being and survival. For instance, if a company's production goals were truly maximized to such an extent that insufficient resources were available for R&D efforts on new products or for marketing and promotional efforts, survival and long-term growth and development would be severely jeopardized. Moreover, if a goal of employee satisfaction were maximized at the expense of production, a similar problem would exist. The use of the goal optimization approach allows for the explicit recognition of multiple and often conflicting goals, as well as for the existence of several constraints on goal effort. Thus, effectiveness is evaluated in terms of how well an organization can attain its *feasible* goals. This focus on feasible, optimized goals appears to be far more realistic for evaluation purposes than is the use of desired or ultimate goals.

Systems perspective. A second aspect of our multidimensional approach to the study of effectiveness is the use of a systems perspective. Although some have argued that the "goal" approach to organizational effectiveness and the "systems" approach are incompatible, it is suggested here that the two can indeed be quite complementary. In fact, it is quite possible—even highly desirable—to examine various factors both within an organization and in the external environment as they relate to each other and as they ultimately affect goal-directed effort. Thus, our own goal approach conceives of goals within a dynamic framework. Goals are not treated as static, ultimate states, but rather they are seen as being subject to change over time. Moreover, the attainment of certain short-term goals can represent new inputs for the determination of subsequent goals. Thus, there is a cyclic nature to goals in organizations when a systems perspective is employed (see also Child, 1975; Etzioni, 1975).

Behavioral emphasis. Finally, the third basic component of our approach includes an emphasis on the role of employee behavior on long-term organizational success. That is, we shall integrate the micro and macro levels of analysis and examine how the behavior of individuals and groups ultimately contributes to or detracts from organizational goal attainment. This approach is taken in the simple recognition that the only way goals are going to be attained is through the behavior of organizational members.

Thus, our approach to the study of organizational effectiveness includes three interrelated perspectives concerning the nature of the relationships among major elements of an organizational system and how such elements interact to facilitate or inhibit the attainment of feasible organizational goals. All three of these dimensions are recognized in the analytic framework discussed below. In fact, as suggested earlier, it is our belief that a clear understanding of the nature of organizational effectiveness can be achieved only by employing all three dimensions simultaneously as we examine the various relevant aspects of the topic.

A Framework for Analysis

An important concern in any examination of organizational effectiveness is specifying the nature of the relationships among major sets of variables as they jointly influence desired outcomes. Although many sets of criteria exist that have been used to evaluate effectiveness, there have been few attempts to integrate such approaches or to investigate in a systematic and comprehensive fashion the actual correlates or determinants of the criteria. Such an undertaking would be a monumental task in view of the many variables that potentially relate to effectiveness. Instead, we must rely on a review of those studies that do exist that examine one or more *facets* of effectiveness (for example, performance, satisfaction) as they relate to predictor variables. Then, based on a composite or synthesis of these findings, we will hopefully be in a position to draw some meaningful conclusions concerning which variables have the most direct impact on the ultimate success or failure of an organization.

This reliance on essentially piecemeal data presents a significant integration problem. First, it is necessary to organize and review the various materials that relate in some manner to certain aspects of goal-directed behavior. Next, these diverse sets of findings must somehow be tied together into a logical, consistent body of knowledge so that useful generalizations can be made concerning the patterns of relationships that exist between major sets of organizational variables as they influence effectiveness. Such is a major task of this book. After examining an analytical framework aimed at identifying the major factors involved in questions of effectiveness, we shall consider systematically our current level of understanding concerning each factor. We will, in short, be building a dynamic model of organizational effectiveness as we progress through the various topics. It is hoped that in this way the logical and empirical foundations of the model will be clearly understood. Following this review of the pertinent research, we shall consider what managers can do in their attempts to facilitate improvements in ongoing organizations. In fact, the crucial role of management in the ultimate determination of organizational effectiveness will be seen throughout our discussions.

Before examining this role, however, let us begin by considering the major sets of variables that potentially have an influence on effectiveness. In essence, the view that is taken here suggests that contributing factors to the ultimate success of an organization can be found in four general domains. As indicated in Exhibit 1-1, these four general areas are: (1) organizational characteristics; (2) environmental characteristics; (3) employee characteristics; and (4) managerial policies and practices.

Organizational characteristics. The first set of variables in our model, organizational characteristics, consists of organizational structure and technology. *Structure* refers to the relatively fixed relationships that exist in an organization with respect to the arrangement of human resources. It is the unique way an organization fits its people together to create organization. As such, the notion of structure includes such factors as the extent of decentralized control, the amount of task specialization, the extent to which interpersonal interactions are formalized, and so forth. Thus, managerial decisions concerning structure represent decisions concerning how people will be grouped for task accomplishment.

On the other hand, *technology* refers to the mechanisms used by an organization to transform raw inputs into finished outputs.

7

EXHIBIT 1-1   Factors Contributing to Organizational Effectiveness

ORGANIZATIONAL CHARACTERISTICS (Chapter 4)	ENVIRONMENTAL CHARACTERISTICS (Chapters 5 & 6)	EMPLOYEE CHARACTERISTICS (Chapter 7)	MANAGERIAL POLICIES & PRACTICES (Chapters 8 & 9)
Structure Decentralization Specialization Formalization Span of control Organization size Work-unit size **Technology** Operations Materials Knowledge	**External** Complexity Stability Uncertainty **Internal (Climate)** Achievement orientation Employee centeredness Reward-punishment orientation Security vs. risk Openness vs. defensiveness	**Organizational Attachment** Attraction Retention Commitment **Job Performance** Motives, goals, & needs Abilities Role clarity	Strategic goal setting Resource acquisition & utilization Creating a performance environment Communication processes Leadership & decision making Organizational adaptation & innovation

Technology can take several forms, including variations in the mechanical processes used in production, variations in the materials used, and variations in the technical knowledge brought to bear on goal-directed activities. As we shall see in Chapter 4, both structure and technology can have a profound impact on organizational outcomes.

Environmental characteristics. The second set of variables relevant to the study of effectiveness center around the task environment in which an organization finds itself. Environment consists of two rather distinct, though related, aspects. The *external environment* refers to those forces that arise outside an organization's boundaries that affect internal organizational decisions and actions (for example, economic and market conditions, government regulations). The influence of such environmental factors on organizational dynamics is generally believed to consist of the following: (1) the relative degree of environmental stability; (2) the degree of environmental complexity; and (3) the degree of environmental uncertainty. The *internal environment,* known generally as organizational climate, includes a variety of perceived attributes of the work environment (for example, employee centeredness, achivement orientation) that have been shown to be related to certain facets of effectiveness, particularly those measured on an individual level (for example, job attitudes, performance). Environmental concerns are dealt with in Chapters 5 and 6.

Employee characteristics. Third, consideration must be given to the role of individual differences across employees as they relate to effectiveness (see Chapter 7). Different employees possess different outlooks, goals, needs, and abilities. These human variations often cause people to behave differently from one another, even when placed in the same work environment. Moreover, these individual differences can have a direct bearing on two important organizational processes that can have a marked impact on effectiveness. These are *organizational attachment,* or the extent to which employees identify with their employer, and individual *job performance.* Without attachment and performance, effectiveness becomes all but impossible, as we shall see.

Managerial policies and practices. Finally, we shall examine in some depth the role of management in organizational performance (see Chapters 8 and 9). Here we will be concerned about how variations in managerial policies, practices, and style facilitate or hinder goal attainment. In general, it will be shown that managers play a central role in the success of an enterprise by planning, coordinating, and facilitating goal-directed activities. It is their responsibility to insure that the structure of the organization is consistent with and advantageous for the prevailing technol- **9**

ogy and environment. Moreover, it is their responsibility to set up suitable reward systems so that employees can satisfy personal needs and goals while simultaneously pursuing organizational objectives. In fact, this facilitator's role is probably the most important function performed by modern managers. As technological processes become more complex and as environments become increasingly hostile and complex, the role of management in coordinating people and processes for organizational success becomes not only more difficult but also more important.

Each of these four main areas of concern will be examined in detail later in this volume. Before beginning this analysis, however, it is useful to have a thorough understanding of three topics that provide the foundation upon which our analysis of organizational effectiveness rests: (1) the notion of open systems theory; (2) the nature of personal and organizational goals; and (3) the ways in which effectiveness has been conceptualized and measured in various studies on organizations. Open systems theory will be discussed in the remainder of this chapter. The topic of goals will be examined in Chapter 2. Finally, approaches to the measurement of organizational effectiveness will be reviewed in Chapter 3. Based on this discussion, we shall then proceed to an examination of the major determinants of effective organizations.

OPEN SYSTEMS THEORY

Nature of Open Systems

Briefly defined, an *open system* is "a set of elements standing in interrelation among themselves and with the environment" (von Bertalanffy, 1972, p. 417). Following this approach, attention is directed toward "problems of relationships, of structure, and of interdependence rather than the constant attributes of objects" (Katz & Kahn, 1966, p. 18).

The general notion of an open system is simple and is composed of three basic components: inputs, throughputs, and outputs (see Exhibit 1-2). Inputs represent all the factors that are "invested" in an organization by the external environment. Such inputs may include money, new employees, raw materials, new machines, and so forth. These inputs are then transformed (that is, acted upon) in the throughput stage into a variety of outputs that are returned to the environment (such as finished products, profits or return on investment, retiring or terminating employees, and so on). Thus, a system is seen as continually interacting with its environment in a variety of exchange relationships.

More specifically, Katz and Kahn (1966, Chapter 2), who have contributed substantially to our understanding of open systems

EXHIBIT 1-2   A Basic Paradigm for an Open Systems Model

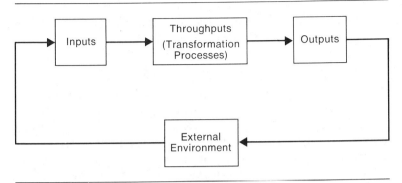

theory, have suggested nine characteristics or properties that are common to all open systems:

1. *Importation of energy* (inputs) from the external environment.
2. *Transformation of energy* (throughput) by means of work activities.
3. *Exportation of transformed energy* (outputs) to the external environment.
4. *Cyclic character* of the transformation processes. Throughput activities produce outputs that, in turn, ultimately become new sources for inputs.
5. *Negative entropy.* Organizations import more energy than they export. That is, systems use energy in the transformation process and store energy for future needs.
6. *Information control mechanisms.* Systems receive information from the environment, employ coding procedures that screen out certain information, and receive feedback from the environment in response to system activities.
7. *Steady state behavior.* Systems tend to maintain, or attempt to maintain, their basic character by controlling or neutralizing threatening external forces for change (that is, "dynamic homeostasis").
8. *Role differentiation and specialization.* As systems grow, there is an increasing tendency toward the elaboration of roles and the specification of function.
9. *Equifinality.* Systems can often reach the same ends by different means. This notion emphasizes the flexibility and adaptability inherent in most open systems.

The emphasis throughout this list is on the dynamic interrelationships that exist among the various components of a system. Not only are most components related to and affected by other system components but in addition the precise nature of such rela- **11** tionships can be expected to change over time in response to environmental changes. As we shall see, viewing work organizations within such a framework of analysis has many advantages, especially when examining the topic of organizational effectiveness.

Organizations as Goal-Seeking Systems

Definitions of *organizations* abound in literature on organization theory. In one of the earliest definitions, for instance, Barnard (1938, p. 73) viewed organizations as "a system of consciously coordinated activities of two or more persons." In other words, organizations have stated purposes, communication systems and other coordinating processes, and a group of people who are willing to cooperate on the tasks necessary for goal attainment. Similarly, Etzioni (1964, p. 4) suggests that organizations are "planned units, deliberately structured for the purpose of attaining specific goals." Moreover, Porter, Lawler, and Hackman (1975) suggest that organizations are generally characterized by five basic factors: (1) social composition; (2) goal orientation; (3) differentiated functions; (4) intended rational coordination; and (5) continuity through time.

Several common threads run through these various definitions of organizations. Most importantly, organizations are viewed as collectivities of people working together for common goals. Inherent in such a definition are the related notions of a goal orientation and a systems perspective. In other words, individuals are viewed as joining together and coordinating their activities (through differentiated functions, rational coordination, and so on) to create a viable system capable of attaining common objectives. Every member may not value all the objectives equally; instead, an individual would probably pursue some less valued (to him) goals in exchange for securing the efforts of others on those goals that are more highly valued by him. Thus, through coalition and cooperation, members of an organization attempt to satisfy their diverse needs and goals to the extent possible commensurate with resources.

Viewing organizations as goal-seeking systems has several advantages for the study of effectiveness. To begin with, it focuses attention on the dynamic interactions among the various parts of an organization; it looks at *relationships*. For instance, we might examine how variations in job technology affect organizational structure and how these two variables jointly affect performance (see Chapter 4). Second, such an approach also focuses attention on the interactive dynamics between an organization and its external environment (see Chapter 5). Third, by focusing on goals and objectives, it becomes possible, as we shall see, to examine effectiveness and efficiency against organizational intentions. Instead of using our own value judgments concerning what an organization should be pursuing, we can study within a more objective framework what an organization is actually trying to do—and how well it succeeds. Finally, viewing organizations as goal-seeking systems allows for a clear recognition of the transitory or changing nature of organizations and their purposes. Not only do organizations become modified over time in terms of structure, technology, and environment but in addition the very goals that they pursue may shift for a variety of reasons. Hence, the use of the systems framework allows for a more thorough examination of how organizations are constructed and how they pursue their objectives in a successful or unsuccessful fashion.

Generic subsystems. It was suggested above that one advantage of viewing organizations within a systems perspective was that it served to focus attention on the various components of an organization, as well as on the interrelationships among such components. With respect to this aspect of organizational systems, Katz and Kahn (1966, Chapter 5) have provided a useful framework for analyzing these various components of organizations. Essentially, it is suggested that organizations possess five relatively distinct—though interrelated—subsystems:

1. The *productive* subsystem, which is concerned with the major functions or work of the system (for example, a department or group of departments that manufacture a product or provide a service).
2. The *supportive* subsystem, which secures needed inputs for the productive subsystem and distributes the system's outputs (for example, the purchasing, marketing, and public relations departments of a company).
3. The *maintenance* subsystem, which focuses on maintaining and protecting the organization's structural integrity and character (for example, training functions, compensation plans, company newspapers).
4. The *adaptive* subsystem, which concentrates on the survival and adaptation of the organization in a changing environment (for example, research and development department, long-range planning functions).
5. The *managerial* subsystem, which focuses on coordinating, controlling, and directing the other subsystems so that maximum effort can be directed toward desired ends.

As we shall see, questions of organizational effectiveness relate to all five subsystems. In fact, a major problem with much of the existing theory and research on the topic is the failure to recognize these distinct but interrelated subsystems and to adequately account for them in model-building attempts. **13**

Requirements of organizations. In order to survive and maintain some degree of stability vis-à-vis the external environment, organizations are faced with a series of requirements that must be met (Etzioni, 1975; Gross, 1965; Yuchtman & Seashore, 1967). The extent to which an organization can satisfy these requirements largely determines its ability to continue the pursuit of its objectives over time. If system effectiveness cannot be maintained—that is, if the organization fails to satisfy these requirements—severe threats to its stability occur that can jeopardize survival and goal attainment. Such threats can take the form of a loss of resources, a loss of legitimacy from the supporting environment, organizational stagnation, and so forth. Thus, when we examine questions concerning the ability of an organization to pursue its stated objectives, concern must also be shown for its ability to satisfy on a continuing basis those intervening system requirements necessary for long-term goal effort. These requirements include the following:

1. *Resource acquisition.* Organizations must be able to compete successfully for scarce and valued resources to serve as inputs for organizational work activities.
2. *Efficiency.* Organizations must strive to secure the most advantageous ratio of inputs to outputs in the transformation process.
3. *Production/output.* It is necessary that organizational systems be capable of steady and predictable delivery of the goods or services it intends to provide.
4. *Rational coordination.* The activities of the organization must be integrated and coordinated in a logical, predictable fashion that is consistent with the ultimate goals of the entity.
5. *Organizational renewal and adaptation.* In most organizations, it is necessary that some resources be set aside and invested in activities that will enhance the net worth of the organization in the future. Without such renewal efforts, organizational survival is easily threatened by short-term shifts in market demands, resources, and so on.
6. *Conformity.* Because of the close interrelationship between an organization and its external environment, it is often necessary that organizations follow the prevalent dictates and norms of the environment. Wide deviation from social norms, laws, regulations and moral prescriptions can result in a variety of sanctions being levied against the organization that serve to reduce its sources of legitimacy and threaten its survival.
7. *Constituency satisfaction.* Organizations are composed of a variety of constituencies, including employees, investors,

consumers, and so forth. It is important for system effectiveness that organizations strive to satisfy the various—and divergent—needs of these constituents if they are to continue receiving necessary support and cooperation. Given the often conflicting demands made by the various constituents (for example, employees want more money, while investors want increased profits and consumers want lower prices), a major function of modern management is to somehow achieve a workable synthesis that at least marginally satisfies all parties.

There is a difference, however, between meeting a set of organizational requirements and the concept of organizational effectiveness. Although the satisfaction of such requirements may be seen as prerequisite to effectiveness, the two should not be equated. Instead, these requirements should be seen as the necessary yet insufficient conditions for success. That is, without such activities an organization cannot hope to continue in its pursuit of its ultimate objectives. But even with these activities, an organization can hope for little more than probable survival. The real question insofar as effectiveness is concerned is whether or not an organization meets its intended goals and, unless survival is its only objective, an organization must do far more than simply meet these requirements in order to be truly successful. This point will be amply demonstrated in the following chapters.

Diversity in organization. A major problem that will continually surface throughout this examination of the nature of organizational effectiveness is the heterogeneity among organizations. Organizations differ not only in their size and shape (for example, tall versus flat structure) but also in the technologies they employ, the environments in which they function, the work climates they create, and the types of goals they pursue. In fact, several organizational typologies have been suggested recently as a means of categorizing such diversity for purposes of organizational analysis (see, for example, Hall, 1972).

It is this property of uniqueness—that is, every organization is an original—that complicates any attempts to draw meaningful generalizations concerning what managers can do to facilitate effectiveness. In fact, a major criticism that can be leveled against much of the present work that has been done on effectiveness is that it often ignores this diversity. Instead, we continually see references to *the* steps to organizational success. The reader should be cautioned at the outset against such generalized and prescriptive approaches to the topic.

It is suggested here that a more productive approach to the study of organizational effectiveness is through a willingness to **15** accept such diversity in organizations and an attempt to deal with it in the form of contingency models of organizations. That is, it may be necessary for both organizational analysts and managers to begin their analysis by gaining conceptual entry into the particular organization under study and then examining major sets of relationships as they affect success or failure. This contingency, or tailored, approach to the study of organizational effectiveness is far more demanding on organizational analysts than are earlier approaches that simply listed ''defining characteristics'' of successful firms. However, the use of a contingency approach in organizational analysis will greatly facilitate the precision of understanding of a given organization's particular characteristics that contribute to ultimate performance and goal attainment. Thus, such an approach will be implemented throughout our analysis.

INDIVIDUAL AND ORGANIZATIONAL GOALS

2

Central to any discussion of organizational effectiveness is the notion of goals. In fact, as mentioned earlier, most definitions of organizational effectiveness ultimately rest on the question of how successful an organization has been in attaining its stated objectives. Because of the importance of goals for an understanding of organizational success, a somewhat detailed examination of the topic is in order here. We shall first examine the nature of personal motives and goals of individual members of organizations. Next, the concept of organizational (or organization-wide) goals will be discussed. Finally, we will examine the interaction between these two types of goals as it influences subsequent behavior and performance in organizations. A major theme that will become apparent here and throughout this book is the contention that effectiveness is best facilitated by finding ways to integrate personal motives and goals with organizational objectives.

PERSONAL MOTIVES AND GOALS

Most employees have fairly specific notions about what they want from their jobs. Such notions may include receiving a certain salary increase or promotion, having a challenging job, making new friends, and so forth. In fact, the very act of going to work has often been conceptualized in terms of an exchange relationship in which individuals contribute their energies towards organizational goal attainment in exchange for the receipt of certain outcomes from the organization that facilitate personal goal attainment (Barnard, 1938). This model, known as the "inducements- **17** contributions theory," suggests that individuals will be inclined to participate in organizational activities only to the extent that they see their rewards (inducement to work) as being commensurate with their efforts (contributions). Thus, personal motives and goals at work become important variables in understanding human behavior and organizational performance.

It is useful for our purpose here to distinguish between personal *motives* and personal *goals*. Motives, or "needs" as they are often called, are internal states within individuals that activate and direct behavior toward specific goals (see Exhibit 2-1). Personal motives may include a need for achievement, affiliation, power, competence, and so forth. Personal goals, on the other hand, and their concomitant goal-directed efforts are external manifestations of inner motives. For instance, a salesman with a high need for achievement (a motive) may set a personal goal for himself of increasing his monthly sales by 10 percent. His behavior is then directed toward this goal in the hopes of satisfying his initial achievement motive. Based on his subsequent performance, he would then receive feedback from the environment concerning the extent to which he met or failed to meet the goal.

Personal motives and goals can thus represent a significant influence on the behavior of individuals in organizational settings. Because of this fact, it is necessary to acknowledge and account for such goals in any discussion of *organizational* goals. The concept of organizational goals (that is, the goals that are set for an organization as a whole) is useless for purposes of management unless they can be translated into individual task goals that will be acceptable to employees. If these task goals are in conflict with personal needs and goals and if management is unwilling or unable to offer sufficient inducements to mollify the conflict, then there is little reason to believe that employees will want to contribute toward organizational goal attainment. (See Chapter

EXHIBIT 2-1 A General Model of the Basic Motivational Process

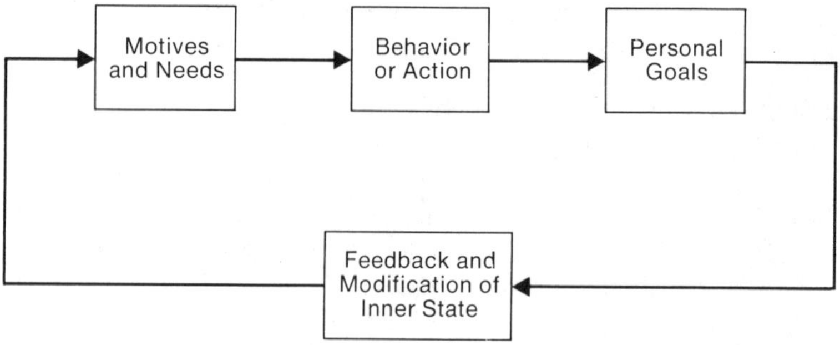

7 for an extensive examination of the role of personal goals in individual behavior.) Before examining the nature of such conflict in detail, however, we shall first look at the notion of organizational goals.

NATURE OF ORGANIZATIONAL GOALS

The Goal Concept

A defining characteristic of organizational systems is their goal-seeking nature. Physical, financial, and human resources are generally organized for the pursuit of fairly clearly defined organization-wide objectives. In fact, it has been suggested that the goals an organization pursues often provide insight, not found elsewhere, into an organization's character and thus to its behavior (Perrow, 1970). They give the student of management a useful frame of reference for understanding and evaluating organizational activities.

On the surface, an *organizational goal* may be defined as a desired state of affairs that organizations attempt to realize (Etzioni, 1964). In other words, goals serve to answer the question of where the organization is going. A company whose basic objective is to make a profit would tend to direct its resources and energies into areas that would ultimately result in corporate income. A non-profit hospital, on the other hand, might organize its resources toward improving community health or patient care. In this sense, goals may represent policy statements concerning how an organization intends to organize and utilize its scarce resources.

This simple approach to the concept of goals leaves several questions unanswered, however. For example, when we speak of an organization's goals, whose goals are we talking about? Do we mean the goals set forth by executive management, or is it more appropriate to define goals in terms of the desired future states of *all* members of the organization? Moreover, there is the problem of multiple—and often conflicting—goals. Few organizations pursue only one goal. A business enterprise, for instance, may wish to seek a profitable return on investment while improving social welfare in its community. Thus, a question arises as to how an organization will determine which goals are more important to pursue than others, given limited resources.

In short, although the simple definition of goals with which we began may be useful on a fairly abstract level, it lacks the precision that is necessary if we are to understand more fully the relationship between organizational goals and organizational effectiveness. A more detailed understanding of the goal concept results from examining the purposes to which goals are put in **19** organizational settings. Hence, let us briefly examine several positive *and negative* consequences that result from the existence of goals in organizations.

Functions and Dysfunctions of Organizational Goals

The existence in an enterprise of formally stated objectives can affect organizational behavior in a multitude of ways. This impact can be felt not only on an organization-wide level (for example, executive decision making) but also on the level of the individual employee. Moreover, although such goals can at times lead to very positive results for an organization and its members, their very nature can also sometimes result in negative consequences vis-à-vis organizational performance and effectiveness.

Functions of goals. We shall begin by considering the more positive functions served by organizational goals on both an organization-wide and an individual level (Etzioni, 1964; Steers, 1971; Zald, 1963). As indicated in Exhibit 2-2, goals can serve at least five functions for the *organization* as a whole. (1) To begin with, goals often focus attention or provide direction for managers in their attempts to acquire and utilize organizational resources. That is, goals become defined as being organizationally relevant (that is, legitimate), thus providing sanctioned guidelines for the activities of the membership. (2) Goals often serve as a rationale for organizing. The activities, practices, and processes necessary for goal attainment can impose numerous restrictions and constraints on the behavior of individual members and groups. Such basic social processes as communication patterns, authority and power structures, division of labor, and status relationships can thus be largely dictated by the chosen goals of an organization. (3) Goals can serve as a standard of assessment for an organization, against which judgments can be made as to the effectiveness and efficiency with which an organization achieves (or fails to achieve) its purposes. For example, a company that sets its primary goal as making a profit can determine fairly easily at year's end whether or not—or the degree to which—it has succeeded in goal attainment. (4) Goals often constitute a source of legitimacy for an organization that justifies its activities and its very existence to such diverse groups as investors, members, customers, and the public at large. In this sense, goals are centrally involved in the process of adaptation and innovation in a dynamic and uncertain environment. (5) Finally, goals can assist the organization in acquiring needed human resources. People who identify with the humanitarian goals of the Red Cross, for example, may join that organization at very low salaries because of their agreement and/or identification with the organization's objectives.

20

EXHIBIT 2-2   Functions and Dysfunctions of Organizational Goals

	For Organization	For Individual
Functions	Focus attention	Focus attention
	Rationale for organizing	Rationale for working
	Standard of assessment	Vehicle for personal goal attainment
	Source of legitimation	Personal security
	Recruitment through identification	Identification and status
Dysfunctions	Means to end can become real goals	Rewards may not be tied to goal attainment
	Measurement stresses quantitative goals at expense of qualitative ones	Difficulty in determining relevant performance evaluation criteria
	Goal specificity problem (Ambiguous goals fail to provide direction; highly specific goals may constrain action and creativity)	Inability of individuals to identify with abstract, global goals
		Organizational goals may be incongruent with personal goals

In summary, then, goals can indeed serve several useful functions for an organization as a whole. Likewise, such goals can also be functional for *individual* members of the organization. (1) On an individual level, goals can provide direction on one's job, thereby allowing an employee to focus his attention and efforts more clearly toward specific corporate objectives. (2) Organizational goals often provide a rationale for working and at times provide a sense of meaning to an otherwise pointless job. They can answer the question, "Why am I doing this?" (3) Organizational goals may serve as a vehicle for *personal* goal attainment. A commission-based salesman can satisfy both his own monetary goals and his company's profit goal by increasing his sales. (4) In addition, goals may assist individuals by providing a sense of psychological security; they provide a feeling that the organization is going somewhere and, hence, that it will remain in operation for some time to come. Although such may not in fact be the case, the perception of organizational longevity or continuity into the future can serve to provide comfort and security to an employee in an ever-changing, unstable environment. (5) Finally, goals can provide a source of identification and status for employees. How often, when you asked someone what he did for a living, did he reply: "I work for XYZ Company"?

It is doubtful that any one goal of an organization would simultaneously serve all these organization-wide and individual functions. Instead, various goals would probably serve different functions for different individuals at various points in time. For example, an employee may join and remain with a company primarily because he or she feels that the organization is doing more to help society at large than are its competitors and ignore the profit motives of the company. However, the executive management of the same company may feel it has a greater responsibility to its stockholders to make a profit than it does to engage in social welfare. Thus, although a given company may claim to have both these goals (profit and social welfare), the goals might be functional for different elements of the organization for quite different reasons.

Dysfunctions of goals. An issue often overlooked in organization theory is the dysfunctions that can result from the existence of stipulated goals. In fact, a major problem for many managers and organizational researchers is the assumption that the specification and elaboration of organizational goals is entirely positive in effect. This assumption ignores certain negative aspects of goals (see Exhibit 2-2).

Several dysfunctions of organizational goals can be identified both on an organization-wide and on an individual level. First, let us consider several *organization-wide* dysfunctions: (1) It is possible that the means set forth for attaining an organization's goals can themselves become goals. This is usually called a *means-ends inversion.* For example, a city that has a goal of improving traffic safety may install a quota ticketing system among its policemen, requiring them to issue so many traffic tickets per month. Although the quota originally was intended as a means to an end (that is, public safety), it is highly likely that the quota itself could become the goal in the eyes of organizational members (the police), thus shifting the focus and effort away from the original objectives. (2) A second dysfunction centers around the notion of measurement. As Etzioni (1964) has pointed out, measurement tends to stress the measureable. Hence, qualitative goals (for example, improve employee morale) may tend to become ignored by managers while such highly quantitative and measureable goals as profit and sales become accentuated. (3) A final problem with goals on the organizational level deals with the degree of goal specificity. Goals that are stated too ambiguously may fail to provide needed direction, while highly specific goals can serve to constrain creative and innovative behavior (see Chapter 7). Thus, a problem exists in formulating intended or desired objectives so they are sufficiently specific without being overly constraining.

22 Although many of these organization-wide dysfunctions would also apply on an *individual* level, other problems emerge that are unique to individual employee behavior. Some of these problems do not necessarily follow from the mere existence of goals, but their behavioral implications are closely related to it. (1) To begin with, where reward systems (for example, pay and promotional policies) are not designed specifically to reward goal-directed behavior, we would not expect goal attainment to be necessarily maximized. Instead, employees will tend to pursue those activities that have the greatest payoffs with respect to personal needs and goals. (2) Moreover, even where reward systems do attempt to reflect goal-directed performance, it often becomes difficult to identify those performance criteria that are directly related to the ultimate attainment of organizational goals. Consider the example of a personnel manager in a large company. If profit is the company's main goal, how does one evaluate a personnel manager based on criteria that are relevant for organizational goals? (3) Furthermore, another individual problem arises where employees fail to identify with broad, abstract goals. For example, how can a factory worker contribute to a company goal of organizational growth? (4) Finally, occasions may often arise where the goals of the organization are in conflict with the personal goals of various employees. This conflict can be seen time and again in arguments between management and unions as to whether stockholders or employees should receive an increased proportion of corporate income.

We have attempted here to review briefly several of the functions and dysfunctions served by (or related to) organizational goals on both an organization-wide and an individual level. Although such factors certainly would not apply in all cases, their presentation here is meant simply to focus attention on the pervasive influence of goals and objectives on the behavior of groups and individuals in organizational settings. Of particular note throughout this discussion is the issue of *goal relevancy*. That is, although certain goals may be important to particular segments of the organization (for example, executive management), they may simply not be important enough to other segments (for example, line workers) to justify time or effort. In such cases, as we shall see, other means must be devised in an effort to secure employee support and participation in goal-directed activities.

Goal Typologies

To this point, the concept of organizational goals has been discussed in rather general terms. Based on this discussion, it is now possible to differentiate several types of goals and consider how such types can affect behavior in ongoing organizations.

The most common distinction among types of organizational

goals is that of official, operative, and operational (March & Simon, 1958; Perrow, 1961; Porter et al., 1975). *Official* goals represent formal statements of purpose made by executive management concerning the nature of an organization's mission. They are typically vague and aspirational in nature (for example, maximize profit, contribute to community welfare, and so on), usually have an infinite time horizon, and are set forth more for purposes of securing support and legitimacy from the external environment than for facilitating actual task accomplishment.

In contrast, *operative* goals represent the real intentions of an organization. That is, they reflect what an organization is actually trying to do irrespective of what it claims to be doing. Thus, official goals may be operative or inoperative to the extent that they accurately reflect actual organizational intentions. Operative goals may or may not be widely publicized. In fact, in some cases, appealing and widely publicized official goals are used by management as a subterfuge to cover less attractive operative goals.

Finally, *operational* goals are those goals for which there are agreed-upon criteria for evaluating the extent to which organizational activities contribute toward goal attainment. Thus, an operative goal is said to be operational to the extent that management can specify in a fairly precise fashion how its attainment will be measured. Operative goals such as "maximize profit" or "manufacture electronic equipment" would therefore not be considered operational; "manufacture and sell one million televisions this year" would. The latter goal has clearly measurable standards (for example, volume, time) for purposes of assessment, but the former two goals do not. The focus of the remainder of this book will be on operative and operational goals and the relationship between them because it is against these types of goals that organizational effectiveness must ultimately be judged.

Other typologies attempt to subdivide the various goals and objectives into categories based on either the functions they serve or their referent. For example, Perrow (1970) has suggested that an organization's goals may be classified according to whose point of view is being recognized. He sets forth five categories of goals:

1. *Societal goals.* Referent: society in general. Examples: produce goods and services; maintain order; generate and maintain cultural values. This category deals with large classes of organizations that fulfill societal needs . . .
2. *Output goals.* Referent: the public in contact with the organization. This category deals with types of output defined in terms of consumer functions. Examples: consumer goods; business services; health care; education . . .
3. *System goals.* Referent: the state or manner of functioning of the organization, independent of the goods or services it produces or its derived goals. Examples: the emphasis on growth, stability, profits, or upon modes of functioning, such as being tightly or loosely controlled or structured.

4. *Product goals.* Referent: the characteristics of the goods or services provided. Examples: an emphasis upon quality or quantity, variety, styling,
availability, uniqueness, or innovativeness of the products . . .

5. *Derived goals.* Referent: the uses to which the organization puts the power
it generates in pursuit of other goals. Examples: political aims; community
services; employee development; investment and plant-location policies
which affect the state of the economy and the future of specific communi-
ties. . . . (pp. 135–36)*

First- and second-order goals. A separate though related aspect of goals concerns the importance, or preference ordering, of the various goals to management. It was pointed out earlier that organizations simultaneously pursue multiple goals. Greater insight into an organization's nature and character can be derived if one can differentiate those goals that are more important to the organization from those goals that are less important. Consider, for example, the findings of a survey carried out by England (1967) in which business managers were asked to rate the importance of a series of potential corporate goals. As can be seen in Exhibit 2-3, organizational efficiency and high productivity were much more important goals for these managers than were employee welfare or social welfare.

Such findings clearly indicate that increased understanding of organizational intent can result when the goals that a given organization pursues are divided into what can be termed *first-order* and *second-order* goals. Given scarce resources, it is highly likely that most managers would initially pursue first-order goals. Then, if resources allowed, second-order goals would receive attention. It is therefore important when considering statements of operative and operational goals to ask which goals are of the first order and which are not. Such questions provide still further clues concerning an organization's intention and actions.

Goal Formulation Processes

The simple approach to the concept of organizational goals that we began with earlier in this chapter becomes even more complex when we consider the various factors that can influence the selection (and modification) of goals over time. This notion of goal formulation is ultimately interwoven with the issue of organizational effectiveness because our approach to effectiveness is to view it largely as the degree of organizational goal attainment. Hence, the inputs into the determination of such goals—their nature, quality, and rationality—can have a major influence on the chances for goal attainment and long-term effectiveness.

EXHIBIT 2-3   Organizational Goal Preferences of U.S. Managers

Type of Goal	% Rating Goal as Highly Important	% Indicating Goal is Significant for Corporate Success
Organizational efficiency	81	71
High productivity	80	70
Profit maximization	72	70
Organizational growth	60	72
Industrial leadership	58	64
Organizational stability	58	54
Employee welfare	65	20
Social welfare	16	8

Source: G. W. England, "Organizational Goals and Expected Behavior of American Managers," *Academy of Management Journal*, 1967, *10*, p. 108. Reprinted by permission.

There are at least two ways to view the goal formulation process (see also F. Hall, 1975, 1976). One approach involves focusing on those factors outside the organization that can influence the selection and modification of organizational objectives. The second approach focuses primarily on those factors and processes within organizations that can affect such objectives. As will be seen, both sources of influence can have a profound effect on the ultimate determination of goals. Two models of goal formulation will be examined here to provide a clearer understanding of the basic processes involved. The first model, by Thompson and McEwen (1958), deals with external forces on goal formulation, and the second, by Cyert and March (1963), deals principally with internal forces. Following this discussion, consideration will be given to summarizing and integrating the major variables—both external and internal—that can affect in some manner the goals of an organization.

Thompson and McEwen model. Taking a fairly abstract approach to the topic, Thompson and McEwen (1958) have suggested that the goal formulation process is best understood by looking at the relationship between an organization as a whole and its external environment. Environment is used here to mean those factors outside the organization (for example, market and economic conditions, competitors, government agencies and regulations) that have the potential to influence organizational actions and success. Under this model, goal formulation is viewed primarily as a process in which the managers of an organization seek to establish and maintain a favorable balance of power with the organization's external environment. The more power the organization has, the more autonomy it has in making decisions concerning future actions.

In stressing the close interrelationship between goal setting and the environment, Thompson and McEwen suggest a continuum of organizational power in environmental relations. This continuum ranges from total organizational control over the environment to complete environmental control over the organization (as shown in Exhibit 2-4). It is suggested that all organizations can be placed somewhere along this continuum depending upon how much power they have in dealing with their environment. For example, a multinational oil company, which has a large amount of resources and produces products that are vital to a modern society, would typically possess a considerable amount of power in dealing with its environment (such as governmental agencies, environmental protection groups, and so forth). Hence, such a firm would be placed toward the left end of the continuum in Exhibit 2-4. On the other hand, a "grass roots" consumer group, which relies on the often uncoordinated efforts of many small but interested parties of concerned citizens, would typically have little power in dealing with its environment. A review of the many unsuccessful attempts by consumer groups to secure desired legislation demonstrates this point. Such a group would be placed toward the right end of the continuum. Other organizations (for example, small businesses, public utilities, political parties, and so on) would be found more toward the center on the power continuum.

The amount of power an organization possesses, in turn, largely determines the optimum bargaining strategy that it should use in dealing with its environment. Most organizations must bar-

EXHIBIT 2-4   Power Continuum in Organizational-Environment Relations (after Thompson & McEwen, 1958)

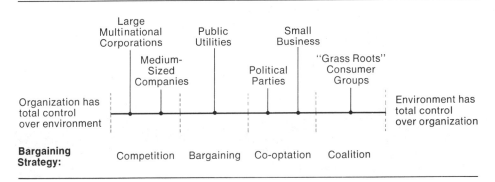

gain with their environment in order to fulfill their goals. For instance, organizations need to secure resources for their inputs
and markets for their outputs. According to Thompson and Mc-
Ewen, the choice of the proper bargaining mode is vital to the
success of the effort. Four bargaining strategies are identified,
depending upon the amount of power an organization has. When
an organization has a great deal of power vis-à-vis its environment
(such as in the case of a large multinational corporation), the
model suggests that the optimum strategy is one of *competition*
with the environment. In other words, the organization is generally
free to determine its own goals and pursue them with little concern
for outside factors. However, as the forces in the external environment assume a larger share of power, management must shift
its strategy toward one of increasing cooperation with the environment. Without such cooperation, the organization would be unable
to secure the resources needed for goal attainment. Depending
upon the relative distribution of power, this cooperation can take
one of three modes: (1) *bargaining,* by which the organization
attempts to engage in exchange relationships with the environment; (2) *co-optation,* by which new and possibly hostile elements
are absorbed into the leadership of an organization in order to
avert threats to its stability or existence; and (3) *coalition,* when
two or more organizations join for a common purpose.

The utility of this model for our purposes here becomes clear
when we examine its implications for goal formulation. In essence,
Thompson and McEwen point out that the manner in which management formulates its objectives is largely determined by the relative
bargaining position of an organization. That is, goal formulation
is seen as a strategic problem. The more power an organization
has, the less its management must rely on the inputs (and controls) from outside sources.

The element of rationality plays a crucial role here in that
environmental support is only "purchased" as one moves from
competition toward coalition at the cost of organizational autonomy. In other words, organizational independence and power become the currency, or medium of exchange, with which an organization purchases needed support from its external environment.
The ability of an organization to select that bargaining strategy
most suited to its relative power position is a function of its capacity to successfully "sound out" the environment for possible support. The more accurate the assessment, the greater amount
of currency that is saved for future bargaining situations (see
Chapter 5).

History is filled with examples of organizations that failed to
assess accurately their relation to their external environments and
28　that suffered severe consequences because of it. Consider, for

example, the case of a labor union deciding whether or not to vote a strike. If union leaders misjudge the environment and "push" a strike that the union membership fails to support, or if they initiate a strike that has little impact on the company (possibly because of large existing inventories), goal attainment becomes increasingly difficult if not impossible. It is for this reason that most union leaders carefully evaluate each situation before acting, considering the strength of support among its members, the production potential of the company, the popular support of the community, and so forth. The failure of any organization to assess accurately the nature and strength of its environment and to act accordingly thus invites open conflict to the detriment of organizational goal attainment.

Cyert and March model. Notable by its absence in the Thompson and McEwen model is a consideration of the role played by different organizational members in the determination or modification of an organization's objectives. This important role has been acknowledged by Cyert and March (1963). Focusing principally on the internal determinants of goals, they begin their analysis by suggesting that any organization is in reality a coalition of groups and individuals with diverse needs, desires, talents, and orientations. Under this approach, goal formulation is seen as a function of three interrelated processes.

First, there exists within organizations a continual bargaining process, similar to the Thompson and McEwen notion, by which various potential coalition members use *side payments* to induce others to join with them on certain goals. Such side payments can take the form of money, status, power or authority, position, and so on. Any conflicts between coalition members are usually settled through this side payment system; that is, for a price, an employee or group adopts the goals. In exchange for wages, employees produce; in exchange for dividends, stockholders invest; and so forth. The more power any member of a coalition has, the greater the amount of side payments he has at his disposal to facilitate group acceptance of his objectives.

Second, organizational goals are also affected by the prior commitments, policies, and agreements with others that have been made by an organization. These internal control processes serve to constrain major changes in an organization's goals by limiting the resources an organization has (see also Simon, 1964). For example, a company that commits itself to paying generous stockholder dividends may be reducing the amount of financial resources it has to enlarge plant production capacity or to invest in research and development of future products.

Finally, goals are sometimes modified based on experience, **29** when members of an organization agree to alter certain goals in response to changes in the environment. Perhaps the clearest example of this can be seen in the attempts by political parties to shift their "platform" based on what their leadership feels are the important issues of the day.

Inherent in all three of these processes is the notion of organizational slack. *Organizational slack* is defined as the excess of total organizational resources beyond the total necessary side payments. According to Cyert and March, slack consists of those payments to coalition members over and above that which is necessary to maintain an organization. In other words, slack is somewhat like a bank account that can be drawn upon in the future when needed. A company experiencing economic difficulty may institute a moratorium on hiring to reduce its total employment, thereby reducing the "slack" in the system. In more favorable times, the same company may hire more people than it really needs—consciously or unconsciously—in an effort to build up its reserves (slack) once again. Slack can take many forms: paying higher wages than those required by market conditions; executive bonuses; carpeting the employee dining room; and so forth. In most cases, such "investments" are made with the intent of retrieving certain benefits in the form of increased commitment and contribution at some future time.

Summary. A comparison of these two models of goal formulation reveals a high degree of overlap, despite the divergent approaches to the subject that were initially taken. Thus, although both models began in different places in terms of their analysis, their conclusions and implications appear to be largely in agreement.

To begin with, both models provide an explanation for the continual difficulty experienced by most organizations in specifying their operational goals in detail. Given a turbulent environment and given recurring conflicts among coalition members as to their organizational aspirations, it is easy to see why such goals would be in a constant state of flux. Hence, although it may be easy to secure agreement among members on relatively abstract and nonoperational official goals, the clarification of such objectives into more specific and more constraining operational goals can become a sizable task indeed. Such a conclusion has obvious implications for any model of organizational effectiveness: If agreement and commitment cannot be achieved concerning operational goals, how then is it possible to assess the extent of organizational goal attainment?

Moreover, both approaches to goal formulation speak to the implied managerial function in such unstable environments. A basic management role here becomes that of facilitating and maintaining sufficient agreement among coalition members and sufficient external support and resources so that coordinated effort in a given direction can proceed as smoothly as possible. This task of maintaining stability of operations is no simple act, considering the diversity of people and forces—both internal and external—involved in the goal-directed activities. In fact, a major ingredient in the determination of both effectiveness and efficiency must be considered the skill with which management coordinates and utilizes its resources in an appropriate fashion for task accomplishment.

Finally, the two models also bear a resemblance in the key factors that are believed to have the strongest influence on ultimate organizational goals. An integration of these two models leads to the conclusion that two of the most potent forces in the goal formulation process are relative *power distributions* (both within an organization and between an organization and its environment) and the nature of an organization's *prior commitments*. When we discuss the relative degree of external environmental support, the concept of side payments or organizational slack, and the notion of coalitions of organizational members, we are in effect raising questions concerning how power is distributed throughout an organization and its environment. An organization that has little slack, for example, is generally less "powerful" in bargaining with its environment than one that has a great deal of slack. Moreover, where power is concentrated in the hands of a small coalition, its members can issue whatever side payments they chose to gain the necessary support for their plans and goals. Where power is quite diffuse, however, and controlled by many coalitions, goal formulation or modification becomes more a function of compromise. In any event, it can be seen that an individual's (or group's) inputs into the goal formulation process is in large measure based upon the relative strength of his or her power base.

Prior commitments, on the other hand, also play a major role in goal determination and modification. Prior organizational commitments can include a wide range of past decisions or obligations made on behalf of an organization (such as existing plant capacity, commitment to minority hiring policies, sunk investments in R&D, and so on). Such commitments directly affect future decisions on allocation or distribution of available resources. Moreover, these commitments can be made as a result of learned behavior (for example, where an organization made a disastrous investment and vowed to steer clear of that area in the future). In this sense, commitments serve as constraints on organizational decision making that can affect future goal formulation almost irrespective of relative power positions.

In summary, then, we have reviewed two prominent models of organizational goal formulation and have seen how both ultimately rest upon considerations of power and commitments. It has **31** been further argued that the success or failure of an organization rests to no small degree on its capacity to understand the nature of both of these factors and on its ability to act in a manner that is consistent with this understanding. In other words, managers in effective organizations must comprehend fully the nature of their present environment—and be aware of changes in it. They must learn from their past experiences and modify their present and future behavior in the light of such learning if they are to maximize organizational performance and insure survival. We shall return to this point in later discussions of specific models of organizational effectiveness (see Chapter 3).

Goal Succession and Displacement

Inevitably, changes occur in the ends that are sought by organizations. When such changes result from conscious intention on the part of managerial decision makers to shift the course of organizational activities, the process is termed *goal succession*. When such a shift is not intended by management, we usually refer to it as *goal displacement*.

Goal succession. The clearest example of goal succession is provided in a case study of the National Foundation for Infantile Paralysis (Sills, 1957). The foundation's initial primary goal was to secure funding for research to eliminate one specific childhood disease, infantile paralysis. Through its "March of Dimes" campaign, this foundation contributed sufficient resources to ultimately lead to the "cure" of the disease; that is, it attained its primary organizational goal. This goal attainment led to a minor crisis inside the organization because its efforts had eliminated its major purpose for existence! After considerable thought, however, the National Foundation revised its goals and set a new course for itself of funding research into a whole series of childhood diseases. This is an explicit example of intentional goal succession. More subtle examples of succession, or at least partial succession, can be found in the decision by several major business concerns (such as Xerox Corporation, IBM Corporation) to broaden (or shift) their original organizational objectives to focus on several specific social problems of our time and devote a share of corporate resources toward the solution of such problems.

Goal displacement. The phenomenon of goal displacement is much less tangible. Goal displacement occurs when there is a diversion—unintended by management—of organizational energies or resources away from the original goals of the organization. The simplest form of goal displacement is a means-ends inversion that, as mentioned earlier, occurs when rules or subgoals aimed

32

at facilitating goal attainment do themselves become the de facto goals in an organization.

The reasons for goal displacement are many. Several of the more important ones can be summarized briefly:

1. *Need to operationalize abstract goals.* Although it is initially possible to set forth goal statements in broad, abstract tones, organizational members have to act in concrete ways. Thus, the abstract goals must be translated, or operationalized, into language that is of sufficient specificity to allow for employee action and for measurement of results. Often, the concrete decisions, plans, and actions that emerge from the original goals are inconsistent in some manner with (or at least do not contribute to) the original but abstract aims of the organization. For instance, the ostensible purpose of an R&D laboratory may be to engage in basic or applied research that benefits its parent company and, hopefully, society at large. However, this goal may become operationalized in terms of the number of patents it secures in a year or the number of publications of its staff.

2. *Delegation process.* Although the initial process of operationalizing goals is largely horizontal in nature (that is, at only one level of the organization), a problem often arises when the final operational goals are delegated down through the organization to individual employees for purposes of task accomplishment. Sills (1957) refers to the delegation process as the ultimate source of displacement. As employees or groups of employees are delegated various goal-relevant responsibilities, their interpretation of the organization's goals, plans, and policies determine in large measure the true operative and operational goals of any enterprise.

3. *Uncertainty associated with new or intangible goals.* The degree of uncertainty experienced by employees concerning both the nature and implications of new or intangible goals can often result in increased anxiety and insecurity in the job situation. In other words, people tend to fear changes in their everyday activities. As a result, in making decisions on goal-relevant matters, employees often prefer to follow past practices because they are generally "safe" and more comfortable, but not necessarily goal oriented (Merton, 1957).

4. *Necessity for coordinated and controlled activities.* Organizational efforts to coordinate the activities of employees for goal attainment often lead to the establishment of policies, rules, and sanctions to guide and reinforce desired **33**

behavior. Where such control systems are perceived by employees as being excessively strict, unreasonable, or unnecessary, they may respond in a variety of non-productive ways, including slowdowns, strikes, sabotage, or "working to rule" (that is, they may so rigidly comply with the letter of the law that goal progress is slowed by excessive red tape, documentation, and so on).

5. *Measurements and evaluations.* Organizations tend to strive for rationality in their goal-directed behavior. The attempt to measure or evaluate such rationality, however, can result in employee efforts being directed primarily toward satisfying quantitative and measurable goals at the expense of nonquantitative goals, as discussed earlier (Etzioni, 1964). Thus, the more qualitative the goal, the easier it is to become displaced.

6. *Prior commitments and decisions.* As Selznick (1949) has pointed out, the pursuit of organizational objectives requires an organization to make a series of decisions aimed at attaining such objectives. These decisions and actions often later emerge in the form of commitments that themselves can become either de facto goals or at the very least constraints on the existing goal set. Such commitments can divert attention and resources away from the intended goals.

7. *Absence of goal consensus.* Often, various departments within an organization (such as production, marketing, R&D) may place greater value and effort on certain goals that have more relevance or payoff to their own particular department than on other goals that may benefit the organization as a whole. Such *suboptimization* can lead to interdepartmental rivalry and conflict—as well as competition for scarce resources—instead of cooperation on mutual organization-wide objectives.

8. *Personal goals and aspiration levels.* Employees (including executive management) can subvert the original goals of an organization—intentionally or unintentionally—in an effort to satisfy their own personal goals. Such displacement may result from individuals or groups taking actions designed to maintain or enhance their own power positions or from attempts to modify organizational goals in order to obtain support and legitimization either from the environment or from other groups or members. Michels (1949) refers to this behavior among leaders as the "Iron Law of Oligarchy," observing that new revolutionary leaders tend to become more conservative in their objectives once they gain power in an effort to protect and maintain their new positions. Moreover, displacement may occur simply

where the goals of the organization are in conflict with personal goals and individuals choose to pursue the latter instead of the former.

INTEGRATING PERSONAL
AND ORGANIZATIONAL GOALS

Individual-Organization Conflict

As can be seen from the above discussion, many of the reasons for goal displacement result from basic conflicts between individual needs, goals, and patterns of behavior, on the one hand, and organizational needs and goals as determined by management, on the other. Oftentimes, it appears that organizational goals are dysfunctional for individual employees. Why, for example, should an employee increase his or her level of effort on the job in order to increase output if there are no personal rewards associated with such behavior? Similarly, why should an employee change his or her job behavior (which is familiar, comfortable, and "safe") and adopt new patterns of behavior aimed at new goals (which are strange and unknown)? Problems such as these are consistently found in organizational settings and largely explain the difficulty incurred by managers in minimizing goal displacement.

The basic nature of the conflict between the goals of individuals and those of the organization has been summarized by Argyris (1957). Essentially, he suggests that as individuals grow and mature they tend to strive toward certain personal life goals. For instance, they develop from being generally passive in nature to being active, from being dependent on others to being independent, from having a short-term perspective and time horizon to having a long-term perspective, and from having a limited behavioral response repertoire to having a wide variety of behavioral responses.

On the other hand, organizations, in their pursuit or rationality, tend to create work environments (particularly at the blue-collar level) that inhibit such human growth and development. That is, organizations often seek individuals who are passive and dependent on the organization; they essentially want people who will do what they are told. Moreover, many jobs (for example, assembly line jobs) are designed to capitalize on short-term perspectives and limited and routine response patterns. Thus, according to Argyris, a basic conflict exists for most employees: They can pursue either their own goals or those of the organization, but not both. Such conflict often leads to frustration and feelings of failure. Moreover, because of their lack of means with which to resolve such conflicts, employees often respond in ways that are detrimental to organizational goal attainment (including turnover and absenteeism, output restriction, strikes, and so forth). **35**

Goal Integration Mechanisms

Several mechanisms have been proposed to resolve this basic conflict and facilitate goal-directed effort (see, for example, Barrett, 1970). First, some organizational analysts have suggested a *socialization model* in which individual employees would be socialized into accepting organizational goals and values. In other words, managers could attempt through a variety of means to shift employee's personal goals more toward those of the organization. This is the approach that was largely adopted by proponents of scientific management, and it remains popular today among many modern managers. Unfortunately, such an approach is likely to have limited results because it still fails to satisfy the individual's basic needs; instead it serves to cover them up. Thus, we would not expect such an approach to produce the desired results over the long run.

Second, several proponents of organization development have suggested an *accomodation model* that would have management adjust organizational goals so they are more consistent with the personal goals of employees. This approach also appears to have limited application. To begin with, it assumes that all employees have similar goals. Given the diversity (and often conflicting nature) of such goals, it may be impossible for an organization to even attempt to satisfy them. Moreover, assuming management could identify a finite set of personal goals, the pursuit of such goals at the expense of the original organizational objectives may cause a loss of environmental support from such dispossessed groups as stockholders, creditors, customers, and so forth.

The third and most promising approach to conflict resolution is the *exchange model.* Here, individuals and organizations are seen as compromising on goals such that the more important goals of *both* parties are largely satisfied. (The inducements-contributions theory mentioned earlier is basically an exchange model.) Thus, management may get increased effort and production in exchange for providing employees with wage increases, more free time, and so forth. Although neither party may receive everything it wants, both should receive sufficient outcomes to justify a continuation of the relationship.

The exchange model appears to have considerable utility in understanding goal formulation processes and individual behavior. Using this approach, it can be seen that a primary reason for goal displacement is the failure of employees to receive sufficient incentives to adopt the goals of the organization. Thus, a major function of management becomes the identification and understanding of the personal goals of employees, plus the discovery of productive ways in which such goals can be integrated (through compromise and exchange) with organizational objectives. Such integration to the extent possible helps to insure that greater employee effort will be available for organizationally relevant tasks and activities. We shall say more on this topic as we examine the issue of individual motivation and behavior later in the book (see Chapter 7).

3

THE MEASUREMENT OF ORGANIZATIONAL EFFECTIVENESS

We now come to a more detailed look at the nature of organizational effectiveness. This elusive concept is referred to far more than it is studied in the literature on organizations. As a result, although almost everyone agrees that effectiveness represents a desirable attribute in organizations, surprisingly few attempts have been made to explicate the concept itself either from a theoretical or a managerial standpoint.

In the previous chapter, effectiveness was viewed in terms of a general level of organizational goal attainment (after Etzioni, 1964, and others). It is obvious, however, that from a *managerial* standpoint such an abstract notion is difficult to apply. That is, such a definition by itself says little to managers that would assist them in assessing the quality of their day-to-day work performance. An alternative way to facilitate understanding of this complex notion is to analyze the various ways in which effectiveness has been operationalized in various studies of the topic. In other words, it is possible to examine the specific evaluation criteria that have been used in organizations to measure the construct. This chapter will focus on an examination of various attempts that have been made to derive such measures. Following this, the concept of efficiency is discussed as it relates to the effectiveness construct. Finally, several potential problems in the measurement of organizational effectiveness are reviewed.

MODELS OF ORGANIZATIONAL EFFECTIVENESS

Most writers on the topic of organizational effectiveness have focused primarily on organization-wide phenomena. Effectiveness is typically measured in terms of performance, productivity, profit, and so forth (see, for example, Katzell, 1975). As such, little consideration is accorded to the role played by the various parts, or subunits, of an organization in determining its success. These macro approaches to the study of effectiveness in organizations have tended to take one of two forms. Some approaches, particularly the earlier ones, viewed the concept within a *unidimensional* framework, focusing on only one evaluation criterion (for example, productivity). In contrast, the *multivariate* effectiveness measures employ several distinct criteria treated simultaneously. We shall briefly consider both of these approaches to the study of effectiveness, beginning with the univariate approach (cf. Steers, 1975c).

Univariate Effectiveness Measures

Initial attempts by industrial psychologists and sociologists to measure organizational effectiveness typically viewed the concept in terms of the attainment of some ultimate criterion. Thorndike (1949) identified several of these early criteria as productivity, net profit, mission accomplishment, and organizational growth and stability. When we consider the more contemporary empirical work on effectiveness that has employed univariate measures, it must be concluded that little has changed since Thorndike's initial assessment. For example, a recent review by Campbell (1973) of various measures employed to determine organizational success resulted in the identification of nineteen variables that were widely used (see Exhibit 3-1). The most prominent of these were: (1) overall performance; (2) productivity; (3) employee job satisfaction; (4) profit or rate of return on investment; and (5) employee withdrawal. Univariate studies typically employ one of these measures as the dependent variable and compare this variable with other independent, or predictor, variables (such as leadership style) to study the relationships between them.

An analysis of these univariate attempts leads to several conclusions. To begin with, it is difficult to advance a tenable argument in support of the use of several of these variables (for example, turnover) by themselves as comprehensive or even adequate measures of organizational effectiveness. Although turnover rates, for example, may represent a major input into the determination of ultimate organizational success, there is little reason to equate the two concepts as has often been done. In fact, this problem really raises doubts as to the use of the univariate approach in general for evaluating effectiveness.

Second, several of the variables employed to measure effectiveness (for example, satisfaction) appear to represent value judgments by researchers or managers of what "ought to be," instead of objective measures of the ability of an organization to **39**

EXHIBIT 3-1   A Partial Listing of Univariate Measures of Organizational Effectiveness

Overall Effectiveness	The degree to which the organization is accomplishing all its major tasks or achieving all its objectives. A general evaluation that takes in as many single criteria as possible and results in a general judgment about the effectiveness of the organization.
Quality	The quality of the primary service or product provided by the organization. This may take many operational forms, primarily determined by the *kind* of product or service provided by the organization.
Productivity	The quantity of or volume of the major product or service that the organization provides. Can be measured at three levels: individual, group, and total organization. This is not a measure of efficiency, no cost/output ratio is computed.
Readiness	An overall judgment concerning the probability that the organization could successfully perform some specified task if asked to do so.
Efficiency	A ratio that reflects a comparison of some aspect of unit performance to the costs incurred for that performance. Examples: dollars per single unit of production, amount of down time, degree to which schedules, standards of performance, or other milestones are met. On occasion, just the total amount of costs (money, material, etc.) a unit has incurred over some period can be used.
Profit or Return	The return on the investment used in running the organization from the owners' point of view. The amount of resources left after all costs and obligations are met, sometimes expressed as a percentage.
Growth	An increase in such things as manpower, plant facilities, assets, sales, profits, market share, and innovations. A comparison of an organization's present state with its own past state.
Utilization of Environment	The extent to which the organization successfully interacts with its environment, acquiring scarce, valued resources necessary to its effective operation. This is viewed in a long-term, optimizing framework and not in a short-term, maximizing framework. For example, the degree to which it acquires a steady supply of manpower and financial resources.
Stability	The maintenance of structure, function, and resources through time, and more particularly through periods of stress.
Turnover or Retention	Frequency or amount of voluntary terminations.
Absenteeism	The frequency of occasions of personnel being absent from the job.
Accidents	Frequency of on-the-job accidents resulting in down time or recovery time.
Morale	A predisposition in organization members to put forth extra effort in achieving organizational goals and objectives. Includes feelings of commitment. Morale is a group phenomenon involving extra effort, goals communality, and feelings of belonging. Groups have some degree of morale, while individuals have some degree of motivation (and satisfaction). By implication, morale is inferred from group phenomena.

Motivation	The strength of the predisposition of an *individual* to engage in goal-directed action or activity on the job. This is not a feeling of relative contentment with various job outcomes as is satisfaction, but more akin to a feeling of readiness or willingness to work at accomplishing the job's goals.
Satisfaction	The degree of feeling of contentment felt by a person toward his organizational role or job. The degree to which individuals perceive they are equitably rewarded by various aspects of their job situation and the organization to which they belong.
Internalization of Organizational Goals	The acceptance of organizational goals by individuals and units within the organization. Their belief that the organization's goals are right and proper.
Conflict-Cohesion	A bipolar dimension defined at the cohesion end by an organization in which the members like one another, work well together, communicate fully and openly, and coordinate their work efforts. At the other end lies the organization with verbal and physical clashes, poor coordination, and ineffective communication.
Flexibility-Adaptation	The ability of an organization to change its standard operating procedures in response to environmental changes, to resist becoming rigid in response to environmental stimuli.
Evaluations by External Entities	Evaluations of the organization or organizational unit by those individuals and organizations in its environment with which it interacts. Loyalty to, confidence in, and support given the organization by such groups as suppliers, customers, stockholders, enforcement agencies, and the general public.

Source: J. P. Campbell, *Research into the Nature of Organizational Effectiveness: An Endangered Species?* Unpublished manuscript, University of Minnesota, 1973. Used by permission of the author.

accomplish its goals. If an organization sets as its primary goal the improvement of working conditions, job attitudes, and so forth, then such a criterion has relevance for an objective appraisal of effectiveness; if not, it becomes difficult though necessary to separate personal values from objective assessment.

A third and perhaps more serious criticism of univariate measures is an integration problem. As can be seen in Exhibit 3-1, there is no lack of criterion variables associated with the concept of organizational effectiveness. However, although the research literature has generally been fairly rigorous in defining and measuring specific dependent variables, it has been much less specific as to how such variables contribute to a meaningful understanding of the organizational effectiveness *construct*. Defining effectiveness simply as productivity, for example, contributes little to our understanding of the abstract phenomenon called ''effectiveness'' and contributes even less to our efforts to build comprehensive models of such a notion. Katz and Kahn explain the problem as follows:

> There is no lack of material on criteria of organizational success. The literature is studded with references to efficiency, productivity, absence, turnover, and profitability—all of these offered implicitly or explicitly, separately or in combination, as definitions of organizational effectiveness. Most of what has been written on the meaning of these criteria and on their interrelatedness, howev- **41**

er, is judgmental and open to question. What is worse, it is filled with advice that seems sagacious but is tautological and contradictory. (1966, p. 149)

More recent univariate studies published since this assessment by Katz and Kahn have typically failed to contribute toward any improvement in the situation. Productivity is still generally equated with effectiveness, without considering what the organization is actually trying to do. The problem of attempting to equate these two concepts is best demonstrated in the example of the Civilian Conservation Corps of the 1930s. The CCC was not intended to be necessarily productive; instead, its primary goal was to put people to work. Thus, productivity and effectiveness are not always equivalent, although they are often related. Examples such as this one suggest that most univariate attempts to study organizational effectiveness probably suffer from a form of empirical myopia. As such, they contribute little toward building effectiveness models or making meaningful recommendations to managers concerning ways to improve effectiveness.

Multivariate Effectiveness Measures

A more meaningful approach to examining the role of effectiveness in organizations consists of model-building attempts, where hypotheses are generated and tested concerning *relationships* between major variables that can affect organizational success. These models have a distinct advantage over univariate techniques in that they generally represent attempts to study in a more comprehensive fashion the major sets of variables involved in the effectiveness construct and to demonstrate or at least suggest how such variables fit together.

One of the first attempts at a multivariate approach to the assessment of organizational effectiveness was carried out by Georgopoulos and Tannenbaum (1957). These investigators advanced an early argument for the use of systems theory in the analysis of effectiveness:

> For theoretical reasons, however, it is preferable to look at the concept of organizational effectiveness from the point of view of the system itself—of the total organization in question rather than from the standpoint of some of its parts or of the larger society. Furthermore, proposed criteria should be system-relevant as well as applicable across organizations. (p. 535)

Viewing effectiveness in terms of goal attainment, Georgopoulos and Tannenbaum argued that definitions of organizational success must consider not only the objectives of an organization but also the mechanisms by which it maintains itself and pursues its objectives. In other words, an evaluation of effectiveness must deal with the question of means as well as ends (see also March & Simon, 1958).

Since this initial effort, several multivariate models have been proposed to explain the dynamics of organizational effectiveness. Although some approaches represent a priori theoretical statements, most are based on or at least tied to some foundation of empirical research. Typically, such models suggest that successful organizational performance is a function of several specific factors found in or exhibited by organizations.

A representative sample of seventeen of these models is summarized in Exhibit 3-2. An examination of these models reveals the diversity of opinions that can be found concerning how best to evaluate organizational effectiveness. We shall review several dimensions on which these various approaches can be compared to emphasize the diversity of opinions on the topic. These dimensions include: (1) the primary evaluation criteria used in the models; (2) the normative or descriptive nature of the criteria; (3) the purported ability to generalize or apply the criteria; and (4) the bases for determining the criteria.

Primary evaluation criteria. One of the most striking conclusions to be drawn from a comparison of these various models is the apparent lack of consensus as to what constitutes a useful set of measures of organizational effectiveness. Although each model sets forth its three or four defining characteristics (or determinants) of success, there is surprisingly little overlap among the approaches. This point is clearly made when one examines the frequency with which each of the evaluation criteria is mentioned in the seventeen models, as shown in Exhibit 3-3. Of all the criteria, only one (adaptability/flexibility) was mentioned in more than half the models. This criterion was followed by productivity and satisfaction in frequency. In other words, there is a notable lack of convergence among the various models as to what actually constitutes (or leads to) effectiveness.

Besides the differences that exist in the actual evaluation criteria used in these analyses, differences can also be found in the way such criteria are believed to be related. A basic issue here centers around whether the approach taken is relatively static or dynamic in nature. Several investigators view effectiveness as a state that organizations strive to attain. Under this conceptualization, once an organization acquires certain defining characteristics (for example, high productivity, high employee satisfaction and retention, and so on), it apparently "becomes" effective. A contrasting viewpoint on this matter suggests that effectiveness is best understood when one views the entire organizational *system* (see Chapter 1). That is, an organization is seen here as existing in a constant state of flux, continually striving to reach or maintain stability vis-à-vis its internal and external environments (Etzioni, 1960, 1975). In other words, such models focus on the manner **43**

EXHIBIT 3-2   Evaluation Criteria in Multivariate Models of Organizational Effectiveness

Study and Primary Evaluation Criteria	Type of Measure*	Generalizability of Criteria†	Derivation of Criteria‡
Georgopoulos & Tannenbaum (1957) Productivity, Flexibility, Absence of organizational strain	N	A	Ded.; followed by questionnaire study
Bennis (1962) Adaptability, Sense of identity, Capacity to test reality	N	A	Ded.; no study
Blake & Mouton (1964) Simultaneous achievement of high production-centered and high people-centered enterprise	N	B	Ded.; no study
Caplow (1964) Stability, Integration, Voluntarism, Achievement	N	A	Ded.; no study
Katz & Kahn (1966) Growth, Storage, Survival, Control over environment	N	A	Ind.; based on review of empirical studies
Lawrence & Lorsch (1967) Optimal balance of integration and differentiation	D	B	Ind.; based on study of 6 firms
Yuchtman & Seashore (1967) Successful acquisition of scarce and valued resources, Control over environment	N	A	Ind.; based on study of insurance agencies
Friedlander & Pickle (1968) Profitability, Employee satisfaction, Societal value	N	B	Ded.; followed by study of small businesses
Price (1968) Productivity, Conformity, Morale, Adaptiveness, Institutionalization	D	A	Ind.; based on review of 50 published studies
Mahoney & Weitzel (1969) General business model: Productivity-support-utilization, Planning, Reliability, Initiative R and D Model: Reliability, Cooperation, Development	D	B, R	Ind.; based on study of 13 organizations
Schein (1970) Open communication, Flexibility, Creativity, Psychological commitment	N	A	Ded.; no study

Mott (1972) Productivity, Flexibility, Adaptability	N	A	Ded.; followed by questionnaire study of several organizations
Duncan (1973) Goal attainment, Integration, Adaptation	N	A	Ded.; followed by study of 22 decision units

Gibson et al. (1973)
Short-run:
  Production, Efficiency,
    Satisfaction
Intermediate:
  Adaptiveness, Development
Long-run:
  Survival
	N	A	Ind.; based on review
			of earlier models

Negandhi & Reimann (1973)
Behavioral index:
  Manpower acquisition,
  Employee satisfaction,
  Manpower retention,
  Interpersonal relations,
  Interdepartmental relations,
  Manpower utilization
Economic index:
  Growth in sales, Net profit
	N	B	Ded.; followed by study
			of Indian organizations

Child (1974, 1975) Profitability, Growth	N	B	Ded.; followed by study of 82 British firms
Webb (1974) Cohesion, Efficiency, Adaptability, Support	D	C	Ind.; based on study of religious organizations

*N = Normative models; D = Descriptive models
†A = All organizations; B = Business organizations; C = Religious organizations; R = Research and development laboratories
‡Ded. = Deductive; Ind. = Inductive

Source: R. M. Steers, "Problems in the Measurement of Organizational Effectiveness," *Administrative Science Quarterly,* 1975, *20,* pp. 546–58. Reprinted by permission.

in which the evaluation criteria fit together, as well as how they relate to other organizational factors.

This systems perspective can perhaps best be understood if we briefly look at two systems approaches to organizational effectiveness (Katz & Kahn, 1966; Yuchtman & Seashore, 1967). Viewing organizations as open systems, Katz and Kahn (1966, p. 170) begin by defining effectiveness as the "maximization of return to the organization by all means." Two basic factors are seen as contributing in a substantive way to the determination of effectiveness. First, the concept of *efficiency* is introduced as a necessary yet insufficient determinant of effectiveness. Katz and Kahn define efficiency as an energic ratio of inputs to outputs and argue that economic and technical solutions to organizational problems contribute to increased efficiency. (See the discussion on efficiency later in this chapter.) Such solutions assist in the economical transformation of energy and thus assist the organization in growth and survival. Building a better mousetrap (a technical solution) or reducing the cost of an existing mousetrap (an economic solution) are suggested as examples of improving efficiency. Second, Katz and Kahn discuss *political effectiveness* as the second determinant, defining this as short-run attempts to maximize the return to an organization through advantageous transactions and exchanges both with the organization's members and with forces outside the organization. "Like efficiency, political effectiveness contributes to the immediate profitability of the enterprise and to its growth and survival power for the longer term. It leads also to increased control over the organizational environment, as short-term advantages in external transactions are reinforced and made permanent by precedent and legal recognition" (Katz & Kahn, 1966, p. 165).

EXHIBIT 3-3   Frequency of Occurrence of Evaluation Criteria in 17 Models of Organizational Effectiveness

Evaluation Criteria	No. of Times Mentioned ($N = 17$)
Adaptability-Flexibility	10
Productivity	6
Satisfaction	5
Profitability	3
Resource acquisition	3
Absence of strain	2
Control over environment	2
Development	2
Efficiency	2
Employee retention	2
Growth	2
Integration	2
Open communications	2
Survival	2
All other criteria	1

Source: R. M. Steers, "Problems in the Measurement of Organizational Effectiveness," *Administrative Science Quarterly*, 1975, *20*, pp. 546–58. Reprinted by permission.

Organizational effectiveness is thus viewed by Katz and Kahn as a joint function of efficiency and political effectiveness in the short term. Assuming such factors can be maintained over time, an organization will in the long run exhibit the four proposed characteristics of long-term organizational effectiveness: growth, energic storage, survival, and control over the external environment. The major focal point of this model, then, is not so much the end state but the *processes* by which the organization came to arrive (or not arrive) at the end state. Thus, the dynamics of organizational systems are clearly recognized.

A second systems model of effectiveness that has received widespread attention has been proposed by Yuchtman and Seashore (1967; see also Seashore & Yuchtman, 1967). The Yuchtman and Seashore model begins by proposing three approaches to the study of organizational success. First, there is what the authors term the "goal approach," in which organizational analysts compare organizational performance against prestated *official* organizational objectives. Second, there is the "functional approach," which bases the "real" goals or functions of a given organization on the theoretical frame or reference of the evaluator. In other words, goals are ascribed to organizations based upon what function the organization serves in society (Parsons, 1956). Both these approaches are discarded by Yuchtman and Seashore (1967) in favor of what they term a "system resource" approach to organizational effectiveness.

Under the system resource conceptualization, effectiveness is defined in terms of the ability of an organization to secure an advantageous bargaining position in its environment and to capitalize on that position to acquire scarce and valued resources. Building upon the earlier work of Georgopoulos and Tannenbaum (1957), Thompson and McEwen (1958), and others, Yuchtman and Seashore state:

> The concept of "bargaining position" implies the exclusion of any specific goal (or function) as the ultimate criterion of organizational effectiveness. Instead it points to the more general capability of the organization as a resource-getting system. Specific "goals," however, can be incorporated in this conceptualization in two ways: (1) as a specification of the means or strategies employed by members of the organization; and (2) as a specification of the personal goals of certain members or classes of members within the organizational system. The better the bargaining position of an organization, the more capable it is of attaining its varied and often transient goals, and the more capable it is of allowing the attainment of the personal goals of members. (1967, p. 898)

Yuchtman and Seashore, then, like Katz and Kahn (1966), reject definitions of effectiveness that evaluate performance based on the existence of an ultimate goal or imply some larger societal function for the organization (see also Georgiou, 1973). Instead, **47** both models focus on the behavior of organizations as they strive to achieve advantageous bargaining positions in their external environments.

Although such systems-oriented approaches to defining primary evaluation criteria contribute considerably to our understanding of the effectiveness construct, certain reservations have been raised concerning specific aspects of these models. For example, several researchers (see Hall, 1972) have pointed out that the Yuchtman and Seashore typology of effectiveness (the goal, functional, and system resource approaches) may in large measure represent an argument over semantics. More specifically, Yuchtman and Seashore define their "goal approach" in terms of official goals and appear to be defining their "system resource" approach in terms of operative goals. That is, a decision by a business firm to compete actively with other firms for specific valued resources may be viewed as a conscious attempt to move the organization in a particular direction (that is, an operative goal). As Hall (1972, p. 100) points out, "the acquisition of resources does not just happen. It is based on what the organization is trying to achieve—its goal—but it is accomplished through the operative goals." In short, it is argued that the Yuchtman and Seashore model represents an "empirical verification of the operative-goal concept" (p. 100).

A second problem with both the Yuchtman and Seashore and the Katz and Kahn models (and, for that matter, many other models) is their abstractness. Simon (1964) discusses the problem of *reification* in organizational analysis; that is, treating an abstraction—an organization—as a concrete object capable of having its own goals. This problem amply applies to the notion of effectiveness. That is, we tend to discuss the behavior of "organizations" as they try to compete for scarce and valued resources. As pointed out by Cyert and March (1963) and Simon, people pursue various goals; organizations do not. Thus, although most models of organizational effectiveness discuss the way various organizations behave, it is important from a managerial standpoint to realize that behind the organizational facade are scores of individuals often behaving in quite divergent ways although all are theoretically pursuing the same general objectives for the organization. This realization complicates tremendously any simple model of organizational success and ultimately requires the manager or organizational analyst to look within organizations and study the relationship between individual performance and the more abstract notion of organizational effectiveness.

Nature of criteria. A second major dimension along which the various models can be compared is the intended uses to which the models are put. At the risk of oversimplifying, it is possible to identify two major types: (1) *normative* models, which attempt to specify those things an organization must do to become effective (that is, to prescribe desirable behavior); and (2) *descriptive* models, which attempt to summarize those characteristics that have been found in successful organizations.

As noted in Exhibit 3-2, most models are normative in nature. They attempt to prescribe, based on either theoretical formulations or value premises, the requisite conditions under which an investigator or manager can determine the degree of effectiveness. For example, Friedlander and Pickle (1968) state that an organization is effective when it is profitable, has satisfied employees, and contributes something to society. What is usually lacking in such normative models is a rationale or empirical defense as to why the given set of criteria does in fact represent true measures of effectiveness and why it should be applied as such to other organizations.

The descriptive models, on the other hand, typically take a more conservative, empirically based approach, simply describing those characteristics that emerged as a result of investigation. In most cases, such descriptions do not carry normative implications. Mahoney and Weitzel (1969), for example, developed a model of effectiveness based on their study but did not claim that this model should be applied to all organizations. In fact, their important findings indicate that different effectiveness criteria may have differential relevance depending upon the nature of the organization and the technologies involved. In any case, they did not propose their model in terms of what "should" be done, but instead chose to simply describe what their findings entailed.

Ability to generalize criteria. A third important point on which the various models differ is with respect to the purported ability to generalize their evaluation criteria (see Exhibit 3-2). Here we are concerned about the question of external validity; that is, the extent to which the models are valid, or applicable, in other organizational settings. Many models purport to set forth evaluation criteria that can be applied to all organizations (for example, Caplow, 1964). Such models are often called "universalistic" (Child, 1974). Other models, however, have narrowed their applicability and focused instead on one particular type of organization (for example, Lawrence & Lorsch, 1967). In such cases, the effectiveness criteria are believed to be "contingent" upon the type of organization under study (Child, 1974).

Typically, those models representing a special case (such as business organizations) are more specific concerning the nature of the evaluation criteria, while the more generalized models tend to be more abstract and sometimes more theoretical. It may be argued that both types of models—the generalized and the specif- **49** ic—are functional for our understanding of effectiveness in organizations if we invest sufficient time and energy in comparing and synthesizing the various approaches. The practicing manager must, accordingly, demonstrate a capacity to understand these various approaches and to derive from such models those concepts most applicable to his or her own unique situation.

Derivation of evaluation criteria. Although an understanding of the actual criteria used in various attempts to study effectiveness as well as their purported nature and applicability is useful, it is also important to know how such criteria were developed. In an effort to highlight such developmental techniques, two relatively distinct categories were set up and the studies were classified according to the techniques used to derive the criteria (see Exhibit 3-2). The two categories are termed here *deductive* and *inductive*. Although a partial overlap between these two categories may exist in some cases, it was felt that such a classification was useful—perhaps necessary—in identifying general trends in the various ways effectiveness is evaluated.

Deductive models consist of those investigations in which the evaluation criteria were set forth by definition or as a result of a proposed theory. Studies of potential determinants or outcomes of such measures were subsequently examined. For example, Georgopoulos and Tannenbaum began by *defining* organizational effectiveness "as the extent to which an organization as a social system, given certain resources and means, fulfills its objectives without incapacitating its means and resources and without placing undue strain upon its members" (1957, p. 538). Based upon this approach, the researchers initiated a questionnaire study to examine determinants of the a priori evaluation criteria.

In the inductive studies, on the other hand, investigators typically attempted to generate meaningful evaluation *as a result of* their findings in one or more empirical investigations. Several of these studies consist of attempts to review the empirical findings of earlier researchers and to integrate them into a unified framework. Price (1968), for example, reviewed fifty existing investigations that related in some fashion to the concept of organizational effectiveness and attempted to draw some meaningful generalizations concerning the nature of the construct. A second variation of the inductive approach is characterized by the use of quantitative techniques to derive empirically the relevant criteria based on studies carried out by the investigators themselves. The most notable examples of this approach are provided by Lawrence and Lorsch (1967), Mahoney and Weitzel (1969), and Seashore and Yuchtman (1967).

In conclusion, it is clear from the foregoing review that the
50 evaluation of organizational effectiveness has a rich and varied

history. Some approaches attempted to measure effectiveness based on a single dimension (for example, productivity), while others employed multivariate and/or index measures. It was noted that there was little agreement among the various approaches concerning what actually constituted a "true" measure of effectiveness. Some criteria were set forth in a normative fashion, prescribing desirable traits, although other criteria were identified in a purely descriptive manner as statements of what was found to be related to effectiveness in a particular study. Moreover, some criteria were intended to apply to all organizations, but others specified clearly their limited organizational domains. Finally, while several sets of criteria were set forth in a deductive fashion, others employed a variety of quantitative and nonquantitative tools to "calculate" such measures in an inductive fashion.

What remains to be done is to attempt to find a common ground upon which the more rigorous of these models can rest. Before this can be attempted, however, more specific consideration must be given to the role played by efficiency in the above frameworks. As demonstrated above, the concept of efficiency is often interrelated with the notion of effectiveness. In addition, we need to be aware of some general problems that have been found to exist in many earlier attempts to evaluate effectiveness and that should be avoided and/or accounted for in any future attempts. We shall now turn to these two issues, beginning with the notion of efficiency in organizations.

EFFICIENCY

Although effectiveness has been generally viewed as the degree to which operative and operational goals have been attained, the concept of *efficiency* represents the cost/benefit ratio incurred in the pursuit of those goals (Barnard, 1938). In other words, efficiency considers the issue of how many inputs (such as raw materials, money, people) are necessary to attain a given level of output or a particular goal. If two companies making the same product finish the fiscal year with equal production levels but one attained the level with fewer invested resources than the other, that company would be described as being more efficient. It achieved the same level of output with fewer inputs.

Although the concept of efficiency is obviously closely related to effectiveness, the exact nature of that relationship is open to question. Several writers (for example, Katz & Kahn, 1966) argue that efficiency is a necessary yet insufficient ingredient in the determination of organizational effectiveness. Such a viewpoint may represent an oversimplification of the issue, however. The relationship between effectiveness and efficiency may in fact depend upon other organizationally relevant variables, such as the **51** availability and/or cost of the necessary resources. For example, at the close of World War II, a ranking German general observed that the Allies (and, in particular, the United States) had not "beaten" Germany but had instead "smothered" her. The general was in effect saying that, although the Allies had been very effective in attaining their goal, they were not necessarily efficient in the pursuit of that goal.

Consider the more recent example of the U.S. space program. In the early 1960s, the United States set a national goal of attaining a safe lunar landing and return by the end of the decade. In 1969, after eight years of research and an investment of more than $26 billion, the mission was accomplished; the program was said to be highly effective. However, how does one judge whether or not the program was efficient? Does $26 billion represent a favorable or an unfavorable cost/benefit ratio? Given the magnitude of the problem and the absence of comparative data, it becomes almost impossible to answer this question with any degree of certainty. Several prominent spokesmen at the time, noting the high profit levels of some of the aerospace companies involved in the project, argued that the project could have been accomplished at a much lower (that is, more efficient) cost. Whether such assertions are correct or not appears open to speculation.

The conclusion to be reached from these and other examples is that in at least some cases efficiency is not a prerequisite of effectiveness. If an organization such as the U.S. government has "unlimited" (or at least vast) resources or if they find themselves in an emergency situation (for example, wartime), efficiency may not represent a critical issue (although it may be desirable) compared to the far more vital issue of effectiveness. Where resources are limited or scarce, however, as in the case of most private organizations, efficiency may emerge as a most important factor in facilitating organizational effectiveness. Under such constrained circumstances, efficiency allows an organization to stretch limited resources (increase their "miles per gallon" so to speak), thus allowing for increased productivity, growth, and expansion with the same amount of inputs. In fact, in some highly competitive market situations, efficiency may represent survival potential itself.

A multitude of factors go into the determination of efficiency in a given organization. Such factors can include relative labor costs, productivity per man-hour, costs of raw materials, technological advances, and so forth. In the last decade, many business enterprises have moved their factories from one state to another because of the lower labor costs or because they would be closer to their sources of raw materials and thus reduce transportation costs. Such moves may be seen as attempts at improving efficiency if not effectiveness.

52

From both a theoretical and a managerial standpoint, it is useful to distinguish between two types of efficiency: potential and actual (Katz & Kahn, 1966). *Potential* efficiency represents the optimal efficiency level at which organizations may theoretically function, given their own unique characteristics, processes, products, goals, and so on. *Actual* efficiency represents the cost/ benefit ratio that an organization actually attains. The example of the Interstate Commerce Commission provides a case in point. For many years, the ICC, a bureau of the U.S. government, set forth regulations that many people felt served to reduce competition and led to inefficiencies. For instance, certain trucking firms were required to carry their cargoes from point *A* to point *B,* not by the most direct route, but instead through an out-of-the-way point *C.* Costs were thus increased both to the trucking firms and their customers. In such cases, the actual efficiency level was well below the potential efficiency level of the firm.

Management itself can also have a major impact on the proximity of actual efficiency levels to potential levels. A firm may have sufficient resources in terms of money, materials, and technological know-how, but inept managerial behavior or poor decision making can easily lead to a less than optimal efficiency level. This key role of management is especially apparent in competitive situations between rival industries in which all firms possess sufficient resources. In such cases, the difference between actual and potential efficiency represents that area in which managerial prowess and leadership can have their greatest impact.

The concept of efficiency, then, may be viewed as being closely related to the effectiveness construct. Whether or not it is a determinant of effectiveness apparently depends upon several additional factors, such as the availability or scarcity of resources. In general, efficiency is defined here as the extent to which resources are rationally utilized in the pursuit of organizational goals. In this sense, factors such as employee turnover and absenteeism (that is, the wasting of human resources) may represent more a statement of organizational inefficiency than ineffectiveness, as has been suggested by others. In other words, although such factors may be seen as contributing indirectly to effectiveness, they may not by themselves represent valid evaluation criteria of the construct itself.

PROBLEMS IN MEASURING ORGANIZATIONAL EFFECTIVENESS

It has been shown that a variety of approaches to measuring organizational effectiveness exist. Furthermore, as we have seen, in many cases little overlap exists between these various approaches. (See Exhibits 3-2 and 3-3.) This absence of consistency makes it very difficult to operationalize the concept for the practice of management. That is, if agreement cannot be reached as to what actually constitutes the evaluation criteria, then it is logical to assume that considerable difficulty would be encountered in any attempt to assess the relative effectiveness or ineffectiveness of a given organization or set of organizations. The magnitude of this problem has led some (for example, Reimann, 1975) to suggest that it may be more appropriate to ignore the issue of organizational effectiveness and focus instead on organizational "competence" (that is, the *propensity* of an organization to reach its goals).

This difficulty in assessing effectiveness apparently results because of several problems inherent in the existing models of organizational success (Steers, 1975c). Indeed, these problems may be encountered in any attempt at model building. As will be seen, these problems of measurement are quite diverse both in their nature and their point of origin. Let us examine briefly several of the more important problems.

1. *Construct validity problem.* Throughout this chapter, we have referred to the effectiveness "construct." A construct is an abstract (as opposed to a concrete) hypothesis concerning the relationships among several related variables. It represents a statement of belief that such variables fit together as a unified whole. For example, we speak of job satisfaction as a construct consisting of several related feelings people have concerning their work, their pay, their co-workers, and so forth. Simply put, the problem here is that we really do not know whether the construct of organizational effectiveness is truly meaningful or useful either for managers or organizational theorists. It has been shown, for example, that there is little agreement as to which variables constitute true measures of effectiveness. Moreover, several of the variables that purport to be part of the construct (such as job satisfaction and performance) do not in fact correlate very highly with one another. Thus, little evidence is available at this time to demonstrate the utility of something called an effectiveness construct. Instead, we have various "pieces"' that are somewhat related and that are believed to contribute in some fashion to organizational success. If the construct is to take on meaning, greater efforts are called for in exploring its nature and composition.

2. *Criterion stability problem.* A second major problem encountered in attempting to measure effectiveness in organizations is that many of the evaluation criteria that are employed have been found to be relatively unstable over time. That is, the criteria used to measure effectiveness at one point in time may be inappropriate or misleading at a later time. In sound economic times, for instance, the effectiveness of a business firm may be related

to the level of capital investment. However, under poor economic conditions, capital liquidity may emerge as a more relevant criterion and high capital investment (that is, when the organization's money is tied up) may change from an asset to a liability. This transitory nature of many effectiveness measures is an important fact for managers to realize. Such criteria change as a function of external pressures, demands, and interests. In fact, it is this transitory property that has led some researchers to argue that flexibility in the face of change is, or ought to be, a defining characteristic of organizational effectiveness.

3. *Time perspective problem.* A related problem deals with the issue of which time perspective one wishes to use when evaluating effectiveness. Gibson, Ivancevich, and Donnelly (1973) recognize clearly the time perspective problem in their approach to effectiveness, suggesting that different criteria be employed in the short, intermediate, and long term (see Exhibit 3-2). Although this approach openly acknowledges the importance of the time issue in any consideration of organizational success, problems still persist for the manager who attempts to implement such criteria. For instance, if current production (a short-run effectiveness criterion) is maximized at the expense of research and development investments in future products, an organization may ultimately find itself with outmoded products and threatened for its very survival (a long-run effectiveness criterion). Ford Motor Company's insistence on the continued production of the standard and highly successful Model A ("in any color, so long as it's black") during the late 1920s and early 1930s almost led to financial ruin as its competitors branched out into other and more colorful models to meet public demand (Chandler, 1962). Thus, although the Model A was a highly effective automobile from a production standpoint, long-run market interests ultimately had to supercede short-term productivity concerns. The problem for the student of management, then, is how best to balance short-run necessities with long-run interests in an effort to maintain stability and growth over time.

4. *Multiple criteria problem.* As pointed out earlier, a major advantage of the multivariate approach to evaluating effectiveness is its comprehensive nature, integrating several factors into one unifying framework. Unfortunately, this advantage can simultaneously represent a problem where such criteria are in conflict with one another. For example, consider the two criteria of work productivity and employee satisfaction. Productivity can often be increased in the short run by pressuring workers to increase their effort, potentially resulting in decreased job satisfaction. Satisfaction, on the other hand, could possibly be increased by reducing work pressures and strain or by allowing workers more leisure **55**

time, thus potentially having an adverse effect on productivity. Other examples could be cited (for instance, profit versus contributing to social welfare). The important point here is that, if we accept such criteria for effectiveness, organizations by definition cannot be effective; they cannot maximize both dimensions (Dubin, 1975; Hall, 1972).

5. *Measurement precision problem.* Measurement consists of rules or procedures for assigning numbers to attributes in order to represent such attributes quantitatively. Thus, when we discuss the "measurement" of organizational effectiveness, it is assumed that it is possible to quantify the concept in a consistent and accurate fashion. However, such quantification or measurement is often made difficult due to the complexity and magnitude of the concept under study. If we define effectiveness in terms of performance and satisfaction, for example, how do we accurately measure such factors? Moreover, how consistent are such measures over time? In fact, we tend to operationalize such factors rather loosely, perhaps defining performance in terms of units of output or satisfaction as reduced turnover and absenteeism. These operational definitions can often allow for a considerable amount of measurement error and can result in less accurate evaluations of organizational performance.

Thus, when managers and researchers are considering appropriate criteria to evaluate effectiveness, specific questions need to be raised concerning how such criteria are to be measured. Measuring satisfaction in terms of turnover rates, for example, fails to recognize the potential spurious effects of other relevant variables on withdrawal behavior (for example, turnover rates tend to decline under poor economic conditions when other jobs are scarce—see Porter & Steers, 1973). Given such problems, attempts must be made to identify criteria that can be measured with a minimum of error or to control for spurious effects in the analysis process.

6. *Generalizability problem.* Even if the various measurement problems can be solved, a problem still arises as to how widely one can generalize the resulting evaluation criteria to other organizations. That is, the most appropriate evaluation criteria for a large business firm (such as profitability, market share, and so forth) may be inappropriate for evaluating a public agency, such as a police department or library. Thus, when considering the selection of criteria, concern must be shown for the degree to which such criteria are consistent with the goals and purposes of the organization under study.

7. *Theoretical relevance problem.* A major purpose of any science is to formulate theories and models that accurately reflect the nature of the subject under study (Dubin, 1969). Thus, from

56

a theoretical standpoint, logical questions must be raised concerning the relevance of such models to the study of organizational behavior. What purposes are served by the existence of effectiveness models? Do they allow us to make predictions concerning future behavior? If such models do not assist us in understanding organizational processes, structures, or behavior, they are of little value from a theoretical standpoint. For such purposes, perhaps the more relevant models are those that attempt to develop integrative mechanisms by suggesting how such criteria affect or are affected by other factors found in the structure and behavior of organizations. Katz and Kahn (1966) provide a good example of such model-building attempts in that they relate the concept of effectiveness to such factors as role performance, decision-making processes, communication patterns, leadership, and so forth. In other words, this model looks at relationships between important organizational variables and does so within a systems framework capable of increasing our understanding of organizational dynamics. This approach offers considerably more both to the researcher and to the manager than do the more simplistic and prescriptive lists of what constitutes effectiveness.

8. *Level of analysis problem.* Finally, it should be noted that most models of effectiveness deal solely on the macro level, discussing organization-wide phenomena as they relate to effectiveness, but ignoring the critical relation between individual behavior and the larger issue of organizational success. Thus, there is little integration between macro and what may be termed micro models of performance and effectiveness. If we are to increase our understanding of organizational processes—and, indeed, if we are to make meaningful recommendations to managers concerning effectiveness—performance models must be developed that attempt to specify or at least account for the relationships between processes on both the micro and macro levels. This problem will be discussed further in the remaining chapters.

Influences on Organizational Effectiveness

It becomes readily apparent from the above analysis that the notion of organizational effectiveness is quite complex and that attempts to measure the construct have consistently encountered problems. In spite of such problems, it is still possible to examine our current level of understanding concerning the major influences on effectiveness. Thus, although differences of opinion exist in regard to the utility of various specific evaluation criteria, it should prove useful to attempt to identify some of the more salient factors that have been shown to influence certain aspects of effectiveness in organizations.

In order to accomplish this, four major factors have been identified that have been found to be associated with effectiveness. As noted in Chapter 1, these are:

1. Organizational characteristics
2. Environmental characteristics
3. Employee characteristics
4. Managerial policies and practices

Each of these four topics will be examined at length in the chapters that follow. Although the topics are treated sequentially, it is important to keep in mind that all four factors interact with each other as they jointly influence resulting organizational success or failure.

Chapters 4 through 7 focus largely on developing a conceptual understanding of how individual, organizational, and environmental factors can facilitate or inhibit effectiveness. Chapters 8 and 9 then attempt to build upon this conceptual base and suggest several areas for managerial action aimed at improving effectiveness. It is hoped that this approach will serve to highlight both theory and research, on the one hand, and practical applications on the other. Finally, Chapter 10 attempts to summarize and integrate our existing level of knowledge of this important topic.

STRUCTURE, TECHNOLOGY, AND ORGANIZATIONAL EFFECTIVENESS

4

The role of organizational structure and technology in the success of an enterprise has long been a topic of concern among organizational analysts (Blau, 1955; Dubin, 1958; Woodward, 1958; Worthy, 1950). As such, a great deal of information is available from which to draw conclusions concerning the relationship between these variables and certain aspects of organizational performance and effectiveness. This chapter will examine this information in terms of its implications for the practice of management. First, structural variation will be considered as it influences both individual behavior and organizational success. This will be followed by an examination of the role of technology in the determination of both structure and effectiveness. Throughout, consideration will be given to the interactive effects among these variables as they ultimately determine the success or failure of ongoing organizations.

STRUCTURAL VARIATION AND EFFECTIVENESS

Put most simply, *structure* refers to the manner in which an organization organizes its human resources for goal-directed activities. It is the way the human parts of an organization are fitted into relatively fixed relationships that largely define patterns of interaction, coordination, and task-oriented behavior. Examples of structural variables include such factors as span of control, relative decentralization or centralization of authority and power, the degree of formalization, the amount of functional specialization, and so forth.

Our primary concern here focuses on discovering the extent to which various structural aspects of an organization influence **59** the resulting degree of effectiveness in organizations of various types. In order to accomplish this objective, a good portion of this chapter will be spent on a systematic review of the available research on structural variation as it influences effectiveness. This review will be highly focused; that is, we will not be concerned here with how one aspect of structure relates to another or how such variables as environment or technology relate to structure unless they specifically address the issue of organizational success.

At least six structural factors can be identified that have been found to affect some facet of organizational effectiveness. These six factors are: (1) the degree of decentralization; (2) functional specialization; (3) formalization; (4) span of control; (5) organization size; and (6) work-unit size. We shall examine each of these factors sequentially as they relate to several aspects of successful performance in organizations. It is important to keep in mind here that because of the imprecision found in many of the studies, it is necessary to focus attention on trends across the various findings instead of on any one piece of evidence.

A summary of the studies that have been carried out relating the structural variables to effectiveness is presented in Exhibit 4-1. For each structural variable, this exhibit lists the investigators of the study, the operational definition of effectiveness that was used (or, more precisely, the particular facet of effectiveness under study), the study sample, and the relationships that were found between the structural variables and the effectiveness measures. It is important to remember when comparing this information that there is often a considerable difference between many of the effectiveness measures that were used. Thus, a particular structural variable may be related to one facet of effectiveness but not another. Following this review, these findings will be evaluated in order to assess our current level of understanding concerning the role played by organization structure in the determination of effectiveness.

Decentralization

Decentralization refers to the extent to which various types of power and authority are extended (that is, decentralized) down through the organizational hierarchy. The notion of decentralization is thus strongly related to the concept of participative decision making. The more decentralized an organization, the greater the extent to which the rank and file employees can participate in—and accept responsibility for—decisions concerning their jobs and the future activities of the organization.

Historically, an increase in organization size typically brought with it a concomitant increase in centralization of authority and power in the upper echelons of management. As organizations grew and expanded, the disparity between the relevant sources of information for decision making (which were often located near the bottom of the hierarchy) and the decision makers themselves became greater, often resulting in poor communications, less than optimal decisions, and reduced effectiveness of operation. Although it is not possible to pinpoint precisely when this trend toward increased centralization plateaued, Chandler (1962) has suggested that it may have been during the 1920s when Alfred P. Sloan, Jr., then president of General Motors, introduced the concept of the central office. The idea behind the central office was to concentrate the more important organization-wide *policy* decisions in the hands of the major corporate executives, while decentralizing divisional responsibilities and *operating* decisions to the lowest level possible. Thus, in theory, most decisions would be made closer to their information sources, leading to increased flexibility of operation and increased divisional autonomy, while maintaining corporate control over major policy matters. This initial effort was quickly followed by other corporations who saw decentralization as a key to improving both organizational performance and employee job satisfaction (see, for example, Worthy, 1950).

As shown in Exhibit 4-1, increased decentralization in organizations often leads to improvements in several facets of effectiveness. In particular, it has been found to be related to increases in managerial efficiency, open communications and feedback, job satisfaction, and employee retention. Moreover, decentralization has led in some cases to improved performance and greater innovation and creativity in organizations, although the findings here are not entirely consistent. The rationale behind these findings suggests that decentralized organizations allow for greater autonomy and responsibility among employees at lower levels in the hierarchy, thereby utilizing more effectively an organization's scarce human resources. This explanation is consistent with recent findings among individual employees indicating that increased autonomy and responsibility often lead to increased job involvement, satisfaction, and performance.

It should be pointed out, however, that this close relationship between decentralization and improved effectiveness is not always found in organizations. For example, one study discovered that decentralized control led to improved performance in research laboratories but caused poorer performance in production departments (Lawrence & Lorsch, 1967). Such findings may be attributed to differences in individual or situational factors that can affect the decentralization-effectiveness relationship. It has been shown, for example, that different personality traits and other individual differences can affect the amount of participation that employees seek in decision making (Steers, in press). Thus, some employees **61**

EXHIBIT 4-1   Studies Relating Structural Variables to Facets of Organizational Effectiveness

Structural Variable	Investigator(s)	Facets of Effectiveness	Sample	Relationship
Decentralization	Carlson (1951)	Efficient time utilization	9 corporation executives	Positive
	Weiss (1957)	Retention, attendance, safety record, no. of grievances	34 firms	None
	Read (1962)	Open communications & feedback	104 middle level managers	Positive
	Hage & Aiken (1967)	Program innovation	16 social welfare organizations	Positive
	Lawrence & Lorsch (1967)	Rated performance	R&D labs / Production departments	Positive / Negative
	Sapolsky (1967)	Program innovation	Department stores	Negative
	Carpenter (1971)	Job satisfaction	Public school teachers	Positive
	Negandhi & Reimann (1973)	Profitability; employee retention & utilization	30 Indian firms	Positive
Specialization	Blau et al. (1966)	Reduced labor costs	Health care organizations	Positive (small units) / None (large units)
	Carroll (1967)	Innovation	Medical schools	Positive
	Hage & Aiken (1967)	Program innovation	16 social welfare organizations	Positive
	Child (1973)	Absence of conflict	78 business firms	Negative
Formalization	Blau (1955)	Client service	Govt. employment agencies	Negative
	Aiken & Hage (1966)	Job satisfaction	16 social welfare organizations	Negative
	Hage & Aiken (1967)	Program innovation	16 social welfare organizations	Negative
	Hofstede (1967)	Pursuing high performance goals	NA	Negative

	Study	Outcome Measure	Setting	Relationship
Span of Control	Miller (1967)	Organizational identification	Scientists & Engineers	Negative
	Radnor & Neil (1971)	Efficiency of operation	108 industrial firms	Positive
	Woodward (1958, 1965)	Company performance	100 British firms	Curvilinear
	Ronan & Prien (1973)	Attendance, retention, production costs, injuries, grievances	64 departments of a major manufacturer	None
Organization Size	Grusky (1961)	Orderly executive succession	Business firms	Positive
	Kriesberg (1962)	Orderly executive succession	Business firms	Positive
	Blau et al. (1966)	Reduced labor costs	250 health care organizations	Positive
	Ingham (1970)	Retention & attendance	8 British firms	None (retention) Negative (attendance)
	Boland (1971)	Control over environment	Colleges & Universities	Positive
	Child (1973)	Innovativeness, reduced conflict	78 British firms	None
	Ronan & Prien (1973)	Employee retention	White-collar units / Blue-collar units	Negative / None
Work-Unit Size	Kerr et al. (1951)	Job satisfaction, retention, attendance	Business firms	Negative
	Acton Society Trust (1953)	Attendance	Factories	Negative
	Metzner & Mann (1953)	Attendance	Business firms	Negative
	Cleland (1955)	Absence of labor disputes	Factories	Negative
	Argyle et al. (1958)	Productivity	Factories	Positive
	Revans (1958)	Productivity	Mines; retail stores	Curvilinear
	Baumgartel & Sobol (1959)	Attendance	Business firms	Negative
	Talacchi (1960)	Job satisfaction	Factories	Negative
	Indik & Seashore (1961)	Productivity	Business firms	Negative
	Katzell et al. (1961)	Productivity	Business firms	Negative

may simply want to avoid the added responsibilities that are brought on by decentralization of authority and influence, while other employees may prefer such responsibilities. Moreover, it is conceivable that differing job technologies, work environments, or goals may call for varying degrees of centralization or decentralization in order to be successful. Such a possibility is discussed below in the theories of Burns and Stalker (1961), Lawrence and Lorsch (1967), and others.

In other words, one possible explanation for the divergent findings concerning the influence on effectiveness of decentralization may lie in the intervening nature of other important variables, such as individual or situational differences. We shall return to this point after we have examined the nature of these individual and situational factors.

Specialization

The concept of functional specialization traces its origins to the scientific management movement around the turn of the century. Taylor (1911) and his associates argued that a major determinant of organizational success was the ability of an organization to divide its work functions into highly specialized activities. These writers, looking at effectiveness from the standpoint of industrial engineering, cited Adam Smith's example of the manufacture of straight pins in England as support for specialization. Smith noted that in the late eighteenth century (before the advent of the Industrial Revolution) one worker by himself could make 20 straight pins per day. However, when the tasks required to make such pins were divided into ten separate operations and each worker carried out only one such operation, ten workers could make 48,000 pins per day, or 4,800 pins per worker. Thus, specialization brought about a 240-fold increase in productivity. Examples like this represented a major source of support for Taylor and other advocates of increased specialization.

Specialization may be measured in a variety of ways, including the number of divisions within an organization and the number of specialties within each division (Hall, 1972); the number of different positions and different subunits in an organization (Blau & Schoenherr, 1971); and the number of occupations represented in an organization (Hage & Aiken, 1967). However the concept is operationalized, the hypothesis generally remains the same: Specialization will lead to increased effectiveness because it allows each employee to acquire expertise in one particular area so as to maximize his or her contribution to goal-directed activities.

Unfortunately, few rigorous attempts have been made to examine the applicability of this hypothesis in organizational settings.

64   The evidence that does exist (see Exhibit 4-1) indicates that increased specialization is associated with reduced labor costs and increased innovation and creativity, both inputs into organizational effectiveness. However, specialization has also been shown to be related to increased friction and conflict within organizations. Apparently, increased specialization and job fractionization causes frustration among some employees because it limits their behavior and their attempts to satisfy their personal development goals (see Chapter 2). This frustration then manifests itself in various forms of industrial conflict.

In other words, although specialization may often be beneficial in terms of employee performance, it may simultaneously be detrimental to employees in terms of their job attitudes, mental health, and propensity to remain with the organization. Thus, the benefits derived from specialization in the way of increased productivity may be more than offset by such negative consequences as strikes, sabotage, turnover and absenteeism, and so forth. Again, management must decide how best to balance costs and benefits in its attempt to discover the optimal organizational design with which to pursue its unique objectives.

Formalization

Formalization traditionally refers to the extent to which employee work activities are specified or regulated by official rules and procedures (see, for example, Hall, 1972). The greater the preponderance of rules, regulations, codified job duties, and so on, that govern employee behavior, the greater the degree of formalization. It has often been argued that increased formalization represents a hindrance to effectiveness because managers under highly formalized structures tend to do everything "by the book." Thus, creative, innovative, or adaptive behavior is severely constrained. This problem was believed to be particularly acute in organizations surrounded by changing external environments.

Four of the five studies available relating formalization to some facet of effectiveness tend to support such a notion (see Exhibit 4-1). However, although the trend in these findings is clearly toward a negative relationship between formalization and facets of effectiveness, the strong positive relationship found in the study by Radnor and Neil (1971) cannot be ignored. A possible explanation for these seemingly contradictory results—again pointing to a contingency approach—has been advanced by Zaltman, Duncan, and Holbek (1973) in their theory of organizational innovation. Briefly, it is suggested here that varying degrees of formalization may be functional for an organization depending upon where the organization is in the innovation (or change) process. During the "initiation" stage of innovation, where new sources of information and maximum search behavior for problem solution **65** are critical, organizational flexibility and receptiveness to new ideas or procedures become necessary conditions for successful adaptation. However, once a course of action has been determined, a higher degree of formalized structure may be required for effective program implementation.

This approach is similar to earlier contingency theories such as those advanced by Burns and Stalker (1961) and Lawrence and Lorsch (1967). In essence, the position taken here is that less formalized organization design may be more productive in unstable or unknown environments, but higher degrees of formalization may be preferred in more stable, task-oriented environments. If such a proposition is correct, it must be concluded from Exhibit 4-1 that most of the organizations studied existed in unstable environments because most of the relationships between formalization and some facet of effectiveness were negative. Such a conclusion would be consistent with Terreberry's (1968) contention that organizational environments are, in general, becoming far more complex, thereby demanding greater flexibility and adaptability on the part of management and organizational members. Where such organizational flexibility is not forthcoming in a changing environment, we would expect that goal attainment would be very difficult. If, on the other hand, the environment and technology were relatively constant (as, for example, in the automotive industry), then formalization may be more likely to be associated with increased effectiveness.

Span of Control

Span of control refers to the average number of subordinates per supervisor. Often, the term refers more specifically to the average number of workers reporting to a first-level supervisor. Many early management theorists sought to identify an optimal span of control between a supervisor and his subordinates (see, for example, Graicunas, 1937). The underlying assumption of such efforts was that there existed some desirable superior-subordinate ratio (usually ranging from 6:1 to 15:1) that could maximize effectiveness by maximizing the relative contribution of each member of the work group.

Based on the two studies that are available on the subject, few concrete conclusions can be drawn. Woodward (1958, 1965) found in a study of British firms that a curvilinear relationship existed between span of control at the first level of supervision and company success. Moreover, it was found that this relationship was affected by the nature of the technology employed by the firms. That is, of the firms that were rated more effective, those that employed small batch technology (that is, production of unique units to customer specifications) and those that employed mass production technology both had relatively small spans of control (twenty-three and thirteen per supervisor, respectively). On the other hand, successful firms using continuous process technology (that is, chemical processing, oil refining, and so forth) had an average span of control of forty-nine workers per supervisor. Less successful firms in all three technological categories employed spans of control on either side of these ratios.

More recently, in a survey of structural properties of organizations, Ronan and Prien (1973) found no relationship between span of control and a series of effectiveness measures. These researchers did not, however, consider the potential moderating effects of such variables as technology as Woodward had done.

Organization Size

A good deal of interest has been focused on the issue of how the size of an organization may influence various aspects of organizational success. An examination of the results of several investigations indicates an important pattern of findings. On the one hand, increased organization size appears to be *positively* associated with increased efficiency. Such factors as orderly managerial succession, reduced labor costs, and environmental control may all be thought of as some aspect of getting the job done in an orderly, efficient manner.

On the other hand, size also appears to be *inversely* related to employee attachment to an organization. Here we are concerned about the extent to which employees have positive or negative attitudes toward their employer and the extent to which they wish to remain with the organization. Thus, a trend appears to exist in which increases in the size of an organization may lead to some efficiencies of scale but such efficiency may be brought about at the cost of increased negative employee attitudes toward the organization. Moreover, such efficiency may ultimately lead to an increased unwillingness on the part of employees to remain with the organization.

Work-Unit Size

Finally, consider the effects of variations in the size of a work group (as opposed to the size of the entire organization) as they relate to various effectiveness measures. Here, as with organization size, the size of a work group appears to have different effects on employee attitudes and behavior than on organizational output. For employees, increases in work-group size are consistently associated with lower job satisfaction, lower attendance and retention rates, and more labor disputes (see Exhibit 4-1). However, although these findings indicate a definite trend, they do not pro- **67** vide an answer as to why increases in the size of a work group should be inversely related to various facets of effectiveness. A possible explanation may lie in the increased affiliative opportunities that are typically associated with smaller work groups (see, for example, Cartwright & Zander, 1968). Smaller work groups often allow members to become better acquainted, develop close friendships, and build a high degree of group cohesion. On the other hand, larger groups are often more formal and task specialized and present the individual with fewer opportunities to develop close, satisfying interpersonal relationships. Thus, we would expect job satisfaction to be higher—and turnover and absenteeism to be lower—in the smaller work groups.

The impact of work-group size on productivity is much less clear. Such mixed findings might indicate the potential existence of other important variables (such as technology) that may serve to moderate the impact of group size on productivity (see, for example, Woodward, 1965). It would appear, however, based on the available evidence, that no such moderator variables exist concerning the impact of work-unit size on job attitudes.

Summary

In summary, it can be concluded that several aspects of organizational structure can affect certain facets of organizational effectiveness. When we consider the attitudinal and attachment facets of effectiveness (for example, job satisfaction, retention, attendance), the results point to a negative relationship between such facets and the structural variables of centralization, specialization, formalization, organization size, and work-group size. In other words, employees tend to become more attached to an organization, as well as more satisfied, when they have an opportunity to accept more responsibility, when their tasks provide them with greater variety and involvement, when rules and regulations are kept at a minimum, and when the organization and work group are of a modest size. Such findings are not surprising in light of recent research on the attitudinal implications of variations in the task environment (Hackman & Lawler, 1971; Mowday, Porter, & Dubin, 1974; Porter & Steers, 1973; Turner & Lawrence, 1965).

On the other hand, when we view effectiveness in terms of productivity and efficiency (instead of job attitudes) quite different results emerge. For example, functional specialization and organization size are generally positively related to increased efficiency, program innovation, and so forth. Moreover, decentralization, formalization, and work-unit size all appear to be related to productivity in a contingent fashion; that is, other important variables moderate the impact that these variables have on productivity.

In short, an examination of the available evidence reemphasizes the need to specify clearly what we mean by organizational effectiveness. We have been dealing throughout this section with *facets* of effectiveness. The results of our review indicate that structural variables have different effects on attitudinal facets than they do on productivity-efficiency facets of organizational success. Thus, management must specify its targets and aims—that is, its evaluation criteria—if it is to be successful in modifying the organization to meet these criteria. Moreover, the above findings emphasize the opportunity costs associated with such goal-related decisions. If the evaluation criterion is to be productivity, such a goal may only be achieved at the expense of other potentially worthy goals (for example, job satisfaction). Therefore, it is incumbent upon management to critically analyze its needs and objectives, as well as the costs associated with such objectives, before determining a course of action.

THE ROLE OF TECHNOLOGY

In addition to an understanding of the impact of structural variables on effectiveness, it is also important to know how other important sets of organizational variables affect the ultimate success of organizations. One such variable worthy of examination is technology. The role of technology in the determination of organizational behavior was recognized early by such researchers as Walker and Guest (1952) and Dubin (1958). More recently, several comprehensive investigations have been undertaken to clarify the nature of the role played by technological factors. In particular, these studies have tended to focus on the interrelationship between variations in technology and organizational structure as they jointly determine effectiveness. We shall now turn to an examination of these technological variables.

Nature of Technology

The complexity of the technological dimension becomes readily apparent when we examine the various ways in which the concept has been used in the past. Even a cursory examination of the research and writings on the topic reveals the fact that technology oftentimes means different things to different people. The existence of such a diversity of meanings presents a serious problem for managers and researchers alike when attempts are made to compare and integrate the various findings that are available on the topic. Because of the importance of technology in organizational dynamics, and because of the problems created by such diverse approaches to the concept itself, it should prove useful **69** to begin our consideration of technology by examining the various ways in which the topic has been studied.

Although a detailed examination of the variety of definitions goes beyond the scope of our discussion here (see Lynch, 1974), several examples should point up the diversity of approaches to the topic. In recent investigations, the concept of technology has been operationalized in terms of the extent of task interdependence (Hickson, Pugh, & Pheysey, 1969), automation of equipment (Blau & Schoenherr, 1971), uniformity or complexity of materials used (Mohr, 1971), the degree of uncertainty in the task environment (Lawrence & Lorsch, 1967), and the degree of routineness of work (Hage & Aiken, 1969; Perrow, 1970), to name a few. It should be evident from this partial list of definitions that when researchers and managers discuss technology, they are not always focusing on the same issues.

A search for convergence among this diversity of opinion reveals at least two important points. First, there appears to be general agreement that the technology dimension involves either mechanical or intellectual processes by which an organization transforms inputs, or raw materials, into outputs in the pursuit of organizational goals. When we discuss the role of technology in organizations, we are focusing our attention on "who does what with whom, when, where, and how often" (Chapple & Sayles, 1961, p. 34). In short, technology refers to the transformation process in organizations where mechanical and intellectual energies are brought to bear in the efficient utilization of scarce resources.

A second important point worthy of note in these definitions—and, indeed, perhaps a major reason for the diversity of definitions—centers around the level of analysis taken in the various studies. Some investigations examined technology at an organizational (or system-wide) level, while others viewed technology at the individual job level. For example, Woodward (1958) classified the firms in her study into small batch, mass production, or continuous process technologies and then studied differences in structural variations between the organizations. It was assumed here that the nature of the manufacturing processes in each firm would affect both structure and effectiveness in the entire organization, even in those areas not specifically related to production (such as marketing and finance). On the other hand, several other studies (for example, Hage & Aiken, 1969) used such variables as noise level, task interdependence, and routineness of tasks on an individual (or at least a group) level as a measure of technology. The assumption of this latter approach is that technologies may vary from department to department or even work group to work group. Thus, there may be a different relationship between tech-

70

nology and structure or effectiveness for an R&D laboratory than for an accounting department or a production unit (see, for example, Mahoney & Frost, 1974).

If we compare the various definitions of technology with the level of analysis of the various studies, it appears as if such definitions are at least in part a function of the level of analysis one wishes to employ. System-wide studies focus on the general type of production technology used throughout a department or organization; individual-level studies are typically concerned with job technology. Such a finding cautions the organizational analyst against drawing general conclusions concerning the effects of technology without specifying in advance the particular aspect—as well as the level—of technology with which one is dealing.

Technological Typologies

The necessity of recognizing both the level of analysis and the operational definition of technology in organizations raises the issue of how various types of technological applications can be organized for purposes of study. If we can clearly identify several categories to which the various technologies can be assigned, it becomes possible to study more precisely how different "types" of technology affect structure, performance, and effectiveness. Toward this end, several researchers have suggested typologies into which the majority of technological variations can be classified.

One of the earliest and most widely used typologies was developed by Woodward (1958, 1965). Focusing specifically on industrial firms, Woodward suggested three categories of technology based largely on the level of technical complexity of the production process. These three categories are:

1. *Small batch, or unit, production.* Product is "custom-made" on small scale to consumer specifications (for example, airplanes, locomotives, printing). Operations performed on each unit are typically nonrepetitive in nature.
2. *Mass production.* Product is manufactured in assembly-line fashion (for example, automobiles). Operations performed are repetitious, routine, predictable.
3. *Continuous process production.* Product is transformed from raw material to finished good using a series of machine, or process, transformations (for example, chemicals, oil refining).

Woodward argued that the technical complexity of an organization increases as it moves from unit, through mass, to continuous process production. Although such a trend may occur in many cases, it is easy to envision exceptions. For example, one would **71** argue that the development and production of a DC-10 or a Boeing 747 (small batch technology) is far more complex technologically than either mass production or continuous process production. Thus, it may be necessary to differentiate standard or routinized from non-standard forms of small batch production technologies when discussing technical complexity. Although the printing process may employ fairly routine production techniques, the design and manufacture of an airplane certainly does not.

A different approach to the classification of technological diversity has been proposed by Thompson (1967). This typology is based on the manner in which individuals or units are organized for task accomplishment:

1. *Long-linked technology,* characterized by serial interdependence of a number of different operations or departments. Roughly equivalent to Woodward's (1958) "mass production" technology, where various pieces are "added" to the product as it moves through manufacturing process.
2. *Mediating technology,* characterized by a linking of otherwise independent units or elements of a system, where the various units are mediated (that is, made compatible) through the use of standard operating procedures. Examples include a bank where customers are classified into depositors and borrowers and then each is dealt with accordingly based on standardized procedures.
3. *Intensive technology,* characterized by uniqueness of task sequence. Here, the choice of techniques and the way they are used to alter an object are varied and are largely influenced by feedback from the object itself (that is, how it responds to what happens to it). Organizations using intensive technologies include hospitals, where a variety of techniques, services, and skills exist and are applied in varying combinations depending upon the particular illness of the patient and his or her response to treatment.

A comparison of Woodward's (1958) typology with the one proposed by Thompson (1967) reveals that the latter is capable of including a wider variety of organizations than the former. Woodward addressed herself specifically to the industrial-manufacturing domain; Thompson sought to include almost every type of work organization. Perhaps broader still is the typology proposed by Hickson et al. (1969). In their analysis of British organizations differing considerably in size, shape, and purpose, they suggested the following categories of technology:

1. *Operations technology,* which focuses on the techniques used in the "work flow" activities of an organization (for example, handcrafting versus mass production).

2. *Materials technology,* which focuses on the types of materials used in the work flow.
3. *Knowledge technology,* which focuses on the amount, quality, level of sophistication, and dispersion of information relevant to decision making and production in an organization.

In contrast to Woodward and Thompson, the Hickson et al. (1969) categories are not mutually exclusive. That is, organizations may exhibit some form of all three technologies at the same time in the same place. For example, one organization may employ a highly advanced manufacturing process (operations technology) on a relatively simple raw material (materials technology); moreover, such a process may require highly skilled, well-educated, versatile employees with a high degree of interdepartmental communications (knowledge technology).

Other typologies could be mentioned (for example, Perrow, 1967). The important point here is the recognition that technology, which has been shown to represent an important influence on structure and behavior in organizations, should not be viewed in simplistic global terms. On the contrary, managers and researchers have an obligation to understand the nature, variations, and intricacies of the technological processes employed in a particular organization under study. In fact, it appears to be far more appropriate to talk about *technologies* instead of a single technology in most modern organizations. Such a fact should be kept in mind when examining the various research findings on the topic.

TECHNOLOGY, STRUCTURE, AND EFFECTIVENESS

Given the complexities of the technological dimension, the difficulty of carrying out research on the topic as it relates to structure and effectiveness becomes apparent. Even so, several attempts have been made to clarify the role of technology in organizational performance and success. Three of the more important investigations will be reviewed here in some detail. Following this analysis, several additional studies that are generally of a supplementary nature will then be reviewed briefly. Finally, an attempt will be made to draw relevant conclusions based on these findings concerning the role of technology and structure in the success or failure of complex organizations.

Woodward

One of the earliest detailed examinations of the relationship among technology, structure, and organizational success was carried out by Joan Woodward and her colleagues (Woodward, 1958, 1965). **73**

Woodward, a British sociologist, began her research in the early 1950s by addressing the question of whether "the principles of organization laid down by an expanding body of management theory correlate with business success when put into practice" (Woodward, 1958). In an effort to provide relevant information bearing on this question, Woodward and her associates surveyed one hundred British manufacturing firms, varying in size from around one hundred to over one thousand employees. None of the firms were particularly large, however. Information was collected concerning a variety of structural variables (such as span of control, organization size, levels of authority, degree of formalization, and so forth), and the relative success or effectiveness of the various enterprises.

Initially, Woodward focused her attention on the relation of organization size to structure. However, no consistent pattern of relationships emerged. (This absence of relationship may have been accounted for by the relatively restricted range in the sizes of the firms, as noted above.) Moreover, no association was found between either size or other structural variables and organizational success. These findings led Woodward (1958) to question the validity of the early "principles" of management; indeed, they did not appear to have universal applicability in all types of organizations.

In an effort to account for the variations in managerial practices and the absence of a clear structure-effectiveness association, the researchers decided to classify the organizations in their survey *by technology* into small batch (or unit), mass production, and continuous process categories (described above). Following this classification, a reanalysis of the data yielded several important findings (see Exhibit 4-2 for details):

1. There was no significant relationship between technological complexity and organizational size.
2. The span of control of first-level supervision increased from unit to mass production technology but then decreased markedly from mass production to continuous process technology.
3. The span of control of the chief executive increased with increasing technological complexity (from unit to mass to continuous process).
4. The number of levels of authority in an organization increased somewhat with increases in technological complexity.
5. The ratio of administrators to workers increased with increases in technological complexity.
6. The ratio of supporting staff and specialists to workers increased with increases in technological complexity.

EXHIBIT 4-2   Relationships Between Technological Variables and Organizational
Structure (after Woodward, 1965)

Structural Variables*	Unit, or Small Batch	Mass	Continuous Process
Supervisory span of control	23	48	15
Executive span of control	4	7	10
Number of levels of authority	3	4	6
Ratio of administrators to workers	9:1	4:1	1:1
Ratio of staff/specialists to workers	8:1	5:1	2:1
Relative labor costs	high	medium	low
Degree of formalization	high	low	high

*Data reported are median scores.

7. Relative labor costs decreased with increases in technological complexity.
8. Formalization (clear definitions of duties, rules, amount of
paperwork) was greatest under mass production technology, tapering off considerably under unit and continuous
process technologies.

Next, Woodward (1965) asked what impact these findings had
for the study of organizational effectiveness. Firms were classified
according to relative degree of success and, again, structure and
technology were compared. The surprising conclusion resulting
from this analysis was that "the organizational characteristics of
the successful firms in each production [that is, technology] category tended to cluster around the medians for that category as
a whole, while the figures of the firms classified below average
in success were found at the extremes of the range" (1965, p.
69). In other words, there appeared to be an optimal level for
several structural characteristics (such as span of control) for
successful firms in each of the three technological categories.
Less successful firms in each category exhibited structural ratios
that were either too large or too small. It is important to stress
here that the optimal level for success was different for each technological category.

Woodward (1965) concluded from these findings that "the
fact that organizational characteristics, technology, and success
were linked together in this way suggested that not only was the
system of production [that is, technology] an important variable
in the determination of organizational structure, but also that one
particular form of organization was most appropriate to each system of production" (pp. 69-71). In short, Woodward was arguing
in favor of a contingency approach to management whereby different technologies required different structures and interpersonal
styles. This *technological determinism* approach to a contingency
theory of management essentially proposes that under mass pro-

75

duction technology, a more highly structured, formalized, bureaucratic managerial style may be more appropriate for organizational success. However, at the two ends of the technological continuum (unit and continuous process), more successful firms employed less structured, less formalized managerial styles with fewer rules and controls and a greater degree of interpersonal interaction. As we shall see below, not all investigators have agreed with this position.

Pugh, Hickson, and Associates

A second major study that has focused on the relationship of technology and structure has been underway for over a decade by several British social scientists led by Pugh and Hickson. Collectively, this research team has become known as the "Aston Group" because much of the early research was carried out at the University of Aston. Although a good deal of this research has focused on relationships among structural variables alone, our primary focus here is on that part of the findings pertaining to the structure-technology relationship and organizational performance (Hickson et al., 1969; Pugh, 1973).

Hickson et al. (1969) view technology in terms of a general factor called *work-flow integration.* Included in this concept are such variables as the degree of task interdependence, the rigidity of work-flow sequences, the automation of equipment, and the specificity of evaluation of operations. The greater the automation, task specificity, and so forth, the greater the extent of work-flow integration. Using this concept, Hickson and his associates surveyed forty-six firms and calculated a numerical index of work-flow integration for each organization. Hickson et al., like Woodward, carried out their analysis on an organization-wide basis; that is, it was assumed that each organization employed only one general type of manufacturing or service technology.

Their index of work-flow integration was then compared to a variety of structural variables with several interesting results. To begin with, no general relationship was found between technological complexity and structural characteristics (specialization and standardization). This finding was in direct contradiction to the earlier findings by Woodward. "In general, our studies have confirmed that the relationship of technology to the main structural dimensions in manufacturing organizations are always very small and play a secondary role relative to other contextual features such as size and interdependence with other organizations. . . ." (Pugh, 1973, p. 32).

On a more detailed level of analysis, however, technology was found to be related to various aspects of structure in a number **76** of highly specific job ratios (termed *configurations* by Pugh and

Hickson). Specifically, Pugh, Hickson, and their associates found the same curvilinear relationship between span of control of first-line supervisors and technological complexity that had been found by Woodward. Moreover, the ratio of quality inspectors and maintenance personnel to workers was also greatest in mass production and tapered off for both unit and continuous process technologies.

When the findings of the Aston Group concerning technology are considered as a whole, however, there appear to be two related conclusions. First, the evidence indicates that "only those [structural characteristics] directly centered on the production workflow itself show any connection with technology. . . . Away from the shop floor, technology appears to have little influence on organization structure" (Pugh, 1973, p. 33). In other words, technology appears to affect organization structure only in those departments actually *using* the technology (for example, production); other departments (such as accounting or marketing) appear to be largely unaffected, according to these data. Second, and almost a corollary of the first point, the evidence appears to support the position that "the smaller the organization the more its structure will be pervaded by such technological effects; the larger the organization the more these effects will be confined to variables such as job counts of employees on activities linked to the work flow itself, and will not be detectable in variations of the more remote administrative and hierarchical structure" (Hickson et al., 1969, pp. 394–95).

Thus, Pugh, Hickson, and their associates interpret their findings within a contingency framework, whereby technology can affect the structural design of an organization but only as moderated by additional intervening variables, such as organization size or departmental function. In small organizations, technology largely dictates structure; in large organizations, technology dictates structure *only* in production-related units. Such findings raise questions concerning the validity of the technological determinism point of view advanced by some (including Woodward) that suggests that technology determines structure. The findings of the Aston Group would argue that such determinism is contingent upon several mediating variables (for example, size of organization, departmental function) that may serve to intervene in the technology-structure relationship. Moreover, it is possible that technological determinism may be operative for only specific aspects of structure (such as formalization, span of control) and not for others (complexity of department, levels of authority). In any event, although some disagreement exists concerning the exact role of technology, both studies clearly point to the relevance of this variable in any consideration of the determinants of organizational effectiveness.

77

Mahoney and Frost

Building upon the works of Woodward, the Aston Group, and others, Mahoney and Frost (1974) have attempted to further our understanding of the role of technology in organizational effectiveness by building an empirical model of effectiveness on the basis of variations in technology. They begin by suggesting that technological variation is best understood and studied on a department-to-department level, instead of an organization-to-organization level. Thus, in contrast to Woodward and the Aston studies, the Mahoney and Frost study clearly recognizes and accounts for the fact that different departments of an organization may employ different technologies.

Their study included 297 organizational units (departments and divisions) from business and industrial firms. Managers were asked to provide information on the units reporting to them concerning work processes and functions performed, size, and skill levels of employees. In addition, they were asked to rate their units on twenty-four specific facets of unit effectiveness (such as planning, development, initiative, cooperation, and so forth) and one global measure of overall unit effectiveness. Each of the units was then classified according to technology following the typology proposed by Thompson (1967): long-linked, mediating, and intensive technology.

Initially, attention was focused on the general relationship between effectiveness and technology. As hypothesized, no direct relationship was found between these two variables. Instead, an indirect relationship was found in which the more important facets of effectiveness varied with the technology of the organizational unit. That is, of the twenty-four facets of effectiveness used, managers saw different ones as being more closely related to *overall* unit effectiveness for each type of technology.

The results of this analysis are summarized in Exhibit 4-3. This exhibit lists in rank order those factors that were seen by managers as being most strongly related to overall effectiveness for units in each technological category; the less important factors (those contributing less to overall effectiveness) have been omitted from the exhibit.

As can be seen from this exhibit, different dimensions are seen by managers as being more important contributors to overall effectiveness for each of the technological categories. For long-linked technology (for example, stenographic pools, data processing input units), the major contributors to overall effectiveness (in rank order) were planning, efficient utilization of employee skills for task performance, tight supervisory controls, and reliability and predictability. Such a description is consistent with typical descriptions of mechanistic work environments (Burns & Stalker, 1961).

EXHIBIT 4-3 Major Contributing Factors to Effectiveness by Technology (after
           Mahoney & Frost, 1974)

Long-linked Technology	Mediating Technology	Intensive Technology
1. Planning	1. Flexibility	1. Performance
2. Performance	2. Planning	2. Cooperation
3. Supervisory control	3. Performance	3. Development
4. Reliability	4. Supervisory control	4. Staffing

Note: The major contributing factors are listed in rank order of importance as they influence effectiveness.

For mediating technology (for example, clerks in an insurance claims department), on the other hand, effectiveness is seen primarily as a function of planning, performance, and supervisory control, plus an ability to remain flexible and adapt to the particular needs of the moment. Remember that mediating technology is characterized by the existence of a set of standard procedures from which the employee selects the most appropriate for a given task. Thus, flexibility, or the capacity to select the correct alternative, becomes an important ingredient in successful task accomplishment here. Finally, intensive technology, which is characterized by a lack of standardized or repetitious procedures (such as an experimental research laboratory), requires more attention to developing an integrated work team, according to these findings. In order to be effective, such units should be characterized by a high degree of problem-oriented performance, a cooperative "team spirit," an emphasis on developing or training members, and staffing [by which Mahoney and Frost mean "interchangeability of personnel among assignments; promotion from within" (p. 129)]. In short, the ideal intensive technology work environment closely resembles Burns and Stalker's (1961) conception of an organic environment.

In summary, a primary contribution of the research carried out by Mahoney and Frost (1974) lies in its capacity to identify clearly the more important influences on organizational effectiveness by technology as seen by managers. It must be remembered, however, that we are dealing here with managerial perceptions and attitudes concerning what constitutes an effective organization.

Additional Studies of Technological Influence

Several other studies have also examined the impact of technology on organizational processes and performance. These studies, along with the ones reviewed above, are summarized in Exhibit 4-4. This exhibit includes the samples under study, the manner **79**

EXHIBIT 4-4   Studies of Technology, Structure, and Organizational Effectiveness

Investigator(s)	Measure of Technology	Dependent Variable(s) under Study	Findings
Woodward (1958, 1965) 100 British manufacturing firms	Firms classified into small batch (unit), mass production, or continuous process, according to production process.	Structural variables (span of control, levels of authority, ratio of managers to other personnel); effectiveness measure (general level of organizational performance and success—see text for details).	(1) Levels of authority & ratio of managers to personnel increased with technological complexity; (2) labor costs decreased with technological complexity; (3) span of control was related to technological complexity as an inverted U-function; (4) successful firms tended to cluster at the midpoints on various structural continua (e.g., span of control); less successful firms clustered at the end points on such continua. In short, it is argued that effective firms employ structures that conform to their technologies.
Lawrence & Lorsch (1967) 10 industrial firms	Technical rate of change, information uncertainty, & feedback timespan.	Amount of differentiation & integration between departments.	Results interpreted as supporting a strong relation between technological variation & increased differentiation between departments.
Harvey (1968) 43 industrial firms	Firms placed on continuum of "technological diffuseness" (number of product changes, number of products produced).	Measures of internal "structure": (1) degree of specialization; (2) centralization; (3) span of control; & (4) program specification.	Organizations with more stable (i.e. less changing) technologies exhibited higher degrees of structuring on all four dependent variables. Findings held with organization size and other variables held constant.
Meyer (1968) State & local departments of finance	Introduction of automated equipment.	Number of levels in hierarchy, span of control.	Introduction of automated equipment led to increased number of levels & span of control.
Hage & Aiken (1969) 16 social welfare agencies	Routineness of task.	Structural variables of degree of participation in decision making, amount of autonomy, measures of affect & distance between supervisors & subordinates, & formalization.	Significant negative correlation between routine technology & participation in decision making; positive relation between routineness and formalization; no relation between routineness and other structural variables.

Study	Technology variables	Structural/effectiveness variables	Findings
Hickson et al. (1969) 46 service & manufacturing firms	Automation of equipment, rigidity of workflow sequences, interdependence of workflow segments, & specificity of evaluation.	Structural variables of span of control, ratio of managers to total personnel, specialization, standardization of procedures, formalization, centralization.	Weak relationship between technology and structure found. Data suggest that technology may affect structure & effectiveness in small organizations; in large firms, technological influence will be confined solely to production units & should not affect other units.
Fullan (1970) 3 Canadian firms (printing, auto, & oil); $N = 149$ subjects	Firms classified into craft, mass production, & continuous process (after Woodward, 1958).	Amount of perceived worker integration (i.e., co-worker & supervisory relations; labor-management harmony; company identification).	Workers in continuous process technology felt highest degree of worker integration, followed by craft workers; mass production workers felt least integration.
Zwerman (1970) 55 U.S. manufacturing firms	Firms classified into small batch, mass production, or continuous process (after Woodward, 1958).	Span of control, levels of authority, size & other structural variables. Firms classified according to success levels.	(1) No simple structural correlates of operating success; (2) replicated Woodward's findings concerning relation of technology & structural characteristics, except found no relation between technology & span of control (in contrast to Woodward). General conclusion that production technology closely related to structural characteristics.
Mohr (1971) 144 work groups in 13 local health departments	Uniformity, complexity, & analyzability of tasks.	Structural variable (degree of supervisory participativeness); effectiveness variables (attitudes, innovativeness, work output).	Moderate relation found between "task manageability" and participativeness. However, it is argued based on the findings that no relation exists between the degree of congruence between technology & structure & resulting effectiveness.
Hrebiniak (1974) 210 subjects in various departments of a major hospital	Jobs classified according to operations & materials technology (Hickson et al., 1969), task predictability, task interdependence, & task manageability.	Structural variables (job autonomy, participation, closeness of supervision, formalization, unity of control) & supervisory behavior.	No clear relation between technology & structure, although certain technological variables were found to be significantly related to some structural variables when supervisory behavior was held constant.
Mahoney & Frost (1974) 297 organizational units in 17 business firms	Units classified into long-linked, mediating, & intensive technologies (after Thompson, 1967).	14 facets of effectiveness (e.g., performance, planning, reliability, coordination, development, etc.—see text for details).	No direct relationship between technology & effectiveness. However, regression analyses indicated different technologies were related to different facets of effectiveness. Authors suggest different models of effectiveness based on type of departmental technology.

in which technology was measured, the dependent variables (aspects of structure and/or effectiveness), and the more significant findings that emerged from the investigation.

When these results are compared to the Woodward, Aston, and Mahoney and Frost studies, several important conclusions emerge. To begin with, before considering technological variations, no consistent or simple relationship was found between organization structure (that is, variations in the degree of complexity, formalization, levels of authority, size, and so forth) and organizational success (see, for example, Zwerman, 1970). In other words, there is no universally desirable structure that can facilitate effectiveness in any environment. Such a conclusion is generally consistent with the studies reviewed earlier in this chapter and indicates that management must understand the uniqueness of its own organization's situation and structure its resources accordingly.

Second, the evidence is equally clear in demonstrating the absence of any simple relationship between technological complexity and overall effectiveness, although there does appear to be some relationship between technology and worker attitudes (Fullan, 1970). In a study of employees working in a variety of technological settings, Fullan found that workers in continuous process technologies were more satisfied and identified with the company to a greater extent than did employees in mass production organizations.

Third, the majority of the available evidence tends to support the contention that technological complexity or variation affects the resulting structure of an organization to a substantial degree. For example, Harvey (1968) found that the more stable an organization's technology was, the greater was its degree of "structuring" (that is, higher specialization, centralization, task specification, and so on). Thus, an automotive firm, which has a highly stable technology, exhibits far more structuring behavior than an aerospace R&D firm, where the technological state is much more volatile. Similar findings concerning the impact of technological stability on structure have emerged in a wide variety of organizations (see, for example, Hage & Aiken, 1969; Hrebiniak, 1974; Meyer, 1968; Zwerman, 1970).

These findings, which on the surface provide support for the technological determinism hypothesis, appear to be largely in conflict with the findings of the Aston Group. For instance, although Hickson et al. (1969) found support for technological determinism only for small organizations, Harvey (1968) found such support in his study of industrial firms of varying sizes both before and after organization size was controlled for. The majority of the evidence appears to support Harvey's conclusions. Thus, it would

82

appear, based on these findings, that technology does indeed often play a central role in the determination of organizational structure.

Finally, we come to the issue of how technology and structure *jointly* relate to effectiveness. Although it has been demonstrated that neither technology nor structure by itself shows any appreciable relationship to effectiveness, several investigations have suggested the existence of an interactive relationship between these two variables as they affect ultimate organizational success. This contention has been called the *consonance hypothesis* (Mohr, 1971). Specifically, it has been argued that organizational effectiveness is largely a result of the extent to which an organization can successfully match its technology with an appropriate structure. Thus, an organization that employs very routine, repetitive technology, for example, may perform best when it relies on a highly formalized structure. Evidence in support of the consonance hypothesis can be found in several studies (for example, Burns & Stalker, 1961; Lawrence & Lorsch, 1967; Perrow, 1967; Zwerman, 1970).

Others take issue with the validity of the hypothesis, however, arguing that such factors as "social-class traditions" may affect structure far more than technology (Mohr, 1971; Pennings, 1975). Although the data from these latter studies clearly do not reject the hypothesis in its entirety, they do suggest the existence of a series of individual and social factors, which have been ignored in earlier studies on technology, that might influence effectiveness. It may be necessary, therefore, to expand the consonance hypothesis to include a recognition of the role of human behavior. Thus, effectiveness may be seen as a function of an organization's ability to successfully integrate technology, structure, *and* personal characteristics and social factors into a congruent, goal-oriented entity. For instance, not only would the use of assembly-line technology call for a structured approach to organizing human resources but in addition it would suggest the need for individuals who were willing—and had the capacity—to work in such an environment (see, for example, Kornhauser, 1965). It appears that the inclusion of this human variable in any consideration of the technology-structure relation would increase considerably our understanding of organizational dynamics and success. We shall return to this point after we have examined more closely the nature of individual motivation and performance in organizational settings.

5 ENVIRONMENT AND ORGANIZATIONAL EFFECTIVENESS

In addition to organizational characteristics such as structure and technology, a second critical dimension for organizational success is the task environment. These environmental influences can be viewed on two levels. First, there is the external environment, which generally represents those forces outside the organization itself (for example, market conditions, economic conditions, and so on). Second, there is the internal environment, representing those factors inside the organization that create the cultural and social milieu where goal-directed activities take place. This internal environment has also been called "organizational climate." As we shall see, although the external environment is usually characterized by largely objective phenomena (for example, unemployment rates, market share, governmental regulations), the internal environment, or climate, is largely perceptual in nature. These differences will become apparent in the discussions below concerning how each set of factors contributes to or influences organizational effectiveness. This chapter will focus principally on the external environment; consideration of the internal environment is reserved for the following chapter.

The external environment will be examined from three perspectives: First, the various ways in which environment is conceptualized will be considered. The focus here will be on what is meant by environment and what are the relevant dimensions of the concept. Following this discussion, the more important empirical studies that have examined the relationship of environment, structure, and organizational success will be reviewed. Finally, several conclusions will be drawn based on these findings concerning the role of environment in effective organizations.

NATURE OF THE EXTERNAL ENVIRONMENT

There are at least three ways in which to conceptualize an organization's external environment. To begin with, it is possible to view the environment as everything the organization is not. In other words, it is what is "left over" after one defines the boundaries of an organization. Such an approach has several problems, however. First, as noted in Chapter 1, there is an absence of agreement as to what actually constitutes an organization. If we cannot specify precisely the dimensions of an organization, defining its complement as the environment (that is, environment = 1 minus organization) becomes at best an imprecise science. Moreover, as noted by Starbuck (1976), there may in fact be no such thing as an identifiable organizational boundary. That is, if we follow a systems perspective, it is difficult to identify the point where organization leaves off and environment begins. For instance, are stockholders members of an organization or are they part of the external environment? Finally, even if it were possible to specify organizational boundaries in a precise fashion and to identify the components of an organization, such an approach still contributes little to an understanding of the nature or form of the external environment.

A somewhat different approach to the environmental conceptualization problem has been taken by several sociologists and management theorists (Brown, 1969; Dill, 1958; Thompson, 1967). Specifically, these researchers focus on the concept of *task environment*. Task environment is seen as that portion of the total setting which is relevant for organizational goal-setting and goal-directed activities. Examples of the more important aspects of task environment include customers, suppliers, competitors, and regulatory groups. Although some formulations of task environment include both internal and external factors (Dill, 1958), we shall focus principally on external factors in this chapter.

The task environment concept has several advantages over the previous approach. To begin with, it clearly identifies several aspects of environment and allows for greater precision in discussions concerning environmental relations or impact. In addition, it facilitates an understanding of the interactive effects among the components of environment. For example, specifying various components allows for the recognition that competitors (one aspect of environment) may affect one's customers (another aspect of environment), forcing a response from the organization. We shall return to the notion of task environment throughout the remainder of this chapter as we discuss various attempts to put organization-environment relations in perspective.

The third approach to viewing the environment is somewhat more abstract but is useful for comparing one organization's envi- **85** ronment to another's on a more general level. Instead of identifying specific components of the environment, this approach attempts to specify several major *dimensions* of the task environment (Duncan, 1972; Emery & Trist, 1965; Terreberry, 1968; Thompson, 1967). These dimensions are generally viewed on a continuum. Three major interrelated dimensions can be identified: simple-complex, static-dynamic, and environmental uncertainty.

Simple-Complex Dimension

The simple-complex dimension assists us in understanding an organization's external environment by raising questions concerning the complexity and qualitative nature of the evnironment. A simple, or placid, environment is one in which the external factors with which an organization must deal are few in number and are relatively homogeneous. For example, consider a company that exclusively manufactures spark plugs for the major automotive companies. Its product line is restricted, its technology is fairly stable, and its market is relatively constant. Moreover, its customers are few in number. In short, it exists in a fairly simple environment.

Contrast that example with a company that builds commercial aircraft. The manufacture of various components of such aircraft are subcontracted to dozens of other firms, increasing significantly the coordination problems among major production units. Moreover, other components (for example, jet engines) must be purchased from still other companies. The technological aspects of manufacture are tremendously complex and varied. And the final product must meet not only the specifications of domestic and foreign airline companies who purchase such aircraft but in addition a series of government regulations. Such an environment is certainly a more complex one than that of the company manufacturing spark plugs.

Just as the manufacture and sale of a spark plug differs from that of a Boeing 747 aircraft both in terms of complexity and cost (approximately $1 versus $25 million), so, too, are there differences in the manner in which an organization must manage itself in response to such divergent environments. Thus, the degree of environmental complexity can have a significant impact both on organizational behavior and on organizational effectiveness as we shall see presently.

Static-Dynamic Dimension

In addition to the issue of environmental complexity, one must also consider the relative degree of stability in organization-environment relations. For example, compare the stability of our automotive parts company, which will make spark plugs year after year, to an aerospace firm, which may receive a contract to build a satellite one year and modular houses the next. One environment is fairly stable; the other is quite dynamic. Environments that are in a constant state of flux often require quite different organizational structures and approaches to management than do more static, predictable environments.

To complicate the picture further, it should be recognized that the static-dynamic dimension is, in reality, a multifaceted phenomenon. Certain portions of the environment may remain static, while others change radically over time. The automobile companies in the 1970s provide a good example of this. While the production technology of automotive manufacturing has remained very stable, with few new technological breakthroughs, the marketing component of the environment changed dramatically as people shifted from large cars to small cars to no cars and back again. In part, this volatile marketing environment was a function of environmental complexity (for example, oil prices, general economic conditions, governmental regulations). Even so, such environmental turbulence had little effect on the stability of the *technological* environment.

Environmental Uncertainty

We thus have at least two important dimensions on which external environments can be compared as they relate to organizational dynamics. Moreover, it has been pointed out that one dimension can at times affect the other dimension as both influence an organization's capacity to adapt and respond successfully to environmental stimuli.

A major reason for the importance of these two dimensions in understanding organizational dynamics is their influence on the degree of certainty or uncertainty with which organizations can make decisions concerning future courses of action. Environmental uncertainty is a result of three conditions: (1) a lack of information concerning the environmental factors associated with a particular organizational decision-making situation; (2) an inability to accurately assign probabilities with regard to how environmental factors will affect the success or failure of a decision unit in performing its functions; and (3) a lack of information regarding the costs associated with an incorrect decision or action (Duncan, 1972).

In an effort to integrate the stability and complexity dimensions with the issue of uncertainty in organizational decision making, Duncan (1972) has proposed a model that attempts to describe the environmental states resulting from such interrelationships (see Exhibit 5-1). The model builds upon the earlier theoretical formulations of Thompson (1967), Emery and Trist (1965), and **87**

Terreberry (1968). In essence, it is suggested that the "static-simple" environments contain the least amount of uncertainty for organizational planners and decision makers, and the "dynamic-complex" environments contain the greatest amount of uncertainty.

An empirical investigation provided general support for the model (Duncan, 1972, 1973). Not only was the dynamic-complex environment found to be associated with the largest amount of perceived environmental uncertainty but in addition it was discovered that the static-dynamic dimension was a more important contributor to perceived uncertainty than the simple-complex dimension. Commenting on his findings, Duncan (1972) concluded:

> Decision units with dynamic environments always experience significantly more uncertainty in decision making regardless of whether their environment is simple or complex. The difference in perceived uncertainty between decision units with simple and complex environments is not significant, unless the decision unit's environment is also dynamic. (p. 325)

This conceptual framework should help the organizational analyst not only to understand the results of the investigations reviewed below but also to see how such findings fit together to provide useful information concerning the role of the external environment in organizational processes.

EXHIBIT 5-1 Characteristics of Various Environmental States

	Simple	Complex
Static	CELL 1: *Low Perceived Uncertainty* 1. Small number of factors and components in the environment 2. Factors and components are somewhat similar to one another 3. Factors and components remain basically the same and are not changing	CELL 2: *Moderately Low Perceived Uncertainty* 1. Large number of factors and components in the environment 2. Factors and components are not similar to one another 3. Factors and components remain basically the same
Dynamic	CELL 3: *Moderately High Perceived Uncertainty* 1. Small number of factors and components in the environment 2. Factors and components are somewhat similar to one another 3. Factors and components of the environment are in continual process of change	CELL 4: *High Perceived Uncertainty* 1. Large number of factors and components in the environment 2. Factors and components are not similar to one another 3. Factors and components of environment are in a continual process of change

Source: R. B. Duncan, "The Characteristics of Organizational Environments and Perceived Environmental Uncertainty," *Administrative Science Quarterly*, 1972, *17*, p. 320.

ENVIRONMENT, STRUCTURE, AND EFFECTIVENESS

Several important studies have been carried out that have examined in some detail the nature of organization-environment relations as they jointly affect the success of an enterprise. Four of these studies will be briefly examined here in order to determine more precisely the role played by environmental factors in ongoing organizations. Attention should be paid to the concepts of stability, complexity, and uncertainty in each of these investigations. Following this review, an attempt will be made to integrate these findings and assess our level of understanding concerning the importance of environmental variation as a determinant of organizational effectiveness.

Burns and Stalker

In one of the earliest studies of organization-environment relations, Burns and Stalker (1961) surveyed twenty British industrial firms in an effort to identify relationships between certain environmental characteristics and resulting managerial practices. The organizations studied consisted largely of concerns with interests in electronics. The aspect of environment upon which these researchers focused was the rates of change in both the relevant technology and market. In other words, Burns and Stalker focused on environmental stability as it related to managerial behavior.

Based on their analysis, it was concluded that there existed two relatively distinct approaches to management and that these approaches were in large measure a function of the relative degree of stability in the external environment. These two styles of management were called *mechanistic* and *organic*. As indicated in Exhibit 5-2, the characteristics of these two styles are quite different from one another. Mechanistic systems, on the one hand, are characterized by centralization of control and authority, a high degree of task specialization, and primarily vertical (and particularly downward) lines of communication. Organic systems, on the other hand, generally exhibit a higher degree of task interdependence, greater decentralization of control and authority, and more horizontal (that is, between departments) communication. Moreover, mechanistic systems are seen as relatively fixed and inflexible entities, while organic systems are viewed as being more flexible and adaptable.

Burns and Stalker argued that each system of management had its proper place in organizational effectiveness. In highly stable and predictable environments, where market and technological conditions remain largely unchanged over time (for example, automotive industry), the mechanistic system may be the more appropriate design. Because the environment is highly predictable **89**

EXHIBIT 5-2   Comparison of Mechanistic and Organic Systems of Organization

Mechanistic	Organic
1. Tasks are highly fractionated and specialized; little regard paid to clarifying relationship between tasks and organizational objectives.	1. Tasks are more interdependent; emphasis on relevance of tasks and organizational objectives.
2. Tasks tend to remain rigidly defined unless altered formally by top management.	2. Tasks are continually adjusted and redefined through interaction of organizational members.
3. Specific role definition (rights, obligations, and technical methods prescribed for each member).	3. Generalized role definition (members accept general responsibility for task accomplishment beyond individual role definition).
4. Hierarchic structure of control, authority, and communication. Sanctions derive from employment contract between employee and organization.	4. Network structure of control, authority, and communication. Sanctions derive more from community of interest than from contractual relationship.
5. Information relevant to situation and operations of the organization formally assumed to rest with chief executive.	5. Leader not assumed to be omniscient; knowledge centers identified where located throughout organization.
6. Communication is primarily vertical between superior and subordinate.	6. Communication is both vertical and horizontal, depending upon where needed information resides.
7. Communications primarily take form of instructions and decisions issued by superiors, of information and requests for decisions supplied by inferiors.	7. Communications primarily take form of information and advice.
8. Insistence on loyalty to organization and obedience to superiors.	8. Commitment to organization's tasks and goals more highly valued than loyalty or obedience.
9. Importance and prestige attached to identification with organization and its members.	9. Importance and prestige attached to affiliations and expertise in external environment.

Source: Adapted from T. Burns and G. M. Stalker, *The Management of Innovations* (London: Tavistock, 1961), pp. 119–22. Used by permission.

under such conditions, it is possible to routinize tasks and centralize directions in order to maximize efficiency and effectiveness of operation. (Note that Burns and Stalker do not suggest that such a system of management is personally satisfying to employees, only that it is efficient.) Where the environment is in a constant state of flux, however, and where an organization has to change direction constantly to adapt to its environment (such as in the aerospace industry), organic systems appear to be more appropriate because of their added flexibility and adaptability. Thus, Burns and Stalker really argue for what might be termed an *environmental determinism* point of view, where the most effective organization design is determined as a function of external factors. The role of management thus becomes one of properly understanding environmental conditions and adapting organizational structure and practices to meet and exploit such conditions.

Chandler

Taking an historical and evolutionary approach to the study of organizational effectiveness, Chandler (1962) traced the growth and development of nearly one hundred major U.S. business concerns. Based on these case studies, he concluded that each major change in the design or structure of these organizations resulted from environmental shifts that necessitated such changes. More specifically, changes in the external environment (that is, customers, markets, sources of supply, and so on) were seen as creating demands on an organization to modify its strategies (goals and tactics) for dealing with the environment. These strategic changes, in turn, necessitated modifications in organizational structure so that it would be consistent with the revised strategy. As Chandler (1962) describes it:

> Strategic growth resulted from an awareness of the opportunities and needs—created by changing population, income, and technology—to employ existing or expanding resources more profitably. A new strategy required a new or at least refashioned structure if the . . . enterprise was to be operated efficiently. The failure to develop a new internal structure, like the failure to respond to new external opportunities and needs, was a consequence of overconcentration on operational activities by the executives responsible for the destiny of their enterprises, or from their inability, because of past training and education and present position, to develop an entrepreneurial outlook. (pp. 18–19)

Chandler sums up his point by adding that growth or change "without structural adjustment can lead only to economic inefficiency" (1962, p. 19). By way of example, he cites Henry Ford's venture into farm tractors in the late 1930s. In an effort to expand his base of operations and find substitutes for the declining automobile market of the time, Ford and his engineering staff designed and built an inexpensive tractor that had the potential of competing effectively against the existing tractors then on the market. However, Ford attempted to sell his tractors through his car dealerships, which were largely inexperienced in farm needs and which were principally located in cities. The new tractor failed commercially until a new structure (particularly a new marketing structure) was designed that was consistent with Ford's marketing goals and strategy. Chandler concludes: "The incredibly bad management of his enormous industrial empire, which was so clearly reflected by the lack of any systematic organizational structure, not only prevented the Ford Motor Company from carrying out a **91** strategy of diversification but also helped cause the rapid drop in Ford's profits and share of the market" (Chandler, 1972, p. 462).

The point here is not to single out one company for criticism. On the contrary, many examples can be cited in which organizations showed an inability to adapt structure to corporate strategies and goals. Instead, the point is to recognize that a key factor in effectiveness and efficiency is often the ability of managers to properly comprehend their environment, make strategic decisions based upon such knowledge, and then organize their human resources around these strategic decisions.

Lawrence and Lorsch

Following the lead of these earlier studies, Lawrence and Lorsch (1967) carried out an extensive investigation of environmental influences on organization design and effectiveness among a small sample of American firms. They began by posing four specific research questions:

1. How are the environmental demands facing various organizations different, and how do environmental demands relate to the internal functioning of effective organizations?
2. Is it true that organizations in certain or stable environments make more exclusive use of the formal hierarchy to attain integration, and, if so, why? Because less integration is required, or because in a certain environment these decisions can be made more effectively at higher organization levels or by fewer people?
3. Is the same degree of differentiation in orientation and in departmental structure found in organizations in different industrial environments?
4. If greater differentiation among functional departments is required in different industries, does this influence the problems of integrating the organization's parts? Does it influence the organization's means of achieving integration? (p. 16)

In an effort to find suitable answers to these questions, Lawrence and Lorsch studied organization-environment relations in three widely divergent industries: plastics, packaged foods, and standardized containers. Firms in the plastics industry were typically characterized by a high degree of uncertainty and unpredictability concerning their external environment. The rate of technological innovation and shifts in market demands in this industry were quite high, requiring organizations to change products, procedures—and sometimes structures—fairly rapidly. The container industry, on the other hand, was typically characterized by a highly stable and predictable environment. Competition in this industry centered around the quality of the product or service, instead of on product innovation, as was the case in the plastics industry. In between the plastics and container industries in terms of environmental stability came the packaged foods companies. These latter organizations were characterized by a moderate amount of predictability and stability in environmental relations.

The central issue concerning Lawrence and Lorsch in their research focused on how organizations adapted structurally to diverse external environments and which adaptation processes were generally more successful. Structural variations within organizations were defined in terms of the amount of *differentiation* and *integration* existing within each organization. Differentiation, as defined by Lawrence and Lorsch (1967, p. 11), refers to "the difference in cognitive and emotional orientation among managers in different functional departments." Thus, it refers not only to the degree of specialization of labor or departmentalization, but also to what might be termed the "psychological" departmentalization (that is, the extent to which managers in different departments are characterized by different attitudinal and behavioral orientations). The greater the psychological distance between managers in different departments, the greater the differentiation.

On the other hand, integration refers to "the quality of the state of collaboration that exists among departments that are required to achieve unity of effort by the demands of the environment" (p. 11). In short, integration refers to the nature and quality of interdepartmental relations, as well as the processes by which such relations are achieved. Such integration can be brought about by several means, including the creation of rules and standard operating procedures that govern behavior, plans and objectives, and mutual adjustment and agreement.

Several important findings emerged from the investigation. To begin with, as indicated in Exhibit 5-3, organizations operating in more dynamic and complex environments (such as plastics) tended to exhibit a greater degree of differentiation between functional departments than did those firms operating in less turbulent

EXHIBIT 5-3   Average Differentiation and Integration Across 3 Environments*

Industry	Organization	Average Differentiation	Average Integration
Plastics	High Performer	10.7	5.6
	Low Performer	9.0	5.1
Foods	High Performer	8.0	5.3
	Low Performer	6.5	5.0
Containers	High Performer	5.7	5.7
	Low Performer	5.7	4.8

*Higher differentiation scores mean greater differences between functional units; higher integration scores mean higher degrees of integration.

Source: P. R. Lawrence and J. W. Lorsch, *Organization and Environment* (Boston: Division of Research, Graduate School of Business Administration, Harvard University Press, 1967), p. 103. Used by permission of Harvard University, copyright by the President and Fellows of Harvard College.

environments (such as containers). The more effective plastics firm had a score of 10.7 on the differentiation measure, compared to 5.7 for both container firms. The packaged foods firms, which operated in a moderately dynamic environment, exhibited a moderate degree of differentiation. In other words, the greater the instability in the external environment, the more psychological distance was needed between departments in order to be effective.

Second, it was noted that, with one exception, more successful firms within each industry had higher scores on both differentiation and integration. Thus, it would appear that one component of organizational effectiveness, as defined and measured here, is the capacity of an organization to achieve an optimal balance of differentiation and integration that is consistent with environmental demands. One hallmark of less effective organizations, accordingly, is an inability to grant various departments sufficient latitude and autonomy to increase their contribution to organizational goals through functional specialization, as well as an inability to devise sufficient means to integrate and coordinate these diverse departments for the common good.

Finally, it was concluded that different environments call for different structural approaches to integration. In the dynamic plastics industry, the more effective organization employed a formal integrating department, whose function was to insure that the various functional areas worked toward common goals. In the moderately dynamic food packaging industry, the more effective organization used individual integrators; that is, individuals whose primary responsibility was to insure mutuality of purpose. Finally, in the more stable containers industry, integration was facilitated in the more effective organization by direct managerial contact through the chain of command. Thus, when we consider the *effective* organizations in the study, each is characterized by an ability to establish a vehicle for integration that is commensurate with its respective environment. The more complex the environment, the more elaborate the integrative mechanisms.

In summary, Lawrence and Lorsch (1967) emphasize the need for an organization to understand its environment and to structure itself accordingly. Although the nature and scope of these findings are more comprehensive than those reported by Burns and Stalker, Chandler, and others, the basic conclusions are the same. That is, environment does play an important role in the relation between structuring activities and organizational success.

Osborn and Hunt

More recently, Osborn and Hunt (1974) carried out a study that focused specifically on environmental complexity as it relates to
94 effectiveness in a sample of social-service agencies. Environ-

mental complexity was viewed here as being composed of three interrelated variables: (1) the amount of risk involved in organization-environment relations; (2) enviornmental dependency, or the degree to which an organization relies upon elements in the environment for growth and survival; and (3) the nature (that is, favorableness or unfavorableness) of interorganizational relationships. Based on these three dimensions of complexity, several specific research questions were posed:

1. Are the proposed task environment variables significantly related to organizational effectiveness? Specifically, is risk negatively associated with effectiveness, is dependency positively associated with effectiveness, and is interorganizational interaction positively associated with effectiveness?
2. To what extent do combinations of risk, dependency, and interorganizational interaction predict better than each variable alone?
3. To what extent are two- and three-way interactive combinations of risk, dependency, and interorganizational interaction associated with effectiveness? (p. 236)

The results of this study indicated that the degree of risk present in the external environment was unrelated to effectiveness. However, both environmental dependency and interorganizational interaction were found to be positively and significantly related to measures of effectiveness. Of the three environmental variables, though, interorganizational interaction (the ability of an organization to develop favorable exchange relations with its environment) was found to be most closely associated with effectiveness. As Osborn and Hunt (1974) conclude:

Regardless of the level of risk or dependency, one point seems to stand out. The manner in which the organization attempts to link itself with the environment has an important influence on effectiveness. (p. 241)

The major thrust of these findings, then, largely failed to support the initial hypotheses. Instead, the ability of an organization to develop favorable environmental relations and, to a lesser degree, environmental dependency were positively related to effectiveness, while risk was unrelated. (The authors did point out, however, that the degree ot heterogeneity among the task environments under study may not have been sufficient to secure an adequate measure of environmental risk.) In any event, a strong case was made for the importance of a high degree of interorganizational interaction and external support as prerequisites for organizational success.

PREDICTABILITY, PERCEPTION, AND RATIONALITY IN ENVIRONMENTAL RELATIONS

A review of the above studies concerning environmental effects on organizational success reveals at least three major themes, or factors, that are found fairly consistently throughout **95** the studies. These three factors are: (1) the degree of predictability of environmental states; (2) the accuracy of perception of environmental states; and (3) the notion of rationality in organizational actions. It would appear that these three factors, when taken together, represent the critical variables in any discussions concerning the impact of organization-enviornment relations on organizational effectiveness. Moreover, as will be seen below, these three variables seem to be related to one another in a fairly consistent fashion.

Predictability of Environmental States

First, let us consider the issue of predictability of environmental states. When we discuss the degree of complexity and stability in the environment, we are in effect raising questions about the degree of uncertainty in organization-environment relations. The greater the uncertainty, the less the predictability. The capacity of an organization to successfully adapt to its environment is facilitated to a large extent by its ability to know what the external environment is going to be like in the future. The more certain managers are about future environmental states, the more opportunity they have to respond accordingly. For example, managers in the plastics firms discussed by Lawrence and Lorsch (1967) were not unduly hampered by the instability of their market so long as their organization was structured in such a way as to accommodate market changes with relative ease (that is, they had the appropriate amount of differentiation and integration).

Thus, environmental instability is not necessarily detrimental

EXHIBIT 5-4   Hypothesized Environmental Influences on Organizational Effectiveness

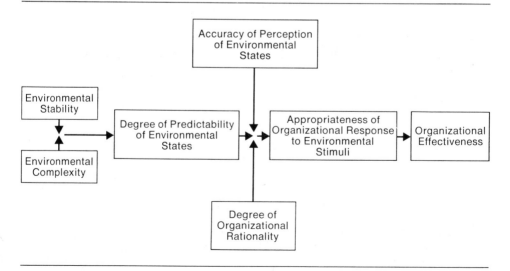

to effectiveness. Instead, its impact on organizational adaptation appears to be more a function of the extent to which the instability (and the direction of such changes) can be predicted in advance with some degree of certainty. Recent research would indicate that if the environment is highly unpredictable, a more organic structure may be more effective, and a mechanistic structure may be more appropriate for predictable environments. In conclusion, then, it would appear that the greater the predictability concerning environmental states, the greater the *potential* for appropriate organizational response (see Exhibit 5-4).

Perception of Environmental States

There appear to be at least two "filters" that may affect the ultimate response of an organization to the existing environmental state. First, there is the problem of the accuracy with which management perceives the environment. As pointed out by Weick (1969) and others, managers respond to what they perceive and such perceptions may or may not correspond to objective reality. Weick calls this the "enacted" (or created) environment. If management accurately perceives the degrees of complexity, stability, and uncertainty existing in the external environment, the probability of appropriate organizational response and adaptation would appear to be enhanced. If, on the other hand, an organization "enacts" an unrealistic environment (either through managerial myopia, lack of expertise, insufficient time, or whatever), the negative effects on organizational success could be substantial.

The real question concerning perceptions of environment is which cues are picked up by organizational decision makers. Managers both as individuals and as a group often exhibit certain response biases concerning what they see or how they see it. This phenomenon has been alternatively referred to as the "organization man" syndrome, the "corporate mentality," "group-think," and other such phrases (Whyte, 1956). Executive managers work together, socialize together, and often think along similar lines. Thus, it is not surprising that their perceptions of the environment may be filtered by similar work experiences and professional associations. When these perceptions are in error, or when only part of the relevant cues are received from the environment, decisions concerning appropriate responses are made on the basis of distorted or incomplete information. Such behavior can severely constrain the utility of organizational response.

Degree of Organizational Rationality

A second problem that can affect managerial reaction to environmental events deals with the extent to which managers behave **97** in a rational manner in environmentally-relevant decisions and actions. Although organizations may strive for rational behavior, it has long been recognized that the attainment of such rationality is often impossible. Because of insufficient information for a particular decision or because of a decision maker's inability to adequately process all the relevant information, managers more than likely engage in some form of *bounded rationality* (Simon, 1957). That is, they attempt to optimize instead of maximize on the quality of their decisions. The concept of rationality is important here for the following reason. No matter how predicatable the environment and no matter how accurate the perceptions concerning environmental states, organizations and managers still have to determine a course of action to respond to changes in the environment. Hence, the more rational the choice processes are in terms of selection among viable alternatives, the greater the probability is that the chosen response will be appropriate to meet environmental demands.

This point should become clearer when we consider the example of the Women's Christian Temperance Union. During the era of prohibition, the WCTU was an active and powerful foe of the legalization of any type of alcoholic beverages. However, as environmental demands changed and popular support shifted in favor of the legalization of liquor, the WCTU remained firm in its opposition. Even though the environment in which this organization operated had changed, and even though it clearly recognized the change, it made a decision to continue its support of prohibition. As a result, the organization lost must of its popular support and virtually all of its power. One might argue here that a more "rational" decision for the WCTU under the circumstances would have been to compromise on the issue while it could still bargain from a postition of strength. Instead, the organization chose to remain firm in spite of environmental changes with the obvious consequences in terms of effectiveness.

In conclusion, it would appear based on the available evidence that predictability, perception, and rationality are all important factors in effect environmental relations. Moreover, there is a pattern to this relationship, where the actual degree of predictability of environmental states is "filtered" by organizational decision makers by their accuracy of perception and by their rationality of behavior. The resulting selection of a particular course of action can then be seen as leading to organizational effectiveness to the extent that it is appropriate for a given environment. If the environment is in fact highly unpredictable (suggesting an organic design) but management perceives it to be stable and employs a mechanistic design, we would not expect a high degree of organizational success over the long term. Similarly, if the environment is unpredictable (and is acknowledged as such by management), but management chooses to ignore the fact for whatever reason, we would again not expect a high degree of success. Only when accurate perception and high rationality of decision making are both present, then, would we predict that an organization's response to environmental conditions would be optimal, thus contributing to effectiveness.

WORK ENVIRONMENT AND INDIVIDUAL BEHAVIOR

An examination of the role of environmental variation in performance and effectiveness would not be complete without considering the nature of the *internal* enviornment. Recently, increased attention has been directed toward achieving a better understanding of how differences in the way an organization is seen by its members affects their attitudes and behavior at work. This perceived environment, or *organizational climate* as it is often called, has long been thought to interact with the individual characteristics of employees to determine such behavior (Lewin, 1938).

The issue of organizational climate is indeed a controversial one (Guion, 1973). Not only are there disagreements over what is meant by climate but in addition it is difficult to reach consensus concerning the exact role of climate in determining organizational performance. Therefore, we shall first examine what is meant by the concept itself—including its relevant dimensions—and how it relates to other organizational variables. Following this, a model is proposed concerning the role played by climate in determining individual behavior and job attitudes. Several examples of recent investigations of the topic are then examined to determine the appropriateness of the model. Finally, several critiques of the construct itself are considered in the light of current research evidence.

NATURE OF ORGANIZATIONAL CLIMATE

When we discuss the concept of organizational climate, we are talking about the perceived properties or characteristics found in the work environment that result largely from actions taken consciously or unconsciously by an organization and that presumably affect subsequent behavior. In other words, climate may be thought of as the "personality" of an organization as seen by its members. Several important things should be noted about this definition. First, we are dealing in a perceptual realm; the climate of a particular organization is that which its employees believe it to be, not necessarily what it "really" is. If employees perceive the climate to be highly authoritarian, for example, we would expect them to act accordingly, even if top management made every effort to be democratic or employee-centered.

A second important feature of this definition is the suggested relationship between other organizational characteristics and actions and resulting climate. It is generally believed that characteristics unique to a given organization, along with the actions and behavior of management, largely determine the climate of an organization. Finally, it is further believed that the climate that does emerge within an organization represents a major determinant of employee behavior. Given this central relationship between organizational characteristics and actions, climate, and behavior, it becomes readily apparent why climate has received such widespread attention in recent years.

The variables that constitute the climate construct are the defining characteristics that distinguish one working environment from another *as seen by* members of the organization. These variables are thought to be measureable and manipulable to some extent (Litwin & Stringer, 1968). Moreover, climate ostensibly serves as a basis for individuals to interpret and understand their surroundings and to determine reward-punishment relationships (Forehand & Gilmer, 1964; Pritchard & Karasick, 1973).

Dimensions of Organizational Climate

A major difficulty that has arisen in attempts to understand the role of climate in organizational settings has been a general inability among analysts to agree on what actually constitutes the construct. That is, although it is relatively easy to agree on a general definition, there is widespread disagreement concerning which specific dimensions or components are involved. Part of this problem lies in the diversity of environments that have been studied (for example, business organizations, R&D laboratories, elementary schools, government agencies). It is difficult to identify several core dimensions that have relevance for all these organizations. A second problem that exists in the work on climate is that a priori climate scales are typically set forth by one investigator with little concern for how this set of scales relates to other sets. Moreover, little concern has been shown in many cases for the validity **101** and reliability of the various scales used in research projects. The result is that scales purporting to measure dimensions of climate proliferate while considerable difficulty is encountered in any attempt to draw meaningful conclusions or generalizations from the various sets of findings.

One of the more promising avenues of research on climate dimensions is represented by Campbell and his associates (Campbell & Beaty, 1971; Pritchard & Karasick, 1973) in their attempt to develop relatively independent scales of several climate dimensions. By using cluster analysis on their original questionnaire, these investigators identified ten dimensions of climate on an organization-wide basis. These dimensions are:

1. *Task structure.* The degree to which the methods used to accomplish tasks are spelled out by an organization.
2. *Reward-punishment relationship.* The degree to which the granting of additional rewards such as promotions and salary increases are based on performance and merit instead of other considerations like seniority, favoritism, and so forth.
3. *Decision centralization.* The extent to which important decisions are reserved for top management.
4. *Achievement emphasis.* The desire on the part of the people in an organization to do a good job and contribute to the performance objectives of the organization.
5. *Training and development emphasis.* The degree to which an organization tries to support the performance of individuals through appropriate training and development experiences.
6. *Security versus risk.* The degree to which pressures in an organization lead to feelings of insecurity and anxiety on the part of its members.
7. *Openness versus defensiveness.* The degree to which people try to cover their mistakes and look good rather than communicate freely and cooperate.
8. *Status and morale.* The general feeling among individuals that the organization is a good place in which to work.
9. *Recognition and feedback.* The degree to which an individual knows what his supervisor and management think of his work and the degree to which they support him or her.
10. *General organizational competence and flexibility.* The degree to which an organization knows what its goals are and pursues them in a flexible and innovative manner. Includes the extent to which it anticipates problems, develops new methods, and develops new skills in people before problems become crises.

This set of climate dimensions is illustrative of the variety of factors commonly included in other conceptualizations of climate (see, for example, Halpin & Croft, 1962; Litwin & Stringer, 1968; Schneider & Bartlett, 1966; Taylor & Bowers, 1972). Although some differences exist between these formulations, the dimensions proposed by Campbell and his associates generally subsume the various dimensions found in earlier formulations. As such, this formulation will be used in the present discussion for the purpose of consistency. (The reader is referred to Campbell et al., 1974, for a detailed comparison of the various approaches to the study of climate.)

Before exploring the relationship between organizational climate and facets of effectiveness, it is important to understand how the notion of climate differs from that of organizational structure. Although some overlap obviously exists [for example, Campbell & Beaty's (1971) notion of "task structure"], it is still possible to differentiate the two concepts. Structure generally refers either to the physical arrangement of people in an organization (for example, work-group size, span of control, and so forth) or to the extent of work "structuring" that is imposed on individuals by an organization (Campbell et al., 1974). In both instances, we are concerned with the extent to which individual behavior in organizational settings is prescribed, standardized, and restricted or controlled (see Chapter 4).

Climate, on the other hand, refers principally to the prevalent attitudes, values, norms, and feelings employees have concerning the organization (Payne & Pugh, 1976). These affective responses result largely from the interaction of an organization's structure and the individual's (or group's) goals, needs, and abilities. Thus, on a conceptual level, structure, an objective phenomenon, is seen as a major influence on climate, a subjective phenomenon.

CLIMATE AND ORGANIZATIONAL EFFECTIVENESS

In order to understand the role of climate in organizational effectiveness, we can construct a hypothetical model on a general level that specifies the relationships between the major sets of variables. Such a model should provide a useful framework around which to analyze the various research findings as they relate to climate and effectiveness.

We have already mentioned the role of structure as a determinant of climate. Along with structure, we can also include technology, external environment, and managerial policies and practices as important influences on climate. (These relationships are schematically represented in Exhibit 6-1 and will be discussed in greater detail below.) The emerging climate, then, represents the **103** arena where employee performance decisions are made. Where climate is conducive to the needs of individuals (for example, it is employee-centered and achievement-oriented), we would expect goal-directed behavior to be high. Conversely, where the emerging climate is in opposition to personal goals, needs, and motives, we would expect both performance and satisfaction to be diminished (see Chapter 7). In other words, ultimate behaviors or outcomes are determined by the interaction of individual needs and the perceived organizational environment. The resulting level of performance, satisfaction, and so forth, then feeds back to contribute not only to the climate of the particular work environment but also to possible changes in managerial policies and practices.

Following this viewpoint, structure, technology, external environment, and other organizational charactertistics affect ultimate outcomes (such as performance, satisfaction) largely to the extent that they contribute to an appropriate climate. Climate is thus seen as an intervening variable. This intervening nature of climate may explain many of the weak or contradictory findings that result when the structure-performance or environment-performance relationships are examined irrespective of climate (see Chapters 4 and 5).

Several additional points need to be made concerning the role of climate in organizational effectiveness as viewed here. First, because climate is generally regarded as existing on an individual

EXHIBIT 6-1   A Partial Model of the Determinants of Effectiveness-Related Individual Outcomes

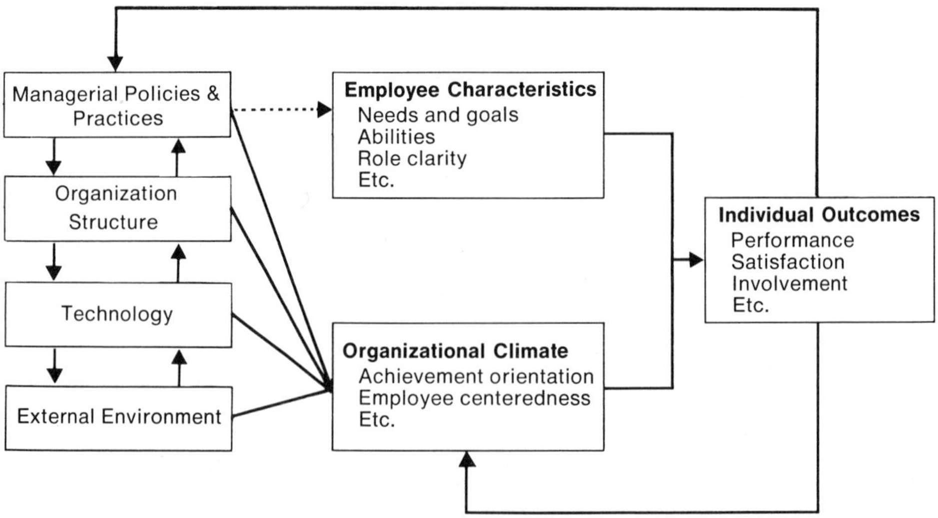

Note: The dotted line from managerial policies and practices to employee characteristics denotes the influence of management on such characteristics through employee selection and training.

or group level (as opposed to an organization-wide level), outcome measures must also be considered on an individual or group level. Thus, instead of talking about climate leading to organizational effectiveness, it is probably more appropriate to talk in terms of individual or group-related facets of effectiveness (for example, job satisfaction, employee performance, organizational commitment, and so forth).

Second, the available information suggests that there is no best, or most suitable, climate. Instead, management must determine what its goals are and attempt to create a climate that is appropriate both for those goals and for the goals and objectives of its employees. If performance is the desired outcome, an achievement-oriented climate may be more suitable; an affiliation-oriented climate may be more suitable if job satisfaction were the desired outcome (Litwin & Stringer, 1968).

Third, it should be noted that the relationships we are discussing here (Exhibit 6-1) should hold only to the extent that employees have control over the attainment of the outcome variables. Where machines control productivity, for example, we would not expect climate to play as large a role in performance, although it most certainly would relate to resulting job attitudes and withdrawal behavior.

Consistent with the framework presented above, investigations of organizational climate have taken one of three approaches. First, some studies examined the potential *determinants* of climate in organizations. Questions were raised here regarding the "causes" of variations in climate dimensions across work environments. A second set of investigations looked at the various *outcomes* that resulted from variations in climate. Particular interest was focused here on how changes in climate affected employee performance and job attitudes. Finally, a third set of studies examined the *intervening* nature of climate as it moderated the relationship between such organizational characteristics as structure and technology and resulting job performance and satisfaction. After examining each of these aspects of the role of organizational climate in work settings, we shall attempt to draw some meaningful generalizations concerning how the research supports the model presented above (see also Hellriegel & Slocum, 1974; James & Jones, 1974).

Determinants of Climate

Exhibit 6-1 suggests that at least four sets of factors can influence in some fashion the climate of a particular organization or work group. In general, these factors originate either in the structure or technology of the organization, its external task environment, or the policies and practices set forth by top management. **105**

The first set of variables that are thought to affect organizational climate are found in the structure of the organization. When taken together, the available evidence indicates that the more "structured" an organization (that is, the greater the degree of centralization, formalization, rules-orientation, and so on), the more rigid, closed, and threatening the perceived environment (see, for example, Marrow, Bowers, & Seashore, 1967; Payne & Pheysey, 1971). Apparently, the more individual autonomy and discretion that is permitted and the more concern management demonstrates for its employees, the more "favorable" (that is, open, trusting, responsible) the work climate. Moreover, this relationship is particularly evident concerning individual discretion in decision making. The results of several investigations indicate that achievement-oriented and trusting climates are highly influenced by the extent to which management allows subordinates to participate in the decisions affecting their jobs (Dieterly & Schneider, 1974; Lawler, Hall, & Oldham, 1974; Likert, 1961; Litwin & Stringer, 1968).

Other structural factors that can affect climate are organization size and the position of one's job in the hierarchy. For instance, one study in a school system found that smaller organizations were consistently associated with a more open, trusting, and dependent climate, although the larger (and more bureaucratized) organizations were perceived to be the opposite (George & Bishop, 1971). Moreover, several studies have found that the location of an employee's job in the organizational hierarchy or in a particular department can affect perceptions of climate to some degree (Hall & Lawler, 1969; Schneider & Bartlett, 1968; Schneider & Hall, 1972). Thus, although research scientists in their section of an organization may see the climate as open, flexible, and dynamic, accountants working for the same firm may view its climate as rigid, routinized, and static. Such findings reinforce the notion that one organization probably has several climates, rather than just one.

The nature of the job technology employed by an organization has also been shown to influence climate. For example, a study by Burns and Stalker (1961), found that routine technologies (such as assembly lines) tended to create rules-oriented, rigid climates where trust and creativity were low. More dynamic or changing technologies (such as aerospace engineering), on the other hand, led to more open communications, trust, creativity, and acceptance of personal responsibility for task accomplishment (see also Litwin & Stringer, 1968).

We know very little about the impact of the external environment on internal organizational climate. One might expect, however, that external events or factors that have particular relevance for employees may indeed affect climate to no small extent. For example, when economic conditions are severe and organizations are forced to lay off (or even consider laying off) some of their employees, those who remain would probably be inclined to see the climate as a threatening one, with little warmth or support and no motivation to take moderate risks (as one would expect in an achievement-oriented climate). Instead, job security would become paramount and creativity, and perhaps productivity, would suffer as people wondered who would be the next to go. Support for such a view of environment as a determinant of climate is provided in a study by Golembiewski, Mungenvider, Blumbery, Carrigan, and Mead (1971), who found that economic and market uncertainties had detrimental effects on perceived openness of climate.

Finally, several investigators have indicated that the policies and practices of management can have a major bearing on climate. For example, it has been shown that managers who provide their subordinates with more feedback, autonomy, and task identity contribute to a significant degree to the creation of an achievement-oriented climate, where members feel more responsible for the attainment of organizational and group objectives (Lawler et al., 1974; Litwin & Stringer, 1968; Marrow et al., 1967; Schneider & Bartlett, 1968). On the other hand, where management emphasized standardized procedures, rules, and job specialization, the resulting climate was not found to lead to the acceptance of responsibility, creativity, or feelings of competence. In other words, it appears that management behavior towards employees, as reflected in the policies and practices that are implemented, does represent a major input into at least certain aspects of climate (such as achievement-orientation). In fact, based on their own research, Litwin and Stringer concluded that management or leadership style represented the single most important determinant of organizational climate. This point will be discussed in more detail in Chapter 9.

In summary, the available evidence is consistent with the model outlined in Exhibit 6-1, particularly insofar as structure and management policies and practices are concerned. Such factors apparently represent major determinants of climate in work settings and, as such, represent important areas of management concern. If climate is related to performance and job satisfaction, then it is incumbent upon managers to consider those variables that can affect climate if changes are to be made that will ultimately contribute to organizational goal attainment. Here again, it becomes apparent that effective managers must exhibit the capacity to recognize clearly the interrelationships between major sets of organizational variables (structure and climate, for example) and **107** to be able to respond to the particular needs of a given organization if they are to contribute to organizational success.

Outcomes of Climate

We now turn to a consideration of the consequences or outcomes of variations in organizational climate. Our focus here will be primarily on individual rather than organization-wide outcomes because of the paucity of information concerning the latter. The two most widely investigated outcomes in this regard are job satisfaction and job performance.

Available evidence indicates that a clear positive relationship exists between climate and job satisfaction. In particular, it has been found that more consultative, open, employee-centered climates are generally associated with more positive job attitudes (Frederickson, 1966; Friedlander & Margulies, 1969; Kaczka & Kirk, 1968; LaFollette & Sims, 1975). Such findings have emerged among a wide range of samples in a variety of institutional areas. Although the magnitude of the relationships between climate and satisfaction is not overly large (indicating that other factors also contribute significantly to overall satisfaction), the findings are consistently in the predicted direction. Thus, it appears that satisfaction on the job results to at least some extent from the manner in which managers show concern for and seek advice and participation from their subordinates. When employees feel that they are an integral part of the organization and that their superiors take a personal interest in their welfare, it is not surprising that they will experience higher degrees of job satisfaction.

The relationship between climate and job performance appears to be somewhat more complex. In a major investigation of this relationship, Litwin and Stringer (1968) concluded that authoritarian climates, in which decision making is centralized and employee behavior is governed largely by rules and standardized procedures, led not only to low productivity but also resulted in low satisfaction and creativity and negative attitudes toward the work group. An affiliative climate, on the other hand, in which good interpersonal relations among employees were stressed, generally led to high job satisfaction, positive attitudes toward the work group, and moderate creative behavior; job performance still remained low. Only in the achievement-oriented climate, where emphasis was placed on goal attainment, were both creative behavior and productivity high. The achievement climate also led to high job satisfaction, positive group attitudes, and high achievement motivation levels. More recent findings by Steers (1975d; 1976b) are consistent with these findings.

It has also been shown that employee-centered climates, with
108 open communications, mutual support, and decentralized decision

making, generally lead to increased employee performance, re-duced turnover, lower manufacturing costs, and reduced training time (Frederickson, 1966; Friedlander & Greenberg, 1971; Hand, Richards, & Slocum, 1973; Marrow et al., 1967). When these find-ings are compared with those reviewed above, a picture emerges in which the most favorable climate for both production and satis-faction is generally one that emphasizes *both* employee achieve-ment and employee consideration. That is, we can generally con-clude that one way for managers to facilitate effectiveness is to bring about a climate that stresses the importance of goal attain-ment while at the same time encouraging mutual support, cooper-ation, and participation on the activities that contribute to goal attainment.

Although creating an achievement-oriented, employee-centered climate may facilitate the desired outcomes, however, it certainly does not guarantee them. Instead, it is also important to look at how the emerging climate interacts with the personal characteristics of employees (for example, needs, abilities, goals) as they jointly affect performance and satisfaction. If employees genuinely are not motivated to perform (perhaps because they see no relationship between performance and rewards) or if they lack the abilities to accomplish their tasks, the impact of climate on performance would be lessened. On the other hand, when the climate is such that it stimulates the achievement motive and provides a vehicle for the satisfaction of a variety of important employee needs, then the contribution of climate to performance and satisfaction would be expected to be substantial (Downey, Hellriegel, & Slocum, 1975; Pritchard & Karasick, 1973; Schneider & Bartlett, 1968; Steers, 1976b).

In summary, climate does indeed represent an important influ-ence on performance and satisfaction. This relationship is ap-parently enhanced by the creation of a climate that emphasizes achievement and consideration for employees. [Although research generally confirms the relationship between variations in climate and both performance and satisfaction, a few studies have indicat-ed that climate has a much more profound influence on satisfac-tion than on performance (LaFollette & Sims, 1975; Lawler et al., 1974; Pritchard & Karasick, 1973).] Moreover, initial findings sug-gest that some personal characteristics (for example, individual need strengths) interact with certain climate dimensions to jointly affect various outcomes. These findings suggest that personal needs, goals, and values must be consistent with—or at least compatible with—the prevailing work environment if desired out-comes are to be maximized. Finally, the general magnitude of the relationships across the various studies suggests a more com-plex process than current research has demonstrated. It seems **109** probable, therefore, to conclude that variables other than the ones encompassed in our partial model also affect performance and satisfaction (see Chapter 7).

Climate as an Intervening Variable

We now come to the third part of the model: the intervening nature of organizational climate. Little is known about this aspect of climate that would guide us in evaluating this facet of the model directly. However, indirect evidence (reviewed above) has demonstrated that several organizational factors (such as structure, managerial style) have an impact on climate and that climate, in turn, influences to no small degree resulting satisfaction and performance. In addition to this indirect evidence, two investigations have been carried out that specifically examined the potential intervening nature of climate. In one study, managerial policies and practices were altered (primarily by replacing top management in a small manufacturing firm), resulting in significant changes in climate (Marrow et al., 1967). The new management, which was described as being more people-oriented, created a climate in which employees felt more important and more responsible for their own actions. The new management style was also seen as being more supportive of employees and more participative on decisions affecting employees' jobs. As a result of such changes in climate, performance increased while manufacturing costs, training time, and turnover all declined.

In the second study, interest focused on how climate served to mediate the impact of both structure and management style on performance and satisfaction (Lawler et al., 1974). In general, it was found that climate was a strong mediator of the relationship between management style and the outcome variables; that is, style influenced climate, which, in turn, influenced performance and satisfaction. In addition, climate also appeared to moderate the impact of organizational structure on the same two outcome variables, although the magnitude of this second relationship was not as high as that concerning management style.

In general, then, the available evidence tends to support the proposed model of the role of climate in organizational dynamics. As shown in Exhibit 6-1, we may conclude that various organizational and environmental characteristics influence the emerging climate of a particular organization and that this climate, along with employee characteristics, influences performance and satisfaction. These outcomes, then, contribute to possible changes in the existing climate and in managerial practices in the form of a feedback loop. Moreover, it would appear that the most desirable climate from the standpoint of meeting both organizational and personal objectives would be one that emphasized both goal achievement and employee consideration. Such a climate represents an exchange relationship between employees and their employer where both work together to satisfy mutual objectives in the long run.

CRITICISM OF THE CLIMATE CONSTRUCT

Due to the rather controversial nature of the climate construct, it would be inappropriate to leave our discussion here without considering several criticisms that have been advanced recently relative to it. Such criticisms should be kept in mind when evaluating the role and utility of climate in modern organizations.

First, several researchers have noted that climate is exclusively a *perceptual* phenomenon. That is, the climate of a given organization is that which an employee *thinks* it is. As Johannesson (1971, p. 30) has pointed out, "there are potentially as many climates as there are people in the organization." Such criticism raises the possibility that organizations do not, in fact, have a climate at all, but rather only a set of feelings and perceptions on the part of the various employees that may change from time to time and from employee to employee (Guion, 1973).

Some have argued that this problem is easily overcome by collecting "objective" data concerning climate instead of using the more subjective self-report data of employees. In other words, we should measure the degree of employee participation, for example, by having trained observers rate quantitatively the extent to which employees have autonomy in decision making. By doing so, it is argued, managers would be more able to determine the precise nature of the climate with which they are dealing. Unfortunately, the problem is not so simple. As pointed out by Vroom (1964) and others, people tend to behave based on how they see their environment and not necessarily how it really is. If employees see their company as employee-centered, they will respond accordingly—even if the company is in fact authoritarian. In other words, whether or not perceptions are accurate, we would still expect them to strongly influence actual behavior. This fact, combined with the knowledge that there may be as many climates as there are employees, significantly increases the difficulty incurred by managers in trying to deal with climate as it relates to desired outcomes.

A second criticism of climate focuses on the relationship between climate and job satisfaction. Specifically, it has been suggested by several people (for example, Johannesson, 1973) that climate is redundant with respect to satisfaction. In short, questions have been raised as to whether or not climate and satisfaction really represent the same thing. Although theoretically climate **111** represents objective descriptions of the work environment and satisfaction represents affective response (that is, positive or negative feelings) to the environment, it is suggested that when the two variables are measured both represent affective responses. LaFollette and Sims (1975) dispute this contention, however, and offer evidence in support of their position. They found that, although climate and satisfaction were related, the two constructs were not related to performance in the same fashion. If the two variables do not relate in a similar fashion to third variables, it is difficult to defend the contention that they do, in fact, represent the same construct. It was concluded by LaFollette and Sims (1975, p. 276) that assertions of redundancy between climate and satisfaction seem "premature and judgmental, and is contrary to the prevailing evidence to date."

As noted by Hellriegel and Slocum (1974), the primary criticisms of the climate construct appear to be directed not at the construct itself but rather at how the construct has been operationalized and measured in organizational settings. However weak the measures, our current understanding of organizational dynamics indicates clearly that there is "something" within an organization's cultural milieu that creates conditions that are conducive to certain attitudes and patterns of behavior. Whether these forces are called climate or something else, their existence and influence on organizational behavior must be recognized and dealt with if organizations are to become more effective in pursuing their chosen objectives.

EMPLOYEE ATTACHMENT AND PERFORMANCE 7

It was pointed out in Chapter 6 that individual behavior in organizations is a function of the interaction of two important variables: the characteristics of the perceived environment and the characteristics of the individual (after Lewin, 1938). The perceived environment, or climate, was examined in detail earlier. In this chapter, the role of individual characteristics is considered as they influence job performance, and, ultimately, the success or failure of an organization.

Several aspects of individual differences and individual behavior are important for an understanding of organizational success. First, we need to have some knowledge of what organizations require from individual members in order to survive and prosper, as well as what individuals expect in return for their efforts on behalf of the organization. (See also Chapter 2.) Second, we must look at the consequences of this interaction between individual needs and organizational requirements. The results of this interaction can be seen as leading to two equally important outcomes: (1) an individual's desire to maintain his membership in a particular organization (termed here *attachment*); and (2) an individual's desire to perform on the job and contribute to organizational goal attainment. Before examining the determinants of such outcomes, however, let us briefly examine the nature of the behavioral requirements that organizations have with respect to their employees.

BEHAVIORAL REQUIREMENTS OF ORGANIZATIONS

In addition to the structural, technological, and environmental influences on effectiveness, perhaps the most direct contribution

to organizational success results from the behaviors of the employees themselves. It is the employees who constitute an organization's structure and who make use of an organization's technologies. Moreover, it is the employees who respond to environmental variations and pressures. In fact, it becomes readily apparent that the key to organizational success lies in the manner in
which the members of an organization work together (or fail to
work together) for goal attainment. when this role of individual
behavior in organizational effectiveness is examined more fully,
it appears that organizations have three important *behavioral* requirements that must be met in order to insure ultimate success
(Katz & Kahn, 1966).

First, all organizations must be able to attract and maintain
a steady work force of qualified men and women. This means
that, in addition to successfully recruiting, hiring, and placing individuals in the system, organizations must be able to hold on to
these employees by offering suitable rewards that are commensurate with individual contribution and are relevant to individual need
satisfaction.

Second, organizations must be able to secure dependable
role performance from their employees. A major component of
organizational efficiency is predictability—both of machines and
of people. Management must know that all employees are going
to carry out their assigned jobs to the best of their ability. Thus,
a company salesman is expected to sell, and a mailroom clerk
is expected to sort and deliver mail. If the mailroom clerk decided
unilaterally that he or she wanted to sell for a while, a major
segment of organizational communications (company mail) would
come to a halt. This problem of dependable role performance
is particularly acute in upper echelons of management where all
too often top managers—who bear primary responsibility for corporate policy making—spend too much of their time on minor
day-to-day decisions and activities that may be fun (or may be
a habit) but are not role relevant. Less time is therefore available
for more appropriate goal-directed activities. Thus, if an organization is to operate effectively, each member must be willing not
only to perform but to perform those specific tasks for which he
or she bears primary responsibility.

Finally, in addition to dependable role performance, effective
organizations also require that employees engage in some form
of spontaneous and innovative behavior. It is obviously not possible for employee job descriptions to be so precise that employees would know exactly what is expected of them at all times.
Job descriptions or instructions seldom take into account emergency situations or unusual opportunities or events. Instead, they
114 represent only general guidelines as to job requirements. In order

to meet emergencies or capitalize on unique opportunities, it is necessary for individuals to act on their own—that is, to make their own decisions—and to respond in accordance with their feelings of what is best for the organization. Simple examples of such spontaneous or creative behavior would include employee suggestions for improving a manufacturing process, an employee decision to ignore a particular rule or procedure where circumstances obviously call for such action, and so forth. Thus, a truly effective organization will attempt to provide a work atmosphere in which employees not only carry out their primary job requirements but also assume the responsibility to think and to act in a creative manner so as to improve both efficiency and goal-directed effort.

When we examine these three behavioral requirements of organizations, it becomes apparent that the first requirement—attracting and maintaining members—focuses on the issue of organizational *attachment*. That is, we are concerned here with why an individual joins a particular organization and what motivates him or her to remain. The second and third behavioral requirements of effective organizations deal more specifically with the level and quality of employee *performance* in organizations. In the study of human behavior as it relates to organizational effectiveness, employee attachment and performance emerge as the key variables to be examined. Although structure, technology, and environment contribute to and often constrain effectiveness, such variables are largely overshadowed by the role of employee behavior. If employees are not motivated to remain with and contribute to an organization, questions of effectiveness become academic. Let us examine more closely the nature of attachment and performance in organizations.

ATTACHMENT TO ORGANIZATIONS

The notion of attachment in organizational settings can be broken down into two major components. First, there is a formal *attachment* to an organization. Here we are concerned about discovering ways to reduce or minimize turnover, absenteeism, and other forms of withdrawal and increase the time one spends in the work environment. No claim is made in the simple notion of attachment that the individual is strongly attracted to or has positive feelings toward the organization—only that for whatever reason he or she maintains membership. *Commitment,* on the other hand, represents a state of affairs where individuals are strongly attracted to (committed to) the goals, values, and objectives of their employer. Commitment thus goes well beyond mere membership in that it includes highly favorable attitudes towards one's **115** employer and a willingness to exert high levels of effort on behalf of the organization in order to facilitate goal attainment.

There is some question as to whether attachment and commitment are contributors to organizational effectiveness or whether they represent the evaluation criteria themselves. That is, on one hand, it can be argued that highly committed employees will contribute a great deal to the attainment of an organization's goals, whatever those goals may be. Conversely, however, it can also be argued that attachment and commitment are themselves desirable ends and thus are realistic measures of effectiveness. The resolution to this problem depends upon the existing goals of a given organization. If the primary objective of a company is to make a profit, for example, then attachment and commitment may be viewed as potentially important influences on such an outcome. However, if the existence of a highly committed work force is itself a major corporate objective, then commitment becomes the evaluation criterion, and we can focus our concern on how to facilitate such commitment. It is highly conceivable that in most work organizations we would be concerned about both the determinants and results of commitment and attachment.

Sources of Attachment and Withdrawal

If we consider attachment or sustained membership a desirable end, then questions are logically raised concerning how such an end is achieved. What exactly are the major factors that influence individuals to remain with and participate in the activities of an organization? A recent review of the research evidence on attachment and withdrawal found that continued attachment is strongly and positively related to experienced overall job satisfaction (Porter & Steers, 1973). However, as was pointed out in the review, such a finding really tells us very little about *why* an employee is satisfied or dissatisfied; nor does it help us determine what must be done to improve satisfaction and attachment.

Employee turnover. In order to identify more clearly the various specific factors that influence an employee's decision to participate, four principal areas, or sources of attachment and withdrawal, were suggested (Porter & Steers, 1973). These four sources are:

1. Organization-wide factors (such as pay and promotional practices, organization size).
2. Immediate work environment factors (for example, supervisory style, peer group interaction patterns).
3. Job content factors (such as task repetitiveness, autonomy, role clarity).
4. Personal factors (age, tenure, personality, vocational interests).

Each of these areas was seen as representing one "level" in the organization, moving from the more general organization-wide factors to the more specific personal factors. In their review of over sixty studies on the causes of withdrawal, it was found that important sources of attachment or withdrawal can be found in all four levels of the organization. It was thus concluded that the contributing factors to attachment are both numerous and diffused throughout the organizational milieu.

Due to the multiplicity (and sometimes conflicting nature) of the findings, an attempt was made to develop a model that was capable of explaining the processes by which attachment decisions were made. Central to the model is the concept of "met expectations." According to the model, each individual is seen as bringing his or her own unique set of *expectations* to a job. For some individuals, it is likely that a high value would be placed on attaining their expectations in the areas of salary, promotional opportunities, supervisory and peer group relations, and so forth. Others may stress having a challenging or prestigious job. These different levels of expectations (that is, the sum total of the things an employee wants from a job) are schematically represented in Exhibit 7-1.

The second part of the model acknowledges the fact that there are differing levels of *rewards* that are potentially available to em-

EXHIBIT 7-1   Hypothetical Example of Expectations × Rewards Interaction as It Relates to Decision to Withdraw

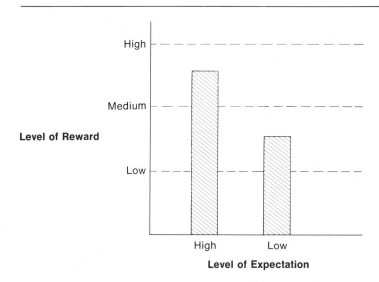

Source: L. W. Porter and R. M. Steers, "Organizational, Work, and Personal Factors in Employee Turnover and Absenteeism," *Psychological Bulletin*, 1973, *80*, p. 172. Copyright 1973 by the American Psychological Association. Reprinted by permission.

ployees in various organizations. These different reward levels are also represented in Exhibit 7-1. The notion of rewards focuses on the level and intensity of the outcomes experienced by each employee. It can be seen in the exhibit that the employee who has higher expectations would be satisfied only by a high reward level, while the employee whose expectations are more moderate would be satisfied by more modest rewards. Moreover, the actual level of rewards may vary as a function of each employee's unique set of expectations. That is, whatever the composition of the employee's expectation set, it is important that *these* expectations be largely satisfied if the individual is to be able to justify continued organizational membership. Doubling the salary of an employee who truly does not value additional money would thus have little impact on insuring continued attachment.

The initial expectations of an employee may change over time in response to events that either occur or are anticipated to occur at work. For instance, during poor economic times, some employees may shift their reward emphasis away from a pay raise and toward job security at almost any salary. Other employees may not, however. In either case, whatever an employee's unique set of expectations, it is toward these factors that we must direct our attention if we are to increase employee attachment in work organizations.

Available evidence in support of the model suggests at least three ways in which the satisfaction of an employee's expectations—and his intent to remain—can be increased. First, in some cases it may be possible to increase the number of rewards available to employees in exchange for suitable performance. These increased rewards could include not only larger pay raises but also improved opportunities for satisfying peer group interactions, improved supervisory relations, and the like. Hopefully, if reward levels could be increased to a sufficient level, employee expectations would be more likely to be met (Dunnette, Arvey, & Banas, 1973; Katzell, 1968; Ross & Zander, 1957). At times, however, this approach may be impractical. (There is a limit to how far pay raises or promotional opportunities can be increased.) In such cases, attempts can still be made to increase the equity or fairness with which such rewards are distributed (that is, make such rewards more contingent upon job performance than on seniority, favoritism, and so forth).

Second, efforts can be made by top management to insure that the expectation levels of entering employees are realistic (Macedonia, 1969; Wanous, 1973; Weitz, 1956; Youngberg, 1963). In many instances, employee recruiters tend to be overly optimistic in describing a job or organization to potential recruits. Such behavior serves to create unrealistic expectations that are almost impossible to meet by the realities of the situation and tend to insure a high rate of turnover and absenteeism. If, instead of creating unrealistic expectations during job interviews, recruiters described the available jobs in realistic detail (and perhaps let the applicant see or experience the job first hand), it should be possible to achieve a better match between employee needs and abilities and the nature of the job. Such actions should improve chances for sustained membership.

Third, organizations may consider the installation of cafeteria-style compensation plans (Lawler, 1971), where employees may choose from among a set of alternative rewards for good performance. Thus, while one employee may prefer to receive a pay raise or bonus in exchange for superior performance, another employee may prefer increased time off to spend with the family.

Employee absenteeism. Withdrawal from organizational activities may take several forms. In addition to complete severance of organizational activities (turnover), an employee may elect to withdraw temporarily through absenteeism. Although some analysts and managers consider these two forms of withdrawal similar in both cause and outcome, it is possible to distinguish between the two on at least three important points:

1. The negative consequences for the individual that are associated with absenteeism are usually much less than those associated with turnover. For example, with the prevalence of company sick leave policies, an employee can miss work (up to a point) without salary loss.
2. Absenteeism is more likely to be a spontaneous and relatively easy decision, while the act of termination can be assumed to be more carefully considered over time in most cases.
3. Absenteeism may sometimes represent a substitute type of behavior for turnover, particularly where alternative employment is unavailable. In this sense, absenteeism may allow for temporary avoidance of an unrewarding situation without the loss of the benefits of employment; turnover, on the other hand, represents a complete severance of the individual from such benefits. (Porter & Steers, 1973, p. 173)

When we examine the available research on absenteeism, it becomes apparent that much less is known concerning this form of withdrawal than is known about turnover. Although many studies have been carried out, the results are often conflicting. In view of the fact that absenteeism may be far more costly to a company than turnover, it is somewhat surprising how little we really know about its causes. The only clear trends that do emerge indicate that absenteeism is fairly consistently and positively related to increases in work-group size and in family problems and inversely related to overall job satisfaction, opportunities for participation in decision making, and increased job autonomy (Porter **119**

& Steers, 1973; Yolles, Carone, & Krinsky, 1975). Although it may be that met expectations play a similar role with absenteeism and turnover, we cannot be certain of such a relationship at present.

Impact on organization. Before leaving the topic of organizational withdrawal, consideration should be given to the impact of such behavior on the organization as a whole. Withdrawal—particularly turnover—often leads to several specific consequences for organizations that have a direct bearing on ultimate effectiveness (cf. Price, 1974). For instance, several studies suggest that increased turnover often necessitates increases in administrative staff in proportion to production personnel (Kasarda, 1973). Moreover, turnover can lead to successively higher amounts of formalization and sometimes successively lower amounts of innovation and creativity (Gouldner, 1954; Grusky, 1960). Finally, high turnover and absenteeism can inhibit the development of work-group cohesion (Burling, Lentz, & Wilson, 1956). In other words, in many instances, increased turnover leads to other undesirable outcomes that can have a direct influence on the success or failure of an organization.

Because of the undesirable outcomes often associated with turnover, many have argued that the reduction of all turnover is a desirable goal. However, such a proposition can be questioned on several grounds (Porter & Steers, 1973). To begin with, from the standpoint of the individual employee, leaving an unrewarding job may lead to the attainment of a more satisfying one, thereby increasing an individual's opportunity for personal goal attainment. Second, from the standpoint of the organization, the loss of an ineffective performer would open a position for a potentially more effective employee. Given a scarcity of human resources –or, more accurately, given the scarcity of funds to hire the necessary human resources—it is important that those employees who are retained are capable of maximum contribution to organizational objectives. Finally, considering the present state of technological flux, some turnover may be considered necessary in order to accommodate rapid change and increased efficiency.

In summary, the issue of withdrawal from organizations represents a multifaceted problem that is not easily resolved. Suffice it to say that a goal of most effective organizations is likely to be to increase or strengthen the attachment of their effective members, while attempting to improve the contribution of their less effective members. In this way, organizations move one step closer to the attainment of a fully integrated, goal-oriented work force capable of contributing effectively toward organizational success.

Organizational Commitment

Although attachment is a willingness to maintain membership in an organization, commitment goes much further to include a strong, positive attitude toward the organization. As defined by Porter and Smith (1970, p. 2), organizational commitment refers to "the nature of an individual's relationship to an organization, such that a highly committed person will indicate: (1) a strong desire to remain a member of the particular organization, (2) a willingness to exert high levels of effort on behalf of the organization, and (3) a definite belief in and acceptance of the values and goals of the organization." Thus commitment—as opposed to attachment—involves an active relationship between an employee and his employer in which the employee is willing to give something of himself in order to contribute to the realization of the organization's goals.

Antecedents of commitment. Much has been written about the possible antecedents of organizational commitment and identification (Buchanan, 1974; Hall & Schneider, 1972; Hrebiniak & Alutto, 1972; Koch & Steers, 1976; Sheldon, 1971; Steers, 1976a). When these various findings are considered, they point to three major areas in which influences on commitment can be found (Exhibit 7-2). These areas are: (1) personal characteristics of employees, including tenure in the organization and variations in need strengths (such as need for achievement); (2) job characteristics, such as task identity and opportunities for co-worker interaction; and (3) work experiences, such as the perceived dependability of an organization in the past and the way other employees talk and feel about the organization.

Managers can learn a great deal from these findings concerning ways to increase employee commitment levels. First, employees must somehow be induced to remain with the organization. This might possibly be done using a series of system-wide rewards for membership, such as relatively high salary levels, good fringe benefits, opportunities for personal growth and advancement through company training programs, and so forth. Such actions should serve to make the organizations more attractive to employees, especially in comparison to other organizations. However, it would not be generally expected that these system-wide rewards by themselves would significantly increase commitment, only attachment.

Based on this increased attachment, however, managers can then attempt to build commitment by placing employees in situations where they have opportunities to achieve goals that are personally meaningful to them. Assuming such goals are organizationally relevant, we would expect overall performance to increase **121**

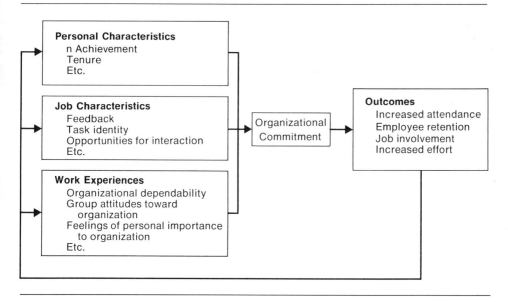

also. Moreover, employees must be shown that management and the other employees are truly concerned about their welfare. It may be possible to modify certain aspects of employees' jobs so they have greater autonomy and responsibility and can identify more with the actual tasks they do. Finally, it is important that employees understand and identify with the objectives and goals of the organization. Such identification may be brought about in part by the modification of operative goals so that they encompass several of the personal goals of employees (Chapter 2). In other words, it is necessary to create an atmosphere of mutual trust and support between employee and employer where both contribute something to the attainment of the other's goals and where such an exchange is made with adequate consideration for the employee's needs and desires. Unfortunately, as can be imagined, it is much easier to describe such prerequisites for commitment than to actually bring them about.

Outcomes of commitment.   Far less is known about the attitudinal and behavioral consequences of organizational commitment. Based on our current level of understanding, we would expect that commitment would lead to at least four effectiveness-related outcomes (Exhibit 7-2). First, employees who were truly committed to the goals and values of an organization would probably be more likely to exhibit high levels of participation in organizational activities (March & Simon, 1958). Their attendance would generally suffer only when illness prevented them from actually coming to work. Thus, voluntary absenteeism should be lower for such individuals than for those employees who were less committed (Steers, 1976a).

Second, and relatedly, highly committed employees would probably have a stronger desire to remain with their employer so they could continue to contribute to the attainment of the goals in which they believe. There is empirical support for this position in two recent studies where it was found that commitment represented an accurate predictor of subsequent turnover (Koch & Steers, 1976; Porter, Steers, Mowday, & Boulian, 1974). In fact, both studies clearly indicated that, although job satisfaction may be a better predictor of turnover during the *initial* stages of employment, commitment emerges to become a stronger predictor than satisfaction as time goes on and employees come to identify more with the organization and its goals.

Third, because of their increased identification with and belief in the objectives of the organization, it is highly likely that some strongly committed individuals will become highly involved in their jobs because such jobs are the key mechanism by which individuals can contribute to organizational goal attainment. Such a relationship may not be overly strong, however. For example, it is possible that a nurse's aide would be highly committed to the humanitarian goals of the hospital where he or she worked, but would not become *involved* in the more distasteful aspects of caring for the sick. In such cases, although an employee may remain committed to the organization—and may faithfully perform his or her job in order to contribute to hospital goals—the level of actual job involvement may remain fairly low.

Finally, following from the definition of commitment itself, we would expect that highly committed employees would be willing to expend considerable effort on behalf of the organization. In some cases, such effort may become translated into superior job performance (cf. Mowday et al., 1974), while in other cases the relationship may not be so simple. As discussed in the following section, actual job performance is a joint function of several variables (see Exhibit 7-3). Although employee effort, or motivational level, is certainly one of these variables, such effort may not be sufficient to insure good performance if the employee lacks the requisite abilities or misunderstands the nature of the assigned tasks. Even so, commitment may be seen as an important contributing factor to such effort and, potentially, to resulting job performance.

This partial model of organizational commitment also suggests a feedback loop whereby certain of the outcomes reinforce or modify the determinants of commitment. For example, as shown in the model, a highly committed person would probably have **123** strong intentions of remaining with the organization. Such intentions would then most likely become translated into increased tenure, a determinant of commitment. Moreover, increased attendance combined with increased job involvement may facilitate the development of high work-group cohesion, another determinant of commitment. Thus, once again, the cyclical nature of relationships becomes apparent as we attempt to discover more about the major processes involved in organizational behavior and effectiveness.

PERFORMANCE IN ORGANIZATIONS

When questions of organizational effectiveness are analyzed from the standpoint of individual employees, the importance of good job performance becomes apparent. Without superior performance at all levels of an organization, organizational goal attainment and success become exceedingly difficult, if not impossible. And if an organization is unable to successfully meet its objectives, the probability that individual employees will be able to meet their personal goals also diminishes considerably—especially over the long run. Thus, assuming that the improvement of employee job performance is a desirable outcome insofar as effectiveness is concerned, questions are logically raised concerning how such performance is brought about and sustained over time.

Put most simply, it is generally believed that individual job performance is a joint function of three important factors: (1) the abilities, traits, and interests of an employee; (2) the clarity and acceptance of the role prescriptions of an employee; and (3) the motivational level of an employee. Although each factor can be important in and of itself, in combination these three variables largely determine the level of output of each employee, which, in turn, contributes to performance on an organization-wide basis. These three factors will be examined separately to discover how each contributes to job performance. In this regard, we will review a job performance model that attempts to account for all these factors as determinants of individual behavior in organizations. Finally, we will discuss several reasons why employees intentionally behave in such a way as to restrict their output on the job and thus reduce overall levels of organizational effectiveness and efficiency.

Abilities, Traits, and Interests

Employee abilities, traits, and interests represent those individual characteristics that largely determine an employee's *capacity* to contribute to an organization, as opposed to employee motivation, which largely determines an employee's *will* to contribute. These attributes are thought to be relatively stable over time, although some changes are possible through outside intervention (such as training). Our concern here is not so much with a detailed examination of the range of human attributes or their measurement but rather with the implications of variations in such attributes as they affect performance and effectiveness in organizational settings. (A more detailed discussion of the influence of employee abilities, traits, and interests on behavior can be found in Dunnette, 1976).

Employee abilities can affect job performance in a variety of ways. For example, research has shown that managerial success is closely related to the level of one's intellectual capabilities (for example, verbal comprehension, inductive reasoning, memory). In fact, it has been suggested that the higher up one is in the organizational hierarchy, the more important intellectual abilities are for managerial performance (Ghiselli, 1966). Such findings appear to be self-evident and have clear implications for recruitment and selection so long as the organization is in a position to offer such employees work that is sufficiently challenging. Hiring employees of superior intellectual capacity and then placing them on dull, routine jobs would not only stifle their performance potential but could in addition hasten their withdrawal from the organization.

In addition to abilities, job performance can also be influenced by personality traits and employee interests. For example, a series of studies over the past twenty-five years has focused on the need for achievement as it relates to job performance. This need has been consistently found to be highly related to performance among a variety of employees (Atkinson, 1958; McClelland, Atkinson, Clark, & Lowell, 1953; Steers, 1975d). Moreover, in the review of research on employee withdrawal from organizations discussed earlier (Porter & Steers, 1973), it was found that individuals manifesting certain personality traits in extremely high or low quantities tended to leave organizations far more often than did employees with more moderate trait levels. It was also found that employees whose vocational interests were not congruent with the realities of the job left more frequently—and were poorer performers while they remained—than those whose vocational interests were congruent with the job (see also Dunnette, Wernimont, & Abrahams, 1964; Holland, 1976).

The conclusion to be drawn here is that individual job performance is influenced to no small degree by a variety of personal characteristics unique to each individual. If an employee simply does not possess the abilities necessary for a particular job, or if he has little interest in the job itself, there is little reason to believe that his performance level would be high. On the other hand, if management can recruit and train workers whose abilities, **125** traits, and interests are largely congruent with the demands of the job, we would expect the probability of good job performance to be substantially improved. Thus, a major function of management becomes that of insuring a proper fit between employee characteristics and the demands of the job.

Role Clarity and Acceptance

The second major contributing factor to performance deals with the degree of understanding and acceptance of an individual concerning his assigned tasks. Put most simply, the more clearly an employee understands his job requirements and work objectives, the more energy he will have for goal-directed activities— assuming, of course, that he accepts such role prescriptions. Support for such a conclusion is widespread (French, Kay, & Meyer, 1966; Locke & Bryan, 1969; Porter & Lawler, 1968; Steers, 1975d). Moreover, role clarity or specificity has also been found to be related to increased goal commitment, work-group cohesiveness, and job involvement and satisfaction (see, for example, Graen, 1976; Locke, 1976; Raven & Rietsema, 1957; Steers, 1976b).

In the day-to-day activities of organizational life, however, there are two role-related problems that can serve to diminish job effort. The first of these is *role ambiguity,* where individuals are not provided with sufficient information concerning the nature of their required tasks. As noted by Kahn, Wolfe, Quinn, Snock, and Rosenthal (1964), role ambiguity in organizational settings can be brought about by three factors: (1) rapid organizational change; (2) increased organizational complexity; and (3) managerial philosophies concerning communications (that is, policies and actions that lead to poor communications). Because most modern organizations are continually undergoing change caused by a turbulent environment, are becoming larger and more complex, and are often plagued by communications breakdowns, it is not surprising that role ambiguity is rather commonly found in organizations. This role ambiguity is particularly acute in managerial positions, which tend to be far less concrete in nature and require more abstract thinking and decision making than do blue-collar positions. Prolonged periods of role ambiguity can often lead to feelings of futility, poorer job performance, increased anxiety, and general job dissatisfaction among employees. Such feelings can ultimately lead to withdrawal from organizational activities, psychologically if not physically (Kahn et al., 1964).

The second role-related problem is *role conflict.* Role conflict exists when an individual is confronted with two sets of role demands that are incompatible. For instance, a carpenter working on a housing project may want to practice his trade to its fullest and build a quality product, while his boss may want the houses constructed in the simplest and cheapest manner possible. Similarly, an employee's supervisor may stress the need to increase production output, while his co-workers are emphasizing the need to maintain output at its present level. Role conflict has a direct influence on organizational effectiveness to the extent that the goal-related role prescriptions of employees are in conflict with other demands placed on them. Thus, a major concern of management is to discover mechanisms whereby such conflicts can be reduced or eliminated. One way to do this is through attempts to integrate personal or group goals with organizational objectives, as discussed in Chapter 2. Such an integration helps to satisfy both sets of demands, thereby alleviating the conflict.

In summary, it can be seen that one aspect of good job performance consists of clarifying for employees the exact nature of their tasks and then securing their acceptance of the tasks. Where role ambiguity and role conflict can be reduced, greater energies are available for goal-directed effort. All that remains now to complete our understanding of determinants of job behavior is to examine the concept of motivation. Assuming that employees have the requisite abilities and traits and understand clearly the nature of their tasks, they still must be motivated to pursue such tasks. Thus, motivation becomes the link between knowing what to do on a job, having the ability to do it, and actual job performance.

Motivation and Performance

Motivation refers to the process by which behavior is energized, directed, and sustained over time (Porter & Lawler, 1968; Vroom, 1964). As will be noted in this definition, there are three important facets of the concept of motivation. First, there is the notion of an energetic force within individuals that "drives" them to behave in certain ways. Second, there is the notion of goal orientation; that is, behavior is generally directed toward certain ends. Finally, there is a systems orientation to such a view of motivation. Forces both within the individual and the external environment feed back to the individual either to reinforce his present course of action or to cause alternative courses of action to be taken.

Theories of motivation and work behavior have proliferated in recent years. Among the more popular theories are the need hierarchy theory (Maslow, 1954), achievement motivation theory (Murray, 1938), dual-factor theory (Herzberg, Mausner, & Synderman, 1959), equity theory (Adams, 1963; Homans, 1961; Weick, 1964), behavior modification theory (Nord, 1969), and expectancy/valence theory (Cummings & Schwab, 1973; Porter & Lawler, 1968; Vroom, 1964). Each of these models views the basic

127

motivational processes from a somewhat different perspective. For instance, Maslow (1954) focuses on individual needs as the prime motivator, while Herzberg et al. (1959) focus on job design. [See Lawler (1973) and Steers & Porter (1975) for a detailed discussion of the various theories and the research in support of each.] The specific dynamics of the various theories goes beyond the scope of our concern here. Instead, we are interested in a more general model capable of describing the various factors and processes that contribute to an employee's decision to produce on the job. Such an attempt is made in the job performance model described here (after Porter et al., 1975). This model has an advantage over the more specific theories mentioned above in that it attempts to incorporate the major features of many of the theoretical approaches to the study of motivation and performance and to view them within a systems framework.

The job performance model begins with the clear recognition that factors that contribute to motivation and performance come from both the individual and the organization. Individual factors can include abilities, traits, interests, and role perceptions, as discussed above. Organizational factors can include task structuring, climate, managerial style, reward systems, and so forth. These two sets of factors are incorporated into one systems view of work behavior, which is shown in Exhibit 7-3. Those factors contributed by the organization are shown in the top half of the diagram; the bottom half shows those factors contributed by individuals. As outlined by Porter et al. (1975), the model proceeds through six stages.

Stage I: Perception and appraisal of organizational demands. As noted earlier, all organizations have goals and objectives that management has set forth as a rationale for organizing. Moreover, organizations also have many needs that must be met if the organization is to be successful in meeting its goals (such as the need for coordination, specialization, control, and so on). These goals and needs (represented in Exhibit 7-3 by circle A) create a set of objective organizational demands that it expects individuals to fulfill (circle B). Such demands represent the role expectations of employees from the organization's standpoint. For instance, management may feel that it must attain a certain level of output from its production workers or a certain level of sales from its salesmen if the organization is to satisfy its needs and accomplish its goals.

These demands are then perceived and appraised by individual members of the organization in the light of their own unique personal goals, needs, and values (circle E). In some (perhaps most) cases, these individuals will tend to alter or distort the initial organizational demands so they are more compatible with their

EXHIBIT 7-3   A Model of Individual Performance in Organizations

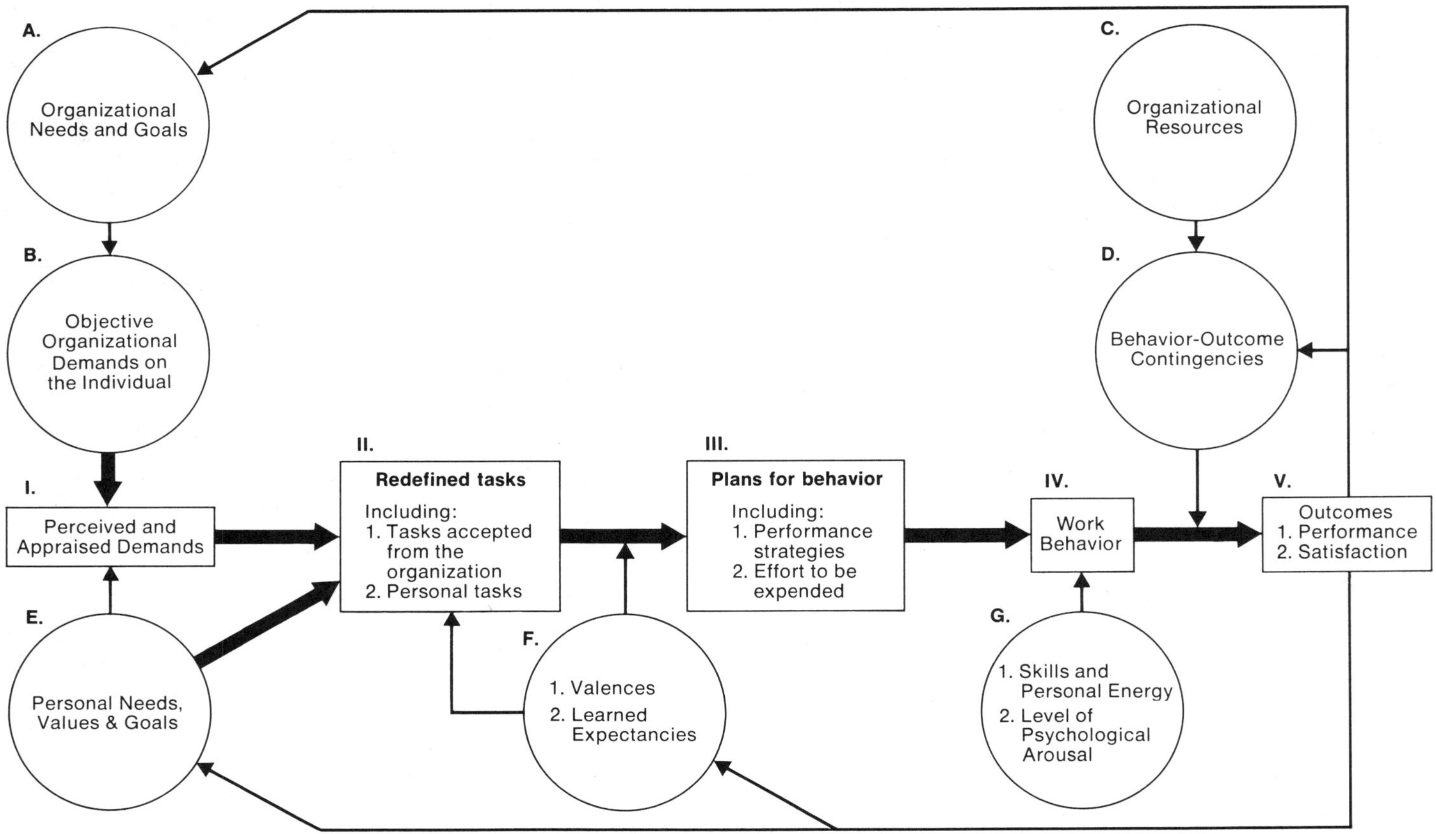

Source: L. W. Porter, E. E. Lawler III, and J. R. Hackman, *Behavior in Organizations* (New York: McGraw-Hill, 1975). p. 121. Reprinted by permission.

own needs and goals. For example, a salesman with a high need for affiliation may stress those organizational demands that deal with interpersonal behavior (for example, he may "overdo" the social requirements of the job) at the expense of other job-related organizational demands. The combination of personal goals and organizational demands, then, creates the "perceived and appraised demands" (box *I*), which are those demands individuals actually see and understand. It is highly likely here that different employees (with different personal needs and frames of reference) would perceive similar organizational demands quite differently, thereby contributing to goal displacement.

Stage II: Task redefinition.   Based on these perceived demands, individuals may decide to redefine the assigned tasks before accepting personal responsibility for their attainment (box *II*). Here we are talking about the "aspiration levels" of individuals. If an employee is assigned a task of producing thirty electronic components per hour, for example, but decides for whatever reason that he is only going to attempt to produce twenty, this twenty becomes the employee's aspiration level (the level for which he is actually trying). Assuming he controls the production technology, there is no reason to believe that his resulting performance would be above this level.

Task redefinition is influenced by several factors. The most important of these, however, are the perceived demands made by the organization and the employee's personal needs and goals. Where these two factors are congruent (for example, the organization demands high output and the individual has a high need for achievement), the tasks would probably be accepted by the employee. Where personal needs and organizational demands were in conflict, however, the individual must select a compromise strategy that at least partially fulfills both sets of needs without jeopardizing his or her job. (Many feel that labor unions often serve an important function here by "protecting" individuals from sacrificing too many of their personal needs in order to meet high levels of organizational demands.)

A further influence on task redefinition is the nature of the expectations individuals have concerning the outcomes or consequences of accepting or rejecting organizational demands, as well as the valences (values) individuals attach to each outcome (circle *F*). Assuming a series of conflicting demands made by the organization, we would expect individuals to accept and work towards those demands that had the highest payoff for the individual. Thus, if an employee has to choose between a dull task such as completing paperwork) and an exciting one (such as meeting new clients or customers), we would predict that he would concentrate his efforts on the latter, so long as the undesirable consequences of ignoring or postponing the former were not too great.

Stage III: Developing a behavioral plan. After an employee has redefined his tasks so they are at least minimally acceptable to him, he then must select an appropriate strategy for task accomplishment. This is done through the development of a behavioral plan (box *III*), whereby individuals reach decisions on how they will organize their goal-directed efforts, as well as how much effort they are willing to expend on such efforts. Although various jobs may offer quite different levels of personal autonomy in developing such plans, it can be assumed that individuals will utilize to their fullest those opportunities that do exist for individual discretion on the job. Here again, the concepts of expectancies and valences enter the process (circle *F*). That is, we would expect that an employee's behavioral plan would be devised in such a way as to maximize effort on those activities that were expected to have the highest return on investment to the employee in the form of desired outcomes.

Stage IV: Work behavior. The behavioral plans of individuals can be seen as leading directly to actual work behavior (box *IV*) as moderated by individual abilities, skills, role clarity, and so forth (circle *G*). Thus, it would be logical to assume that employees who set a rigorous behavioral plan for themselves (that is, high output or performance) would generally outperform those who set less rigorous plans, assuming equal skill levels. Where the necessary skills for task accomplishment are lacking, or where personal needs and goals (such as need for achievement) are unaroused, however, sizable discrepancies may occur between behavioral plans and actual work behavior.

Stage V: Obtaining outcomes. The outcomes that result from work behavior can take many forms. The two most prominent forms from the standpoint of organizational effectiveness are job performance and job satisfaction, as indicated in box *V*. This relationship between behavior and outcomes is modified, however, by the amount of resources (including money) that organizations have (circle *C*) and by the contingencies set up by organizations on the behavior-outcome relationship (circle *D*). That is, in some organizations, rewards may be directly related to performance (as in a piece-rate incentive system), while in other organizations rewards may be determined almost exclusively by seniority. In the first example, there is a strong relationship between behaviors and outcomes, and hence we would expect outcomes to be high (high effort leading to good performance and satisfaction). In the second example, where there is a weak behavior-outcome bond, **131**

we would not expect outcomes to be so high. In other words, where employees do not see desired rewards as being contingent upon performance, there is no reason to believe that employees would maximize their performance-directed efforts.

Stage VI: Feedback. Finally, the proposed job performance model contains a series of feedback loops that can affect both organizational and individual actions. As far as the organization is concerned, the level of outcomes (particularly performance) are evaluated by management to determine the extent to which they meet (or fail to meet) organizational needs and goals. Based on this evaluation, management must then decide whether to alter the demands it makes on individuals (either up or down depending on performance levels) or change the organizational goal levels (goal succession). Moreover, outcomes can also affect the way management structures the behavior-outcome contingencies, as for example when management redesigns the pay incentive system so it more accurately reflects and rewards performance instead of tenure.

On an individual level, outcomes can influence to no small degree the extent to which personal needs and goals are satisfied. An individual with a high need for achievement, for example, may be able to satisfy this need through superior performance, and an individual with a high need for affiliation may be able to satisfy the need through the friends made during work. Where such personal needs are not met to a substantial degree, however, we would expect to see reduced output levels, largely because an individual would redefine his tasks (and aspiration levels) downward (box *II*). Moreover, outcomes can also affect the expectancies and valences of individuals. If an employee consistently receives (and perhaps is satiated by) certain rewards or outcomes that he once highly prized (friendly co-workers for example), he may eventually decrease the valence placed on this particular reward. In addition, if an employee continually receives what he perceives to be a disproportionately low level of rewards in exchange for his efforts, he may lower his expectancies. Because fewer rewards would then be expected, the individual would probably reduce his level of effort so it would be commensurate with his expected reward level, thereby reducing subsequent performance.

Although the model described in Exhibit 7-3 is admittedly a general one, it does serve to illustrate on a simplified level the major factors involved in the determination of organizationally-relevant outcomes, as well as how such factors fit together within a systems framework to affect one another over time. Given the central importance of performance and satisfaction in any consideration of organizational effectiveness, it becomes imperative that managers understand the basic nature of such processes and how they can intervene in the process to facilitate the enhancement of such resulting outcomes.

Reasons for Restriction of Output

The model outlined in Exhibit 7-3 attempts to describe the general processes involved in job performance. As is evident from an examination of the various factors and contingencies that are involved in the process, however, there are many ways in which maximum—or even optimal—job performance can be stymied. Although some of these reasons for poor performance eminate from organizational or managerial problems (such as lack of resources, poor coordination, and so forth), others are the result of conscious decisions on the part of employees *not* to produce. The reasons behind such intentional restrictions on output are many. Some of the more prominent ones are the following:

1. *Potential rewards unappealing.* As noted in the job performance model (Exhibit 7-3), employees place different values or valences on different outcomes. In some cases, the employees may simply not place a high enough valence on the rewards available for increased performance to justify the effort (as, for example, when a manager prefers to spend his extra time with his family instead of doing the "homework" necessary to get ahead).

2. *Weak performance-reward linkage.* Similarly, employees may not see a strong linkage between increased performance and the receipt of additional rewards. It can be very difficult to measure performance accurately on many jobs—particularly managerial positions. Because of this, there are many opportunities for inequities to emerge in the reward system so that good performance is not rewarded to the extent that it should be. Where employees do not see good performance leading to high reward levels, a major motivating force is lost.

3. *Distrust of management.* Particularly on blue-collar jobs, employees often distrust management and feel that increased performance will only lead to increases in the quotas or production rates that are required of them. Such distrust serves to neutralize the incentive system. Moreover, many workers feel that increased performance will lead to a reduction in the work force. (They will "work themselves out of a job.") Such fears can create group pressures to maintain an "acceptable" (that is, moderate) level of performance and to punish "ratebusters" as a threat to the welfare of the entire group.

4. *Desire to have control over one's job.* On a personal level, a major cause of output restriction can be the desire to **133**

maintain at least some control over one's own behavior at work. As jobs become increasingly automated, individual job autonomy is severely reduced. In an effort to resist becoming merely "a cog in the wheel," individuals may try to leave sufficient "slack" in their work schedule (through intentional underproduction) so they can vary their work methods somewhat or do other things to reassure themselves that they have some control over what is happening to them. Such actions can be seen as increasing at least to some extent individual feelings of self-worth and independence by increasing one's freedom of action, and such feelings may more than offset the reduced income that may result from output restriction.

5. *Lack of job involvement.* Finally, a simple dislike of the job can also represent a reason for output restriction. When an employee lacks involvement in his job and prefers to be doing something else, it is difficult for him to focus his total energies on task accomplishment. Moreover, such situations can easily lead to absenteeism and other forms of withdrawal (such as alcoholism) in addition to output restriction, adding further to performance problems.

When we consider these reasons for restriction of output on a job, it becomes apparent that the pressures for such behavior are quite diverse. Some pressures are the result of individual differences between employees (for example, differing valences attached to rewards, differing levels of need for autonomy or control over one's behavior); others are the result of group pressures caused principally by a distrust of management. Such a conclusion highlights the need for managers to recognize clearly the needs and desires of employees in the selection and placement process, as well as in designing or redesigning jobs. Moreover, such a conclusion also focuses attention on the need for managers to deal openly with employees, to state their expectations (and available rewards) clearly, and to attempt to develop trust and rapport with employees at all levels. When employees see their employer as dependable and trustworthy, a major cause of restricted output is substantially reduced.

MANAGING EFFECTIVE ORGANIZATIONS
Part One

8

Up to this point, our primary emphasis has been on an examination of the nature and quality of organizational effectiveness. It was suggested that a systems approach to the topic allows for greater insight into how various organizational and environmental factors jointly influence ultimate organizational success. It was also pointed out that effectiveness is perhaps best understood in terms of the attainment of optimized goals; that is, organizational effectiveness can be viewed as the extent to which an organization can acquire and utilize its available resources to attain feasible operative and operational goals. Throughout, consideration was given to the important roles played by structure, technology, environment, and personal characteristics as they relate to effectiveness of operations.

Based on this examination, we are now in a position to look at the role of the modern manager in facilitating organizational effectiveness. In the final analysis, it is the manager who largely determines the policies, procedures, and actions that influence the ability of an organization to attain its goals over time. Thus, attention will be focused in this and the following chapter on what managers can do to enhance effectiveness.

Opinions differ markedly concerning the role of management in improving effectiveness in organizations (see, for example, Katzell, 1975). However, if effectiveness is viewed in terms of the attainment of operative and operational goals, then it becomes clear that a primary responsibility of managers is to insure that maximum effort is directed toward these goals, whatever they may be. Our review of the various influences on effectiveness leads **135** to the identification of at least six general areas of management concern that are seen as facilitating such goal attainment and effectiveness. These areas are:

1. Strategic goal setting
2. Resource acquisition and utilization
3. The performance environment
4. Communication processes
5. Leadership and decision making
6. Organizational adaptation and innovation

Because these factors largely determine the extent to which an organization's resources are efficiently applied toward long-term organizational interests, it is suggested here that managerial behavior and performance be evaluated in the light of these factors. That is, where managers specify tangible goals for their departments, act to insure the proper acquisition and utilization of resources, create suitable performance environments, and so forth, their contribution toward securing an effective level of operation is maximized. In this sense, organizational effectiveness is not seen as an end state. Rather, it is seen as a continual state that organizations strive to achieve and maintain. Hence, we speak of an organization being relatively effective or ineffective, instead of being entirely one or the other. The job for management, then, is to utilize the tools under its control to improve the relative degree of goal attainment and effectiveness over time.

STRATEGIC GOAL SETTING

If organizations are viewed as goal-seeking systems, then it becomes evident that a major ingredient in organizational success is the ability of management to clearly identify the specific nature of the goals and objectives it wishes to pursue. Without such goal specification, decisions concerning the allocation of scarce resources can easily become suboptimal. In the absence of clear goals and plans, each manager in an organization must decide for himself how to use the money, equipment, and human resources at his discretion. This "individualized" approach to management can easily lead to conflicting efforts and wasted energies.

There are many reasons why managers often fail to plan their activities adequately and to set specific targets and goals for performance: (1) To begin with, there is the issue of accountability; that is, the more specific managers are in setting forth their plans and goals, the more clearly performance deviations from these goals stand out. (2) Moreover, managers are often so preoccupied with present problems that they do not have time to focus on the future. (3) Reward structures in organizations often reward

short-term performance at the expense of long-term planning and development. (4) Managers sometimes lack the patience to engage in detailed planning and goal-setting efforts. (5) Finally, some managers simply do not believe goal setting is worthwhile, particularly in the more dynamic industries that must constantly change course.

On the contrary, however, research has indicated that managers who do engage in planning and goal setting are more productive and generally more satisfied with the results than managers who do not (Comrey, High, & Wilson, 1955; Hemphill, 1964; Locke, 1968; Shure, Rogers, Larson, & Tassone, 1962). Moreover, on an organization-wide level, it has been shown that company performance (including financial success) is strongly related to the extent of planning and goal-setting activities (Thune, 1967). Therefore, a convincing case is made for the benefits to be derived from such efforts for organizational performance.

In recent years, strategic goal setting and planning have become increasingly important for organizational success and survival because of a series of changes in the environments in which organizations must deal (Webber, 1975): (1) The required lead times between initial goal specification and goal attainment have increased for a variety of reasons, providing increased opportunities for goal displacement to occur. (2) As organizations have become larger, the problems of coordinating the various departments and resources for goal-directed effort have increased. (3) Increasing technological complexity requires greater investments of time and money with little guarantee of subsequent payoff; thus, resources must be invested more carefully. (4) Increased task and manpower specialization often reduces the flexibility of an organization to shift priorities at will. (5) Environmental uncertainty has increased in a variety of areas (for example, market, legal, economic), reducing the confidence managers can place in decisions and requiring greater information on which to base decisions. (6) In general, things simply cost more than they previously did. Thus, not only must organizations invest greater amounts initially to begin a project but the potential losses that could be incurred in the event of failure are also greater. Because of reasons such as these, it is important for managers to devote increased time and effort toward clearly defining the goals of an organization and then translating their available resources into goal-directed energies.

Goal setting in organizations can be seen as consisting of two related processes. Initially, on an organization-wide level, management must determine its operative goals and specify measurable operational objectives that will contribute to goal attainment (see Chapter 2). This process, referred to as a *means-ends analysis,* typically results in fairly specific, tangible objectives that **137** can be used for purposes of allocating the available resources (March & Simon, 1958). Next, however, a way must be found to translate these organization-wide goals into smaller segments that can be successfully managed by individual employees. Thus, the second phase in strategic goal setting consists of extending the means-ends analysis down vertically through the organizational hierarchy. This process is shown in Exhibit 8-1. In essence, it is suggested in this exhibit that if sufficient attention, planning, and coordination are employed in the successive identification of goals as one moves down the hierarchy from departments to groups to individuals, then subsequent employee effort should be largely directed toward organizational goal attainment. That is, if individual task goals are specified correctly, employee effort toward such goals should contribute substantially toward the larger goals of the organization. In this way, management can enhance the extent to which organizational requirements can be met (see Chapter 1).

RESOURCE ACQUISITION AND UTILIZATION

Once the strategic decisions have been made concerning the primary direction of an organization, managers then bear a major responsibility for insuring that every effort is made to attain the stated objectives. Efforts must therefore be directed toward securing the necessary resources and utilizing these resources as efficiently as possible in goal-directed activities. At least three related concerns must be dealt with here: (1) system integration and coordination; (2) the role of management policies; and (3) organizational control systems.

System Integration and Coordination

In Chapter 1, five subsystems of organizations were discussed: productive, supportive, maintenance, adaptive, and managerial (Katz & Kahn, 1966). An important part of the managerial role in organizational effectiveness is the nurturance and coordination of these diverse subsystems so that they work together to facilitate goal attainment. In other words, each subsystem must be provided with sufficient resources so that the subsystem itself can maintain itself. In addition, however, the manager's role is that of facilitator and coordinator in integrating the five subsystems so that they perform as a unified whole. For example, the supportive subsystem (which assists in the acquisition of needed raw materials) must be coordinated so that the productive subsystem has the materials it needs to manufacture finished products. Moreover, the maintenance subsystem (which includes a variety of training functions) can assist the productive components by insuring that personnel

138

EXHIBIT 8-1 A Paradigm of Goal-Setting Processes in Organizations

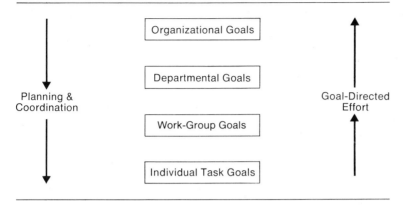

Planning & Coordination

Organizational Goals

Departmental Goals

Work-Group Goals

Individual Task Goals

Goal-Directed Effort

have the latest technological know-how to complete the assigned tasks. The research and development departments, part of the adaptive subsystem, help the organization by contributing new products or services to insure long-term stability of operations. By coordinating the various subsystems, then, maximum energy and expertise are available for organizational activities.

Similarly, efforts can be made to adjust existing organization structure so it is most suited to the demands of a particular technology or environment. For instance, the Burns and Stalker (1961) study found that mechanistic (highly structured) organization design tended to be more suitable for stable environments such as the automobile industry, while organic organization design was more suitable for more dynamic environments like the aerospace industry (see also Chandler, 1962; Lawrence & Lorsch, 1967). Thus, one avenue to improving organizational effectiveness is for management to utilize available information concerning the nature of the external environment and technology to design organization structures that are best suited to demands of a particular situation (see Chapters 4 and 5).

The Role of Policy

A basic responsibility of managers is to establish and implement standardized policies and practices that govern to a large extent the formal activities of an organization. Although such policies have often been justly criticized for being too rigid, arbitrary, and unresponsive to individual needs, there still remains a legitimate place for policy concerns in the pursuit of effectiveness.

Specifically, formal organizational policies can serve several useful functions in organizations: (1) Policies provide guidelines for routine decision making by employees, thereby reducing search behavior for problem solutions and insuring some degree of uniformity of behavior and decision quality. (2) Policies can **139** improve interdepartmental coordination by clearly identifying the domains or spheres of interest of each department or work group. (3) Policies facilitate continuity of action over time by building upon past experiences, thereby reducing the need to make the same types of decisions over and over. (4) Policies often reduce the chances that earlier mistakes will be repeated by setting forth corrective procedures. In essence, then, the role of policy guidelines in organizational effectiveness is to insure that an organization benefits from past decisions and actions and that it minimizes the amount of waste or overlap between the various segments of an organization.

Policies can also have a negative influence on effectiveness, however, when they lead to the continuation of dysfunctional behavior (such as needless red tape) or where they stymie efforts at innovation and adaptation to a changing environment. For instance, the continuation of a policy by one bank not to remain open for business on Saturdays may jeopardize its growth and income if its competitors begin a Saturday banking policy. Thus, policies by management can represent both positive and negative influences on organizational effectiveness, depending upon how they are implemented and how rigid they are. To the extent that managers can use policy guidelines as instruments for goal-directed efforts, their role in facilitating effectiveness is clear. Where the policies themselves assume primary control and managers "do things by the book," their existence can represent an unnecessary impediment to effectiveness.

Organizational Control Systems

All systems are based on the idea of built-in feedback and control loops that provide for a continuous monitoring of system activities. This feedback can be used to keep the system "on target" by noting exceptions so corrective action can be taken. Formal control systems in organizations can take many forms, including financial, physical, and human (Price, 1968). Financial controls include a wide variety of budgetary and reporting procedures, such as profit and loss statements, return on investment, and so forth. Physical control systems include the maintenance and inspection of equipment, inventory control, and so forth (see Newman, 1975, for a detailed discussion of such control systems).

Controls on human resources often take the form of performance appraisals, personnel audits, reward systems, personnel selection and placement procedures, and so forth (Dunnette, 1976; McCormick & Tiffin, 1974). In essence, these human control systems are aimed at insuring that an organization's human resources are best suited for the required tasks and that their development and utilization is consistent with the needs and goals of the organization. For instance, if favorable job attitudes or employee retention are deemed desirable outcomes by management, then consideration may be given to monitoring such attitudes on a fairly regular basis with morale or climate surveys. By doing so, substantial drops in attitudes can be detected and corrective actions can be taken before such negative attitudes lead to poor performance or increased turnover and absenteeism.

Other approaches have attempted to integrate both financial and human resources control systems. One such technique that has become increasingly popular in recent years is *human resource accounting* (HRA). This technique attempts to reflect investments or changes in human resources on the organization's balance sheet (Brummet, Flamholtz, & Pyle, 1968; Rhode & Lawler, 1973). For example, if a company invests heavily in employee training and development that is intended to lead to improved job performance, such investments would be treated the same as investments in new machinery for purposes of computing profit or loss. Moreover, a high turnover ratio among skilled employees would represent a tangible loss to the company that would also be reflected in accounting records.

Although many problems exist in using HRA (for example, it is difficult to reach agreement on what the termination of one employee actually costs an organization), it still holds promise for contributing toward organizational effectiveness in several ways. In particular, the use of HRA or similar procedures allows for a clear reflection of where investments in personnel are being spent, as well as what type of return on investment is being realized. Moreover, HRA represents a relatively straightforward way of identifying the value of those human resources under a particular manager's control; the manager can then be evaluated based on the extent to which these assets have been preserved and enhanced. Where such feedback and control systems can be utilized as reporting procedures for goal-directed effort, their contribution toward organizational effectiveness should not be underestimated.

THE PERFORMANCE ENVIRONMENT

A recent poll of over four thousand U.S. employees on various jobs revealed that 57 percent of those surveyed felt they could easily produce more on their jobs if they wanted to (Opinion Research Corporation, 1972). The survey found that many people simply saw no reason to increase their output at work. The implications of these findings for organizational effectiveness are clear: if the majority of employees are not motivated to maximize their contribution to organizational goals, then organization-wide per- **141** formance and effectiveness will suffer considerably. Consequently, it is important for managers to understand the nature of the performance environment where goal-directed activities take place and to be able to modify this environment where needed to create a more suitable atmosphere for employee effort and performance.

It has been pointed out that behavior in organizations is a function of the interaction of the person and the environment (Lewin, 1938). As such, consideration must be given to improving the person-job fit if more effective outcomes are to be achieved. Putting a highly skilled, independent, ambitious young man on an assembly line or on a custodial crew is clearly not the most appropriate matching procedure. Nor is it the best utilization of an organization's human resources. Hence, effectiveness in organizations can be improved considerably by creating a situation where the characteristics of the job are in tune with the characteristics of the job incumbents, and where both are aimed at improving task-relevant behavior and performance.

Four principal strategies exist for developing a goal-oriented performance environment: (1) employee selection and placement; (2) training and development; (3) task design; and (4) performance appraisal and rewards. In concert, such activities can contribute substantially to improving the work environment where organizational effectiveness is ultimately determined.

Employee Selection and Placement

If management wishes to have a work force that is highly skilled and highly motivated, one factor under its control that can influence such outcomes is the employee selection and placement process. By selecting only those people with higher abilities and skills and with higher initial motivational levels—and then placing them on suitable jobs—organizations can improve the initial quality of at least some of the human inputs that go into the determination of job performance.

Moreover, as noted by Etzioni (1975), recruitment and selection processes can often serve as a substitute for employee socialization and training. If employees who have the desired characteristics (skills, abilities, attitudes, and so on) can be recruited, an organization does not have to develop these characteristics through training and education. On the other hand, if an organization cannot attract the type of people it wants, it must rely on socialization processes to develop the desired characteristics. Such efforts can be seen in recent attempts to hire and retain the hard-core unemployed, whose initial characteristics (such as work attitudes, skills) were not suitable for organizational needs. As Etzioni suggests, if "desirable" employees can be secured through a combination of recruitment and socialization, employee compliance to the needs and demands of the organization will be higher, and resulting effectiveness should increase. Hence, recruitment, selection, and placement become important influences on subsequent organizational success.

Selection techniques generally include the use of interviews, biographical information, and psychological tests. Although the details of the specific selection techniques are beyond the scope of our concern here (see Cummings & Schwab, 1973; Guion, 1976; McCormick & Tiffin, 1974), it is important to note that the validity of the various methods in selecting personnel can vary considerably depending upon the actual selection technique chosen, the conditions under which the technique is used, and the type of job. For instance, the use of psychological tests for identifying performance potential seems to hold more promise for the selection of managers than for tradespeople (Ghiselli, 1963). Therefore, the various selection devices can assist in improving the quality of personnel choices, but their use must be preceded by a careful validation of the chosen technique for a particular job. Moreover, it is often desirable to use several selection techniques together (for example, using tests and interviews) to provide a check on the accuracy of the information gathered from both sources.

Once new employees have been hired, it is still important to insure that they are placed in jobs for which they are well suited. This matching of person and job has been consistently shown to represent an important influence both on performance and on retention of employees (Dunnette et al., 1973; Porter & Steers, 1973; Ross & Zander, 1957; Wanous, 1973). Performance and retention, in turn, have often been identified as indicators of the effectiveness of an organization (see Chapter 3). If employees understand the exact nature and requirements of a job and if they possess the needed skills and abilities, their chances of remaining in the position and doing suitable work are enhanced considerably.

Training and Development

A second general approach to improving job behavior and performance in organizations involves training employees in a variety of skills. Training can serve to develop the capabilities of employees not only for their present jobs but also for future jobs for which they may be needed. That is, training represents an investment in employees (a talent bank) that can then be drawn upon at a future time as needed. As such, it represents an important avenue to bringing about greater effectiveness of operation.

Employee training programs can take a variety of forms, including information presentation techniques (such as lectures, **143** programmed instruction), simulation exercises (for example, case method, role playing), and on-the-job training (for example, vestibule training, learn by doing). (These methods are discussed in detail in Bass & Vaughn, 1966; Goldstein, 1975; Hinrichs, 1976). The appropriateness of the method is determined by the capacity of a particular technique to bring about the desired change. For example, if a company wants to improve the marketing skills of its salespeople, a method (perhaps role-playing exercises) must be selected that will hopefully lead to increased company sales in the near future.

A major problem with training programs in organizations is that management seldom takes the time to validate the results of the particular program. To use the above example, if a company decides to use role-playing techniques to improve salesperson performance, it would ideally follow the results of the training (and hopefully compare the results against a control group) to insure that the training efforts were worth the investment. Unfortunately, many companies simply send their employees "back to school" or hire a training consultant without regard to the impact of such training on subsequent performance. A more preferable strategy is to evaluate the effectiveness of various training programs on several groups of employees, and then continue the use of the more effective programs. Without such monitoring, training investments may contribute little to improving organizational goal attainment. With such monitoring, however, appropriate developmental techniques can be identified and used to the benefit of both the employees and the organization as a whole.

Task Design

Once an organization has selected and trained high quality personnel, it must still consider the nature of the tasks that it expects these people to perform. Several recent investigations have noted the importance of task design as a factor in both employee performance and satisfaction (Brief & Aldag, 1975; Hackman & Lawler, 1971; Hulin & Blood, 1968; Steers & Porter, 1974; Stone & Porter, 1975; Turner & Lawrence, 1965). It is generally believed that more motivating jobs exhibit greater amounts of variety, autonomy, responsibility, feedback, and task identity (or completeness of task). Such task attributes create a situation in which employees are more challenged and can derive intrinsic satisfaction from accomplishing something important and worthwhile. (See Chapter 7 for a detailed discussion.)

In addition, however, some research indicates that these "enriched" jobs may have a greater impact on certain people than on others. For example, Hackman and Lawler (1971) found that employees with strong higher-order needs (such as need for

144

self-esteem, self-actualization) were more influenced by enriched jobs than employees with weak higher-order needs. (See also Brief & Aldag, 1975.) Performance, satisfaction, and absenteeism were all influenced by such need strengths. Similarly, it has been found that need for achievement can also significantly influence the effects of task attributes on both employee performance and job attitudes (Steers, 1975d, 1976b).

In other words, the effects of task design on performance and effectiveness appear to be two-fold. On a general level, enriching jobs by providing greater autonomy, responsibility, feedback, and so on, can apparently improve performance and satisfaction to some extent for a wide variety of employees. However, such effects appear to have the strongest influence on employees exhibiting high need strengths in achievement, self-esteem, and self-actualization. The problem for the contemporary manager, then, is to be able to understand variations in employee need strengths and personal goals and to redesign the jobs (so far as possible) so that they provide sufficient challenge and meaning to be intrinsically motivating. Although tailoring jobs to fit individuals is certainly not an easy task (and may simply be impossible on many jobs), efforts toward that goal would appear to be well spent in view of the potential positive consequences for organizational performance and effectiveness.

Performance Appraisal and Rewards

Finally, managers also have available to them a variety of methods to guide, direct, and reward employee behavior. In particular, formal performance appraisals and reward systems represent two such methods that can be employed to enhance goal-directed energies.

A variety of performance appraisal systems exist that have been used in organizations (see Campbell et al., 1970; Cummings & Schwab, 1973; Lawler, 1971). Such methods include global performance ratings (from "excellent" to "poor"), ranking techniques, critical incidents (brief descriptions of major events or activities), and management by objectives (where performance is evaluated against predetermined individual goals).

In many organizations, performance appraisals are not used to their fullest potential for a variety of reasons. These reasons include: (1) apathy on the part of either the rater or the ratee; (2) lack of trust or belief in the validity of the rating criteria by ratee; (3) poor evaluation criteria—that is, where the criteria are not directly related to the attainment of task goals; (4) poorly trained raters who do not fully understand the nature and purpose of the evaluation; (5) biased raters who systematically favor particular people or groups of people; (6) an overemphasis on short- **145** term results or behavior at the expense of long-term development; and (7) a failure to involve the employees themselves in the rating process.

Studies have consistently shown that the use of performance appraisals can lead to improved job performance, as well as improved job attitudes, where they are seen by employees as being job relevant and equitable and not based on personal characteristics (French et al., 1966). Thus, the problem for managers is to devise and implement a performance appraisal system that is accepted by employees as being impartial to personality variations, that accurately differentiates among employees in terms of their goal-directed effort and performance, and that allows for some form of employee input or participation. Such a system could also be used for employee counseling and feedback aimed at improving future job efforts.

Employee reward systems also have potential for motivating job performance (see Chapter 7). In fact, the rewards an organization offers its employees represent a major vehicle for meeting the three behavioral requirements discussed earlier: people must join and remain with the organization, people must exhibit dependable role performance, and people must engage in some form of spontaneous or innovative behavior. Rewards, particularly if they are based on behavior, can assist in the satisfaction of all three of these requirements by creating conditions where employees can meet their personal goals by remaining with and contributing to the organization.

There are two general types of rewards in organizations: extrinsic and intrinsic. *Extrinsic* rewards include a wide variety of outcomes that are given to the employee by the organization. Such rewards include pay, promotions, fringe benefits, praise, and so forth. *Intrinsic* rewards, on the other hand, represent those outcomes that are largely self-administered. For instance, an employee may feel rewarded if he achieves a certain level of competence on the job or accomplishes a particularly difficult task (such as when a salesman passes the $1 million mark in sales). A major argument behind job redesign efforts is that enriched jobs often lead to greater intrinsic motivation and rewards.

Several additional points warrant emphasis concerning the effectiveness of reward systems. First, rewards tend to contain greater motivational potential when they are perceived by employees as equitable and fair. If women as a group are consistently paid less then men on a particular job, there is little reason to expect them to be as highly motivated to perform as their male counterparts. Second, rewards tend to be more effective when they are tied directly to job performance and are not based on seniority. Such performance-reward contingencies represent a major aspect of many contemporary theories of work motivation (Porter & Lawler, 1968; Vroom, 1964). Third, rewards tend to be more effective when they are highly valued by individuals. Here we are concerned with the issue of goal integration. If a salary increase is highly valued because it is seen as being instrumental for meeting personal goals (for example, buying a new car), then such a reward would serve an important motivational function for that employee. It cannot be assumed in this example, however, that all employees place the same value on money.

This conclusion leads to a fourth aspect of reward systems. Specifically, if employees want different things from their jobs in terms of outcomes (for example, one employee wants a satisfying job regardless of income, while another is solely interested in money), one way to accommodate such variations is to set up "cafeteria style" reward systems (Lawler, 1971), where employees can choose to some extent the rewards for which they wish to work. Thus, one employee may wish to receive increased time off for good performance, while another may prefer a sizable pay raise or promotion. The use of such variable reward systems allows for greater flexibility of operation and improves the chances that employee motivation will be high because the employee is now working for those things that are valued most by him. However, such techniques are not without their problems of administration and equity, as noted by Milkovich and Delaney (1975).

In summary, managers have available to them a wide variety of tools and techniques that can be used to improve the nature of the performance environment. It has been suggested here that at least four such techniques can be used: improved selection and placement techniques, the use of performance-oriented training and development programs, redesigned and enriched tasks, and greater use of valid appraisal and reward systems. Where these techniques are designed and implemented in such a way that they are related to or contingent upon good performance, their contribution to organizational effectiveness is measurably increased.

COMMUNICATION PROCESSES

In any organizational endeavor, the role of communication is of central importance. This is particularly true in regard to the issue of organizational effectiveness. Communication patterns and processes represent the necessary vehicle by which employee activities become coordinated and directed toward the goals and objectives of an organization. In fact, as Barnard (1938) points out, "in an exhaustive theory of organization, communication would occupy a central place, because the structure, extensive- **147** ness, and scope of the organization are almost entirely determined by communication techniques'' (p. 91). Other important organizational processes like leadership, decision making, and adaptation rely heavily on communication for their implementation and the success of such efforts is largely determined by the effectiveness of the communication techniques that are employed.

It is generally believed that effective communications are particularly important in organizations: (1) that must deal with high levels of uncertainty; (2) that are highly complex; and (3) that employ technologies that do not easily lend themselves to routinization or automation (Hall, 1972). Thus, effective communications may be somewhat more important in large research and development organizations than on an assembly line. Even so, an awareness of communication processes is essential to all organizations if maximum efforts are to be coordinated and directed toward organizational interests.

Influences on Communication

Communication in organizations is influenced by several factors (see Guetzkow, 1965; Hall, 1972; Porter & Roberts, 1976). First, communication is a *social* process. It clearly takes more than one person to complete a communication episode. As such, it becomes evident that a variety of social influences exist that can affect the accuracy of the intended message. For instance, prevailing norms and roles may dictate that different forms of address (formal versus informal) be employed in upward as opposed to horizontal communications. Status barriers between levels in an organizational hierarchy may also influence mode of address and message clarity.

Second, communication is influenced by an individual's *perceptual* processes. An employee's receipt of an instruction from his supervisor, for example, can be affected by his opinion of the supervisor, the extent to which the subject matter is controversial or threatening, other things that are on his mind at the time, his interest in the topic, and so forth. Perceptual processes operate to facilitate or inhibit effective communications in organizations in a variety of ways. Most notable among these processes are ''stereotyping'' and ''halo effects,'' which represent attempts by individuals to organize their perceptual environment by simplification. People or things are simply grouped into general categories (for example, black-white, male-female), and the nature of these categories then serves as a guide to the behavior of the perceiver.

Finally, communication processes are influenced by the very nature and *structure* of the organization itself. A principal argument that is often advanced in favor of decentralized structures is that they facilitate improved communications (see Chapter 4).

When messages must travel through several levels in the hierarchy, the opportunities for message distortion are increased considerably, leading to problems that would have been overcome if face-to-face communication were possible.

Problems in Organizational Communication

Several potential communication problems exist that can inhibit goal-directed efforts in groups and organizations (Guetzkow, 1965; Hall, 1972). These problems include the following:

1. *Distortion.* Communication distortion occurs when the intended message becomes altered as it passes through the information channel from sender to receiver. This can happen because of: *(a)* differing frames of reference of sender and receiver; *(b)* the imprecision of language; *(c)* interpretation errors in the receipt of messages; *(d)* the information condensation process; and *(e)* social distance or status barriers between sender and receiver.
2. *Omission.* When only part of an intended message is conveyed to a receiver, it is called omission. For instance, a machine operator may inform his supervisor that his machine has broken down but omit mentioning that he failed to provide the proper machine maintenance, which caused the breakdown. Omission results both because the sender is unable to grasp the entire message himself and therefore transmits incomplete information or because the sender intentionally "filters" the intended message (possibly out of fear of retribution).
3. *Overload.* Communication overload exists when the receiver is "buried" in information to such an extent that rational decision making and management behavior suffer. As such, overload often contributes to problems of distortion and omission.
4. *Timeliness.* In complex organizations, employees are continually being barraged by information. A major problem concerning the effectiveness of such communication is that of timing. Because communication messages stimulate action, it is important that their transmittal be timed so that they will receive the necessary attention. For instance, providing detailed instructions to workers on a particular job one month before the particular task is to be done may lead to problems of performance failure because of the lengthy time interval between task instructions and task performance.
5. *Acceptance.* Even if all four of the above problems could be overcome, it is still necessary to gain acceptance of **149**

the message by the intended receiver if the message is to be acted upon. If an employee does not accept the message (that is, it "falls on deaf ears"), there is little reason to believe that the message content will affect his or her attitudes or behavior at work. The extent to which communications are accepted is influenced by such factors as employee needs, motives, and experience, as well as by his or her perception of the particular situation. In this sense, a major function of leadership in organizations is to secure the acceptance of task-oriented communications.

Communication and Organizational Effectiveness

If communication is considered an essential aspect of improving organizational effectiveness, then questions are logically raised concerning ways to improve the exchange of needed information in organizational settings. Specifically, the problem for management here is to improve the accuracy, flow, and acceptance of relevant communication so that uncertainty is reduced to its lowest possible level. Remedies to communication problems can be grouped according to the direction of the intended message: downward, upward, and horizontal.

Downward communication. Managers can initiate several steps aimed at improving communication with their subordinates. Some of these techniques are summarized in Exhibit 8-2. In general, these techniques involve clarifying the nature of organizational requirements for employees. The more an employee understands about his job—including what he is to do and why—the less search behavior is required and the more goal-directed effort is available, assuming the employee accepts the task and is motivated to perform it. The use of multiple channels (for example, using written and verbal messages simultaneously) and repetition of messages serve to reinforce the impact of the intended message and insure that it has been received and understood. Moreover, feedback sessions and performance appraisals represent attempts to keep employee effort "on target." In essence, then, most downward communication in organizations is aimed at facilitating improved task performance by clarifying both the objectives and the potential rewards for satisfactory accomplishment.

Upward communication. Perhaps the most important problem in upward communication is information overload. The sheer volume of facts, opinions, suggestions, complaints, and so forth that are transmitted to superiors can easily stifle managerial effectiveness by hampering a manager's ability to act quickly and decisively based on pertinent information. For instance, Allison (1971) has noted that an analysis of the events leading up to the Cuban

EXHIBIT 8-2 Strategies for Improving Communication Effectiveness

Downward Communications

1. Job instructions can be presented clearly to employees so they understand more precisely what is expected.
2. Efforts can be made to explain the rationale behind the required tasks to employees so they understand why they are being asked to do something.
3. Management can provide greater feedback concerning the nature and quality of performance, thereby keeping employees "on target."
4. Multiple communication channels can be used to increase the chances that the message is properly received.
5. Important messages can be repeated to insure penetration.
6. In some cases, it is desirable to bypass formal communication channels and go directly to the intended receiver with the message.

Upward Communications

1. Upward messages can be screened so only the more relevant aspects are received by top management.
2. Managers can attempt to change the organizational climate so subordinates feel freer to transmit negative as well as positive messages without fear of retribution.
3. Managers can sensitize themselves so they are better able to detect bias and distorted messages from their subordinates.
4. Sometimes it is possible to utilize "distortion-proof" messages (Downs, 1967), such as providing subordinates with report forms requiring quantified or standardized data.
5. Social distance and status barriers between employees on various levels can be reduced so messages will be more spontaneous.

Horizontal Communications

1. Efforts can be made to develop interpersonal skills between group members and departments so greater openness and trust exist.
2. Reward systems can be utilized which reward interdepartmental cooperation and minimize "zero-sum game" situations.
3. Interdepartmental meetings can be used to share information concerning what other departments are involved in.
4. In some cases, the actual design of the organization itself can be changed to provide greater opportunities for interdepartmental contacts (e.g., shifting from a traditional to a matrix organization design).

---

missile crisis of 1962 reveals that the Central Intelligence Agency had sufficient information to assess accurately the deployment of missiles on Cuba and take quiet diplomatic steps to remedy the problem long before events reached crisis proportion. The problem was that the CIA possessed so much information that it was months behind in its processing of such intelligence. By the time the information was analyzed, opportunities for diplomatic conflict resolution had long passed.

A commonly used way to reduce overload problems is *screening,* where only the more important aspects of a message are transmitted up the hierarchy. Screening serves to eliminate much of the more peripheral details and opinions and only allow information to be forwarded that is needed for a particular decision. Screening can take several forms. For instance, Dubin (1959) **151** discusses the "principal of sufficiency," where organizations intentionally regulate both the quantity and quality of upward information (for example, where managers at each level in the hierarchy write "summary reports" for their superiors). As these reports go up the hierarchy, they increasingly contain information pertinent to policy decisions and omit details aimed at implementation decisions. A second approach is "queuing," where messages are handled sequentially by managers (often in rank order of importance). Finally, many organizations employ some form of "management by exception," where routine decisions and actions are handled by policy guidelines and only exceptions, deviations, or emergency situations are reported upward.

A second approach to improving upward communication involves attempts to create an organizational climate in which subordinates have little fear about reporting negative outcomes to their superiors. A major problem in upward communication is that bad news often gets filtered out as it moves up the hierarchy so that quick remedial action is inhibited. If conditions could be created in which subordinates did not fear negative consequences from admitting mistakes, more rapid and accurate reporting could result and management could act more promptly to take corrective action.

Other strategies could be mentioned, including the use of "distortion-proof" messages (Downs, 1967), the reduction of social and status barriers, and an increased awareness of potential sources of bias in reporting (see Exhibit 8-2). In general, such techniques aim at improving effectiveness of operation by improving the quantity and quality of the feedback that managers receive. If extraneous materials are screened out of messages, if employees feel more open about reporting events and outcomes, and if managers are sensitive to the potential biases associated with certain messages, then the quality of information for managerial decision making and behavior should be enhanced considerably.

Horizontal communication. If an organization is to make efficient use of its available resources, it is important that a concerted effort be made to coordinate and integrate the efforts of the various departments and work groups. Lawrence and Lorsch (1967) address this issue in their discussion concerning the appropriate levels of integration and differentiation in organizations (see Chapter 5). The success of an organization in achieving these appropriate levels hinges on the effectiveness of their horizontal communication. Several strategies can be identified that are aimed at improving such communication.

For example, efforts can be made to develop higher levels of interpersonal trust and openness between work-group and department members. If such an atmosphere can be created, more spontaneous, creative efforts can emerge, and less energy will be devoted to protecting departmental territoriality. (It will be remembered from Chapter 7 that creative and spontaneous behavior is considered a basic behavioral requirement of organizations.) In addition, reward systems can be designed so that they reward cooperation between departments instead of competition. For example, performance evaluations for managers could include consideration of the extent to which the manager helped *other* departments reach their goals. Such techniques reduce the inclination to conceal information that may be useful to other departments or groups.

Many organizations use some form of department head meetings to share information between departments. Unfortunately, these meetings often become vehicles for mostly downward communications and little effort is devoted to facilitating horizontal information sharing. Instead, efforts could be made to have interdepartmental meetings where all the members of two or more departments or groups (not just the supervisors) could come together to share information and ideas. If each department had more accurate information concerning the needs of other departments, more concerted attempts could be made to integrate employee efforts for mutual goal attainment.

Techniques such as these—if properly designed, implemented, and rewarded—can make a major contribution to improving effectiveness by improving the information-gathering and information-sharing activities of an organization. Where uncertainty can be reduced, the quality of the resulting decisions and the decisiveness of managerial action can be improved measurably to the benefit of organizational stability, growth, and development.

MANAGING EFFECTIVE ORGANIZATIONS Part Two

9

In Chapter 8, four general areas were discussed in which managerial behavior could have an impact on the effectiveness of an organization. These areas were strategic goal setting, resource acquisition and utilization, the performance environment, and communication processes. In this chapter, we will continue our discussion of the role of management in facilitating organizational success by examing the two remaining areas of managerial concern in effectiveness: (1) leadership and decision making and (2) organizational adaptation and innovation. It is argued here that these six topics, when taken together, represent the primary focal points for effective managerial behavior in organizations.

LEADERSHIP AND DECISION MAKING

Nature of Leadership

The concept of leadership in organizations has a variety of meanings. One of the more relevant meanings from the standpoint of managerial behavior has been suggested by Katz and Kahn (1966). They define *leadership* as "the influential increment over and above mechanical compliance with the routine directives of the organization" (p. 302). In other words, leadership occurs when one individual can induce others to do something of their own volition instead of doing something because it is required or because they fear the consequences of noncompliance. It is this voluntary component of leadership that sets it apart from other influence processes such as authority and power.

Functions of leadership. In many ways, it is the quality of managerial leadership that differentiates effective organizations from ineffective ones. Leadership can serve several important functions that are necessary for organizational effectiveness. To begin with, leadership fills the void left by the incompleteness and imperfections of organization design (Katz & Kahn, 1966). Because it is not possible to design the "perfect" organization and account for every member's activities at all times, something must insure that human behavior is coordinated and directed toward task accomplishment. This something is leadership. Second, leadership helps to maintain the stability of an organization in a turbulent environment by allowing for rapid adjustment and adaptation to changing environmental conditions (see Chapter 5). Third, leadership can assist in the internal coordination of diverse organizational units, particularly during periods of growth and change. It can act as a buffer between conflicting parties. Fourth, leadership plays a role in maintaining a stable membership for an organization by facilitating personal need satisfaction and personal goal attainment.

Leadership can be viewed as a multidimensional process, consisting of at least two types of activities. One type of activity is directed toward task accomplishment. Such activities are said to be *instrumental* in that they are aimed at securing employee effort on task-relevant activities. In addition, leadership can serve a variety of *socio-emotional* activities. That is, it is important for a leader to be concerned with maintaining stability in the work group and enhancing the personal need satisfaction of group members. Organizational success is influenced to no small degree by the ability of its leaders to handle both types of activities simultaneously, thus insuring that both organizational and personal goals are largely satisfied (see Chapter 2).

Various models of leadership have been suggested in the literature on organizations (Fiedler, 1965; Fiedler & Chemers, 1974; House, 1971; Hunt & Larson, 1974; Stogdill, 1974; Vroom & Yetton, 1973; Yukl, 1971). In general, these models suggest that leadership effectiveness is a result of a combination of factors, including the characteristics of the individual (for example, leader personality, intelligence, and so on) and the characteristics of the situation (such as relative power distribution between superior and subordinates, nature of the task, time pressures). A major thrust of many of the more recent so-called "contingency models" is that the success of a particular leadership style (for example, autocratic versus participative) depends in large part on the particular situation at the time. When time is short and the outcome of the decision will have little impact on subordinates, a more autocratic style may be more effective to get the job done quickly. On the other **155** hand, when group acceptance of a particular action is important, a more participative style of leadership may be more effective.

Constraints on leadership. An important aspect of understanding how leadership works in organizations is recognizing occasions where it may not work or where it may have a diminished impact. If leadership is viewed as a means of enhancing effectiveness in organizations, the potential constraints on such means must be clearly recognized. Several possible constraints on leadership effectiveness can be identified:

1. The extent to which managerial decisions and behavior are preprogrammed due to precedent, structure, technological specificity, or the absence of familiarity with available alternative solutions.
2. The traits and skills (particularly leadership skills) of the manager. Research has indicated, for example, that effective leaders tend to exhibit certain personal characteristics (such as intelligence, aggressiveness, ''presence,'' good communications skills). Moreover, good leaders typically demonstrate expertise in their own area of endeavor (such as a foreman who can perform all of the jobs of his or her subordinates). The lack of such skills may preclude to some extent effective leader behavior.
3. The inability of a leader to vary his or her behavior to suit the particular situation. More ''rigid'' patterns of behavior may be inappropriate for many situations requiring certain styles of leadership.
4. The extent to which a leader controls rewards that are desired by subordinates (pay raises, promotion, and so forth).
5. The characteristics of the situation (how much power a leader has, the importance of a given decision or action, the quality of interpersonal relations between leader and subordinates, and so forth).
6. The openness of the organization to variations in leader behavior (for example, a participative leadership style may be discouraged or prohibited in a military organization).

These constraints serve to set the stage on which influence attempts take place. The greater the skills and abilities of the leader, the easier it will be for him or her to deal with such constraints and use the available latitude to best advantage in securing subordinate support for task accomplishment.

Decision-Making Behavior

A common characteristic of effective leaders is the ability to make decisions that are appropriate, timely, and acceptable. In fact, the inability or unwillingness to accept such responsibility can easily lead to a loss of allegiance or legitimation by followers. If we are to understand more fully the role of managerial leadership in organizational effectiveness, it is therefore necessary to examine the nature of decision-making processes and the role of management in such processes.

Decision making in organizations is a process of selecting among available alternatives (Shull, Delbecq, & Cummings, 1970). Three stages in the decision-making process can be identified (Simon, 1960): (1) *intelligence activities,* which include problem recognition and search for the causes of the problem as well as possible solutions; (2) *design activities,* which formulate and assess alternative courses of action in terms of positive and negative outcomes; and (3) *choice activities,* or the decision itself. The quality of the resulting decision is seen as being largely influenced by the thoroughness of the intelligence and design phases, as well as by the rationality and goals of the decision makers themselves (see Chapter 5).

By building upon this process, it is possible to examine some general guidelines for improving the manner in which decisions are made in organizations. The improvement in the nature and quality of the resulting decisions should then contribute to effectiveness by improving the allocation and utilization of an organization's various resources for purposes of task accomplishment. One such strategy for improving decision-making effectiveness has been suggested by Thompson (1967).

Briefly, Thompson suggests that decisions in organizations are characterized by two major dimensions: (1) beliefs concerning cause-effect relationships; and (2) preferences among possible outcomes. Taking a contingency approach, it is argued that the selection of an appropriate strategy for a decision is a function of the nature of these two dimensions at the time of decision, as shown in Exhibit 9-1. A different decision strategy is suggested for managers for each of the four possible situations:

1. A *computational strategy* is seen as being most appropriate where both beliefs and preferences are relatively certain. For instance, if a company knew from past experience that increasing its advertising expenditures would improve sales (cause-effect belief) and if there was general agreement among managers that a sales increase is desirable (outcome preference), the decision would be obvious, assuming sufficient resources.

2. A *judgmental strategy* is appropriate where preferences are certain but cause-effect beliefs are not. For example, if management wanted to improve sales but was uncertain whether this could best be accomplished through increased **157**

EXHIBIT 9-1   Strategies for Decision Making

Preferences Regarding Possible Outcomes

		Certainty	Uncertainty
Beliefs About Cause-Effect Relations	Certain	**Computational Strategy**	**Compromise Strategy**
	Uncertain	**Judgmental Strategy**	**Inspirational Strategy**

Source: J. D. Thompson, *Organizations in Action* (New York: McGraw-Hill, 1967), p. 134. Used by permission.

advertising or reduced product pricing, the decision would rest on the judgment or reasoning of the parties involved.

3. A *compromise strategy* is considered suitable where there is relative certainty concerning cause-effect relations but lack of agreement concerning outcome preferences. Here we are concerned about goal conflicts. One manager may prefer to improve product quality or image, for example, while another prefers to increase profits. Although the means to each of these goals may be clear, some compromise or bargaining may be necessary in reaching a final course of action (see also Cyert & March, 1963).

4. An *inspirational strategy* is suggested when both beliefs and preferences are unclear. In other words, when little is known about a situation and few people have clear preferences among available alternatives, the time may be appropriate for either "brainstorming" attempts or for someone to play a hunch. Under such circumstances, it is generally believed that some form of action is preferable to no action at all. Companies often use outside management consultants for such purposes when they know something is wrong but are not sure about the precise nature of the problem. Oftentimes, an outsider can provide a fresh insight and suggest alternatives that have been overlooked by management.

In essence, then, Thompson (1967) suggests some clear guidelines for managers concerning various styles, or strategies, for decision making, depending upon what is known about the situation and what are the particular goals or preferences of management.

Participation in Decision Making

A major issue concerning managerial approaches to decision making is the extent to which managers allow (or should allow) their subordinates to participate in decisions affecting their jobs. Participative decision making represents one attempt to decentralize authority and influence throughout the organization. It is generally thought that such action will often lead to improved decision quality, increased commitment of members to decision outcomes, and increased satisfaction resulting from involvement. Such results are often felt to be associated with effective organizations (see Chapter 3).

Three general levels of shared decision making can be identified: (1) *autocratic decisions,* which are made exclusively by superiors; (2) *consultative decisions,* which are still made by supervisors alone, but after they consult with their subordinates and collect relevant information; and (3) *group decisions,* which are made by the group itself (Vroom & Yetton, 1973). In actual practice, such styles exist on a continuum from autocracy to total abdication by a superior. Most decisions would probably fall somewhere in between these two extremes.

A recent contingency model of participation in decision making (Vroom, 1973) suggests that, instead of using one decision style exclusively, effective managers will employ all these styles, depending upon the particular decision situation. Specifically, Vroom identifies three aspects of a situation that appear to influence the success of a given style: (1) the required quality of the decision; (2) the acceptance or commitment on the part of subordinates necessary to carry out the decision effectively; and (3) the amount of time required to make the decision. Based on this model, Vroom and Yetton (1973) carried out a series of investigations on managerial decision-making behavior. The major findings included the following:

1. Managers tend to be *more* participative when the quality of the decision is important.
2. Managers tend to be *more* participative when subordinate acceptance of the decision is critical for its effective implementation.
3. Managers tend to be *more* participative when they trust their subordinates to focus on organizational rather than personal goals and when conflict among subordinates is minimal.
4. Managers tend to be *less* participative when they themselves have all the necessary information to make a high quality decision.

5. Managers tend to be *less* participative when the immediate problem is well structured or where there is a common solution that has been applied in similar situations in the past.

6. Managers tend to be *less* participative when time is limited and immediate action is required.

The effects of increased subordinate participation in decision making on subsequent performance and satisfaction are also worthy of note. It has generally been found that more supportive, participative styles of leadership lead to increased job satisfaction, lower turnover and absenteeism, lower intragroup stress and conflict, and increased member cooperation (Filley & House, 1969; Steers & Porter, 1974; Vroom, 1964). Moreover, such leadership can lead to improved job performance, although the results are not entirely consistent (Dubin, 1965). In fact, many of the current industrial efforts at redesigning and enriching jobs represent attempts to allow greater subordinate influence and participation in the events surrounding their jobs.

The remaining question is why participation often leads to improved performance and job attitudes. A partial answer to this question has been discussed by Ebert and Mitchell (1975). They suggest four reasons why participative decision making "works": (1) it clarifies organizational contingencies—employees understand better what is expected of them and what the potential rewards are for task accomplishment; (2) it increases the likelihood that employees will work for rewards and outcomes that they value; (3) it increases the effects of social influence on behavior; and (4) it increases the amount of control that an employee has over his own behavior. Thus, participative decision making can represent a useful vehicle for facilitating organizational goal attainment in certain circumstances. However, its implementation should only follow a careful analysis of whether the particular situation warrants such an approach or whether alternative decision strategies are more suitable.

Improving Leadership Effectiveness

Based on this examination of the nature of leadership and decision making in organizations, it is now possible to suggest several ways in which the effectiveness of managerial behavior can be enhanced, thereby contributing to overall organizational effectiveness. Five such ways will be discussed: (1) managerial selection and placement; (2) leadership training; (3) rewarding leader behavior; (4) rewarding subordinate behavior; and (5) organizational engineering.

Managerial selection and placement. Initially, it appears that improved leadership effectiveness can be facilitated to some extent by increasing the likelihood that those in command possess the requisite qualifications to influence their subordinates on task-related activities. Unfortunately, this is much easier said than done. Identifying leadership potential presumes that an organization knows what characterizes good leaders and that it can accurately predict how various individuals will behave in an array of situations. Some research indicates that effective leaders do tend to possess certain identifiable personal characteristics, including high intelligence, sensitivity to situational variation, initiative, self-assurance, and individuality (Ghiselli, 1963). These characteristics are not considered universal, however.

In addition, an awareness of the situation (for example, the relative power distribution between superior and subordinates, the clarity or specificity of the task, the interpersonal relationships between superior and subordinates) is also vital in the selection of effective leaders (Fiedler, 1965). That is, a more authoritarian, task-oriented supervisor may be more suited to a work environment characterized by high task structuring, centralized power, and distant leader-subordinate relations. Conversely, a more people-oriented, considerate supervisor may be most appropriate for situations characterized by task ambiguity, decentralized power and influence, and close leader-subordinate relations. The point here is that the selection and placement of managers and supervisors should, according to these findings, be influenced heavily by both the personal traits of the individual and the work situation into which he or she is to be placed. Such a conclusion is largely inconsistent with the current practice of promoting employees into supervisory positions on the basis of seniority or even on the basis of good job performance alone. Although good job performance may be a desirable trait for supervisors to possess, it does not by itself insure good supervisory abilities.

Leadership training. In addition to improving the selection and placement procedures of supervisory personnel, attempts can also be made to develop such individuals to their fullest potential as managers through a variety of training techniques. (For a detailed discussion of training methods, see Bass & Vaughn, 1966; Campbell et al., 1970; Goldstein, 1975.) In general, training techniques can take two forms. First, it is possible to change an individual so that he or she exhibits greater amounts of a desirable trait (for example, he or she can be made more self-assertive, more decisive, more interpersonally competent). Second, it is possible to show an individual how to modify the work enviornment so it is more compatible with the individual's approach to management. For example, a more authoritarian manager may try to create **161**

a work environment where tasks are clearly defined, the locus of power is centralized, and interpersonal relations have minimal impact on performance (such as a machine-paced assembly line). By far, the majority of existing training techniques have been aimed at modifying the individual instead of the situation on the assumption that these changes are more easily accomplished.

Campbell et al. (1970) have identified five general types of managerial training programs: (1) general management programs, which attempt to develop broad managerial skills; (2) human relations programs, which focus on interpersonal problems in supervision; (3) problem-solving and decision-making programs; (4) laboratory education programs, which use the experiential approach to enlighten managers concerning their own behavior; and (5) specialized programs, which cover a variety of special topics that are important to particular organizations.

Based on their review of the available findings on these various training techniques, Campbell and associates arrived at the following conclusions concerning the effectiveness:

1. Approximately 80 percent of the studies in the general management and general human relations categories yielded significant results on most of the criteria which were used . . . . In general, however, the thrust of these studies reflects an overreliance on one particular class of criterion variables, namely, measures of "human relations mindedness. . . ." [Few studies considered the effects of such training on objective job performance.]

2. The evidence, though still limited, is reasonably convincing that T-group training and the laboratory method do induce behavioral changes in the "back home" setting. This statement is based primarily on results from the studies using the open-ended perceived change measure as a criterion. . . .

3. The small number of research studies dealing with attempts to teach problem-solving and decision-making skills is disappointing. So is the generally negative tone of the results. Either such programs do not produce changes in behavior or we have not yet learned to detect them. . . .

4. Studies comparing the effects of two or more methods [of training] are too few to warrant any attempt at generalization. Similarly, these include just enough studies examining interactions with individual differences to suggest that some are important and some are not and that the overall pattern is a complex one. Both of these research areas deserve a great deal more attention. (1970, pp. 321–24)

In summary, this review leads to very few firm conclusions regarding the most appropriate or effective way to train leaders. Several reasons exist for this lack of consensus. First, as noted by Campbell et al. (1970), most of the studies they reviewed had several methodological problems that could interfere with the validity of the findings. In addition, however, it appears that a major reason for the inability to reach a consensus on the findings is the failure of most studies to recognize situational variations as an influence on behavior and effectiveness. A leadership style that may be appropriate for one situation may be inappropriate for another. Instead, it may be more suitable to develop a manager's repertoire of leadership skills—as well as his capacity to diagnose differences in situations—so the most applicable skills can be used as dictated by the situation.

Rewarding leader behavior. A third approach to improving leader effectiveness involves designing organizational reward systems that are responsive to desired managerial behavior. If pay raises, promotions, and the like were based primarily on the ability of managers to ellicit subordinate efforts on goal-directed activities, then such managers would be more inclined to see effective leader behavior as being instrumental for desired rewards (see Chapter 7). In other words, by manipulating the available rewards, organizations can motivate managers to be more aware of the role of leadership in task accomplishment and to attempt to improve their capacity for such activities.

Rewarding subordinate behavior. Similarly, an organization can structure its rewards so they stimulate rather than inhibit desired behavior on the part of subordinates. In other words, it is possible for an organization to increase the discretion managers have in rewarding subordinates so that following a leader's directives will be seen by subordinates as instrumental to personal goal attainment. Recent "path-goal" theories of leadership reflect this view (Evans, 1970, 1974; House, 1971; House & Mitchell, 1974). These theories suggest that a leader will be effective to the extent that he makes rewards available to subordinates and to the extent that these rewards are contingent upon the subordinate's accomplishment of specific goals.

Following a path-goal approach, the role of a leader in facilitating effective task performance can be seen as consisting of the following activities:

1. Recognizing and/or arousing subordinates' need for outcomes over which the leader has some control,
2. Increasing personal payoffs to subordinates for work-goal attainment,
3. Making the path to those payoffs easier to travel by coaching and direction,
4. Helping subordinates clarify expectancies,
5. Reducing frustrating barriers, and
6. Increasing the opportunities for personal satisfaction contingent upon effective performance. (House & Mitchell, 1974, p. 85)

In other words, by integrating personal and organizational goals, a leader can improve the likelihood that effort toward both types of goals will be increased. Hence, the more effort an employee directs toward organizational goals, the more effort is simultaneously directed toward personal need satisfaction. Because potential goal conflicts are reduced, greater efficiency and effectiveness of operation are therefore possible. **163**

Organizational engineering. Finally, organizations may adopt a more structural (as opposed to a behavioral) approach to improving leader effectiveness by attempting to modify either an individual's job or the way such jobs are clustered (for example, reporting procedures, lines of authority, decentralization). It is thus hoped that such changes in the structure of an organization will be more conducive to goal attainment. In other words, as Fiedler (1965, p. 115) describes it, organizations may want to "engineer the job to fit the manager."

For instance, if a manager had a high level of technical competence but was ineffective in "leading" his subordinates, it may not be feasible—or even desirable—to remove him. (This situation is particularly common among R&D scientists and in the higher echelons of management, where a particular individual is highly competent in one area—and perhaps indispensible—but lacks needed expertise in others.) Instead, the nature of the work situation could be modified so it was more consistent with the individual's behavior. For example, interpersonal problems of the group could be handled on an informal basis by an assistant. Moreover, the manager's position power could be increased by giving him greater controls over rewards and sanctions, increasing his rank, or channeling more information through him. Although this strategy is not an ideal one, it may represent an optimal solution to the problem of utilizing needed personnel who lack certain requisite skills for managing. By modifying the job around such individuals, some degree of efficiency can be maintained while still utilizing the talents of the particular individual.

It can be seen from the above discussion on leadership and decision making that these interrelated processes represent a strong influence on the ability of an organization to organize and utilize its available resources for goal-directed efforts. Not only must quality decisions be made in a timely fashion but in addition such decisions must be accepted and carried out expeditiously if organizations are to maximize their return on investment in human resources. Throughout this process, the role of leadership emerges as a necessary link between reaching decisions or determining courses of action, and actually carrying out the actions as they relate to improving the effectiveness of organizations.

ORGANIZATIONAL ADAPTATION AND INNOVATION

It has been emphasized throughout this examination of effectiveness that the ability of an organization to successfully adapt to a changing environment is a primary characteristic of effective organizations (Duncan, 1973; Georgopoulos & Tannenbaum, 1957; Price, 1968). Such organizational changes must not be random or merely for the sake of change, however. Instead, management has a responsibility to balance the needs of adaptation and innovation with the equally important needs for stability and continuity of operations. As pointed out by Kast and Rosenzweig:

> Management is charged with the responsibility for maintaining a dynamic equilibrium by diagnosing situations and designing adjustments that are most appropriate for coping with current conditions. A dynamic equilibrium for an organization would include the following dimensions:
>
> 1. Enough stability to facilitate achievement of current goals.
> 2. Enough continuity to ensure orderly change in either ends or means.
> 3. Enough adaptability to react appropriately to external opportunities and demands as well as changing internal conditions.
> 4. Enough innovativeness to allow the organization to be proactive (initiate changes) when conditions warrant. (1974, pp. 574–75)

The capacity of management to simultaneously meet these four conditions will largely determine the ability of an organization to survive and grow in a turbulent environment.

Forces for Change

Occasions for change in organizations become apparent when management senses that an organization's current activities, goals, or values are deficient in some way. When such a deficiency occurs (that is, when there is a notable gap between what an organization is trying to do and what it is actually accomplishing), it is incumbent upon management to initiate positive steps aimed at reducing such a performance gap (Downs, 1967). For instance, several years ago many scientists and mathematicians—and a great number of college students—considered a slide rule essential for carrying out the computations required of them. Almost overnight, however, the advent of inexpensive electronic pocket calculators made the slide rule largely a thing of the past. One company alone experienced a 75 percent drop in slide rule sales in just two years. In other words, the technology of calculating instruments changed radically, necessitating a change in those organizations producing such instruments. Only those companies that were aware of future trends and began planning early were able to maintain their position in the market. Other companies either disappeared or have moved on to other fields of endeavor leaving behind a lucrative market.

The causes of performance gaps can be found both within organizations and without. If we are to take a comprehensive view of innovation and adaptation processes, then managers must be cognizant of both types of forces and be able to account for both in their actions and behavior.

External forces. A variety of external forces for change that require organizational action can be identified. These include: (1) changes in economic or market conditions, such as when demand **165**

for a company's products declines suddenly; (2) changes in product or manufacturing technology, such as when a competitor discovers a less expensive manufacturing process; (3) changes in the legal or political situation, such as when a new consumer protection law proscribes current products or practices; and (4) changes in resource availability, such as when a major input (oil, for example) becomes far more costly or simply unavailable.

Such forces create gaps in organizational performance that, if not remedied, can lead to severe threats to organizational stability and survival. For instance, the oil shortage of the mid-1970s and the resulting corporate distribution policies led to the demise of many "independent" service stations that clearly lacked the resources that were necessary to survive and compete with company-owned service stations. Simply put, the independent stations did not have the capacity to respond adequately to external forces for change.

Internal forces. Similarly, several factors within an organization can represent important forces for change. These factors include: (1) changes in the composition and/or personal goals of employees, such as when newer and/or younger employees have a different "work ethic" than more senior employees; (2) changes in job technology, such as when craft-type jobs are replaced by automated equipment; (3) changes in organization structure, such as when a company grows so large it needs to create new divisions; (4) changes in organization climate, such as when mass layoffs create a climate of distrust, hostility, and insecurity; and (5) changes in organizational goals, such as those caused by goal succession. This last reason for change (goal succession) may result either because management realizes its initial expectations are too high, too low, or are misdirected for some reason.

Such forces serve to create unstable conditions within organizations and jeopardize goal-directed efforts. When stability and continuity are threatened, it is necessary for organizations to attempt to adapt their structure or behavior to insure long-term growth and survival. Before considering such change processes, however, it is useful to consider several reasons why change in organizational settings is often difficult.

Resistance to Change

Resistance to change in organizations can be found throughout the organizational milieu. These diverse sources can be categorized into either personal (or individual) sources and organizational sources. Some of the more prominent personal and organizational reasons why change is difficult in many organizations are listed in Exhibit 9–2.

EXHIBIT 9-2   Personal and Organizational Sources of Resistance to Change

Personal Sources	Organizational Sources
1. Misunderstanding of purpose, mechanics, or consequences of change	1. Reward system may reinforce status quo.
2. Failure to see need for change	2. Interdepartmental rivalry or conflict, leading to an unwillingness to cooperate
3. Fear of unknown	3. Sunk costs in past decisions and actions
4. Fear of loss of status, security, power, etc., resulting from change	4. Fear that change will upset current balance of power between groups and departments
5. Lack of identification or involvement with change	5. Prevailing organizational climate
6. Habit	6. Poor choice of method of introducing change
7. Vested interests in status quo	7. Past history of unsuccessful change attempts and their consequences
8. Group norms and role prescriptions	8. Structural rigidity
9. Threat to existing social relationships	
10. Conflicting personal and organizational objectives	

Personal sources.   It can be seen in Exhibit 9–2 that, on a personal level, employees may resist the introduction of new techniques or methods because they feel secure under the existing conditions and fear that the changes will destroy the existing interpersonal relationships that have developed through the years. Moreover, some employees may not fully understand the reasons behind a change or how it will affect their own particular situation. Group norms may operate to resist any change in work procedures for fear of it leading to higher output without commensurate rewards.

In addition, employees may simply not identify with the changes (creating passive resistance) and "drag their feet" in implementation. This last reason has often been cited as a reason for the failure of many "affirmative action" programs that attempt to increase minority hiring; it is often the case that existing non-minority employees are simply indifferent to the goals of affirmative action. It is important to realize here that most personal reasons for resisting change are not the result of any overt intention to interfere with goal attainment. Instead, such resistance results largely from a fear of the consequences of change and a preference for the known over the unknown.

Organizational sources.   The nature and character of the organization itself can also influence the extent to which change is accepted in organizations. For instance, the prevailing reward structure may be designed to favor existing behavior (for example, when an organization pays salespeople solely on the basis of total sales and ignores effort and time investments in developing new customers). Moreover, when various departments view each other **167**

as rivals, they may act to subvert cooperative efforts aimed at change for fear of resulting encroachments on their territory. Managers of organizations may consider themselves bound by past decisions and actions because of previous large investments made in a particular product or technology. It is sometimes easier to live by past decisions than to admit that a mistake was made or conditions have changed. Finally, previous organizational attempts at change may have been ill-conceived and unsuccessful, leading to an absence of confidence in the success of any new attempt.

Other reasons could be mentioned (see Exhibit 9–2). The important point here is that it is incumbent upon management to be aware of the various sources of resistance to change in organizations and to be able to act in such a way that these sources of resistance are minimized. This conclusion implies that managers have an obligation to assess accurately the nature and need for change. They then must lay the groundwork for the implementation of change by examining and dealing with the various possible sources of resistance. In other words, it may be concluded that the manner in which the change is implemented is at least as important for success as the actual change itself.

Planned Change in Organizations

In its ideal form, the change process can be viewed as a series of fairly discreet, sequential steps leading from the recognition of the problem to the introduction and assessment of the change strategy. Although actual change processes may be far more complex, the use of a simplified flow diagram serves to highlight some of the more important steps in the process. The steps in a simplified change process are identified in Exhibit 9–3.

Initially, because of changes in the environment, structure, technology, or membership of an organization, performance gaps emerge. Such gaps may take the form of a loss of sales revenue, reduced productivity, increased absenteeism and turnover, and so forth. Once these gaps are recognized by management, efforts can then be made to create a climate that is conducive to change. If sufficient time and effort are invested initially in eliminating the various causes for resistance to change, then a more open approach can be taken to the change process. Next, management diagnoses the extent of the problem and, based on their analysis, recommendations are made for appropriate adjustments that purportedly will remedy the situation and eliminate or reduce the performance gap. After considering the implications, costs, and benefits of the various alternatives, a decision on a particular change strategy is made and implemented. Finally, once implementation is complete, management can assess the extent to

EXHIBIT 9-3 An Outline of Basic Change Processes in Organizations

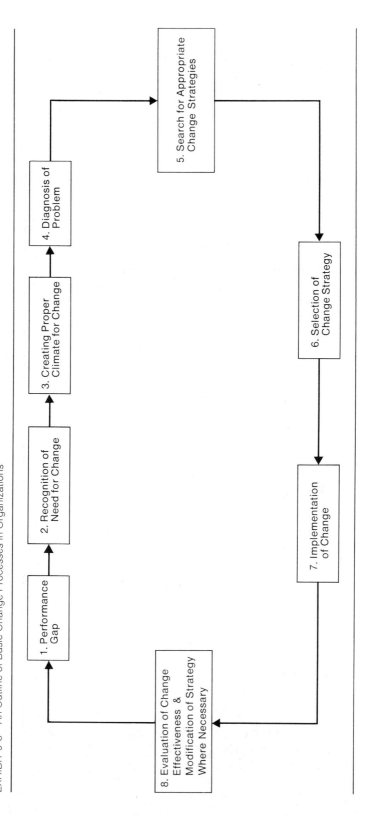

which the change has been successful in reducing the performance gap and can take steps to reinforce and maintain the new program to the extent that it serves the needs of the organization and its members.

Consider the following example. During the past two decades, a major U.S. research laboratory specializing in valves and gauges spent the majority of its time and effort designing hardware for aerospace projects. Most of its income came from government contracts. However, as the government funds became scarce, the laboratory was faced with a clear performance gap. Because no further contracts were seen as forthcoming, management recognized the need for change and began laying the groundwork for a shift away from aerospace engineering. A diagnosis of the situation led to the conclusion that the laboratory's technical expertise could be applied with minimal organizational disturbance to hardware problems in the automotive industry. Thus, management shifted the goals of the laboratory to that of providing precision valves and gauges for automobiles instead of space vehicles. This action opened up new sources of income for the laboratory. A subsequent assessment of the change revealed that the process had been carried out with minimal loss of personnel and that the laboratory now had sufficient revenues to continue operations in an area in which it had ample expertise. In other words, the organization responded to environmental changes by adapting its goals to such changes so that stability and continuity would be maintained.

Strategies for Planned Change

The success or failure of organizational change rests not only with the accuracy of problem identification and the successful reduction of resistance to change but also with the appropriateness of the selected strategy for implementing change. In recent years, a multitude of change strategies have emerged. Although a detailed analysis of the specific methods is beyond the scope of our concern here (see Huse, 1975, for an in-depth discussion), it is possible to identify the major types of approaches. Three general approaches to planned change in organization can be identified. These include: (1) changes aimed principally at individuals; (2) changes aimed at organization structures and systems; and (3) changes aimed at organizational climate and interpersonal style (see Exhibit 9–4).

Individual change strategies. Change strategies aimed at modifying individuals tend to focus on improving employee skills, attitudes, and motivational levels. These approaches assume that

170   behavior in organizations – and ultimately organizational effec-

EXHIBIT 9-4   Comparison of Three General Approaches for Initiating Organizational Changes

Approaches for Initiating Change	Typical Intervention Techniques	Intended Immediate Outcomes	Assumptions About the Major Causes of Behavior in Organizations
Individuals	Education, training, socialization, attitude change	Improvements in skill levels, attitudes, and motivation of people	Behavior in organizations is largely determined by the characteristics of the people who compose the organization.
Organizational structure and systems	Modification of actual organizational practices, procedures, and policies that affect what people do at work	Creation of conditions to elicit and reward member behaviors that facilitate organizational goal achievement	Behavior in organizations is largely determined by the characteristics of the organizational situation in which people work.
Organizational climate and interpersonal style	Experiential techniques aimed at increasing members' awareness of the social determinants of their behavior and helping them learn new ways of reacting to and relating to each other within the organizational context	Creation of a system-wide climate that is characterized by high interpersonal trust and openness; reduction of dysfunctional consequences of excessive social conflict and competitiveness	Behavior in organizations is largely determined by the emotional and social processes that characterize the relations among organization members.

Source: L. W. Porter, E. E. Lawler, III, and J. R. Hackman, *Behavior in Organizations* (New York: McGraw-Hill, 1975), p. 440. Used by permission.

tiveness—is largely determined by the characteristics of the members of an organization. Hence, if these members can be changed in some way, it is assumed that greater efforts will be available for goal-directed activities. Individual change strategies take many forms, including a wide variety of personnel training programs (for example, skills training, communication effectiveness training, decision making exercises), socialization efforts (for example, to develop a "company man"), and attitude-motivation training (for example, to improve a manager's achievement motivation).

Structural and systemic change strategies. A second major approach to change involves attempts to restructure an organization so that it is more capable of utilizing available resources for goal attainment. Structural or systemic changes can include such things as alterations in reporting procedures or decision-making processes, changes in organizational policies and practices, decentralization of authority and power, and modifying technological processes. An example of this latter type of change (changing technologies) can be seen in the recent Swedish experiments in redesigning automotive assembly jobs from the traditional assembly line to the "autonomous work group" concept, where work teams assume responsibility for assembling major parts of an automobile. Initial results of these experiments indicate that, although productivity may not be increased a great deal, there are substantive improvements in quality of workmanship, job satisfaction, attendance, and retention (Lindestad & Norstadt, 1973). Thus, by some standards, such changes in job design have proved beneficial for the organization in terms of organizational effectiveness.

A major purpose of structural or systemic changes is to create conditions in an organization that facilitate and reward goal-directed efforts. For example, a project or matrix organization design may be appropriate where divergent areas of expertise need to be coordinated for a particular project (such as a space satellite project). The assumption underlying this approach to change is that behavior, performance, and effectiveness are largely determined by the way an organization or work group is structured (that is, the specific characteristics of the organization—see Chapter 4). Thus, a more mechanistic design may be most appropriate for organizations dealing in a stable environment, while an organic design may prove more suitable for organizations in less stable environments (Burns & Stalker, 1961).

Climate and interpersonal change stategies. Finally, a series of approaches to change involve attempts to modify employee awareness of themselves and their relations with those around them. It is assumed under this approach that desirable outcomes are largely influenced by the social and emotional processes that characterize the relationships between people in organizations. By changing interpersonal styles, it is hoped that a climate can be created that is conducive to high levels of interpersonal trust, open communications, and reduced conflict and competitiveness. This new climate is then thought to be more favorable both for improved performance and personal need satisfaction.

The techniques used to bring about such changes include team-building exercises (attempts to develop well-integrated, cohesive work groups), survey feedback (where one's perceptions of his or her interpersonal style or a particular climate is compared against the perceptions of others), conflict resolution exercises, T-groups, and so forth (see Huse, 1975). These approaches represent largely experiential approaches to change by which members learn more about their own behavior and role in an organization and are then given opportunities to experiment with new forms of behavior or new roles in the hopes that increased interpersonal competence will result.

The selection by management of the appropriate technique depends largely upon the nature and character of the problem, the particular change goals, the orientations of those implementing the change, and the resources that are available. For instance, where poor communications is seen as a barrier to effective performance, management may decide to make structural changes (such as using a matrix design) to remedy the situation. By changing reporting procedures, lines of authority, and so forth, more interaction and exchange of views may result, thereby improving communications. Alternatively, management may institute communications training programs to improve both interpersonal competence and communications skills. Both approaches may serve to reduce barriers to effective communications, although the techniques and underlying assumptions are quite different. The important point here is that management must assume primary responsibility for recognizing the need for change in organizations, for diagnosing the nature and extent of the problem, and for implementing what it considers to be the most effective change strategy, given the circumstances. Without such leadership, the ability of an organization to respond to internal and external threats to stability and continuity is greatly diminished, reducing the likelihood that an effective level of operation can be maintained.

ORGANIZATIONAL EFFECTIVENESS
A Review

10

Organizations typically exist in turbulent environments where resources are limited and where threats to growth and survival can
be relatively commonplace. Within such environments, they must
not only meet a series of what may be termed organizational
requirements (for example, resource acquisition, efficiency, pro-
duction/output, organizational renewal, constituency satisfaction)
but in addition must satisfy certain behavioral requirements with
respect to their members (for example, a stable membership, dependable role performance, spontaneous and innovative behavior).
The role of management under such circumstances is to organize
and utilize the available resources in a way that minimizes external
threats and pressures and facilitates the attainment of the ultimate
aims of the organization. The way in which organizations and their
managements go about this has been the topic of this volume.

EVALUATION OF ORGANIZATIONAL EFFECTIVENESS

Centrality of Goals

A recurrent theme that has emerged throughout our examination
of the nature of organizational effectiveness is the notion of goals
and goal attainment. Individuals are seen as joining organizations
in order to better accomplish their own personal goals (such as
income, status, meaningful work). Similarly, organizations are seen
as goal-seeking entities that attempt to bring together the collective
effort of their members for the pursuit of specific organization-wide
objectives (for example, profit, growth, productivity). In fact, on
a general level, it has been suggested that effectiveness itself could

best be understood in terms of the extent to which an organization is successful in acquiring and utilizing resources in the pursuit of operative and operational goals.

Facets of Effectiveness

In an effort to make the abstract notion of effectiveness somewhat more tangible (and measureable), several organizational analysts have attempted to identify the more salient facets associated with the construct. Although a wide array of evaluation criteria have been employed (see Exhibit 3-2), the most widely used ones include the following:

1. Adaptability-flexibility
2. Productivity
3. Job satisfaction
4. Profitability
5. Resource acquisition

Variables such as these have alternatively been identified as measures of effectiveness itself and as facilitators or intervening variables that enhance the likelihood that effectiveness will result (Price, 1968).

Much of what is currently known about the nature of organizational effectiveness has resulted from piecing together the findings of various studies using such criteria. Unfortunately, a major problem exists with this approach in that there is little agreement among investigators concerning which criteria represent useful (that is, valid) indicators of effectiveness. In fact, in seventeen investigations (reviewed in Chapter 3) that attempted to identify evaluation criteria, only one (adaptability-flexibility) was mentioned in more than half the models (Steers, 1975c).

Not only do differences exist with respect to the specific criteria that are felt to be important for effectiveness but in addition differences can be found in the ways such criteria have been derived and their purported applicability to organizations. For example, several models of effectiveness tend to be normative or prescriptive in nature, attempting to specify what an organization must do to be successful. On the other hand, other approaches are largely descriptive in nature, simply summarizing the characteristics that have been found to exist in successful organizations. Moreover, some investigators argue that their list of criteria apply to all types of organizations (businesses, R&D laboratories, educational institutions, and so on), while others are more conservative and limit the types of organizations for which their criteria are thought to be applicable. Finally, as noted in Chapter 3, some models use a deductive approach to identify their evaluation criteria; that is, the criteria are set forth either by definition or as **175** part of a proposed theory based on earlier work. Other models tend to be more inductive, determining the relevant criteria as a result of empirical investigation.

A possible explanation for the lack of agreement on evaluation criteria and for the diversity of approaches to the subject may lie in recognizing the existence of several problems that hamper measurement attempts. These problems include the following: (1) existing evaluation criteria are often unstable; (2) different criteria may be relevant for different time perspectives (short versus long term); (3) multiple criteria often conflict with one another; (4) some criteria are not applicable to certain types of organizations; and (5) some criteria (for example, adaptability) may be difficult to measure accurately. Other problems could be mentioned (see Chapter 3). The point here is that any attempt to evaluate the current level of effectiveness of an organization must be preceded by a careful analysis of the possible constraints or sources of error inherent in such evaluation attempts. If inappropriate criteria are employed, the resulting assessment may be of little value for managers. Thus, if such criteria are to be used by management as indicators of success or failure, considerable effort is required to select only those criteria that accurately reflect the stated objectives of the organization.

A PROCESS MODEL OF EFFECTIVENESS

Because of the abstract nature of the topic, a model has been proposed in an effort to facilitate an understanding of the nature of organizational effectiveness. The model places an emphasis on the major *processes* related to effectiveness, instead of looking at effectiveness as an end state. It thus recognizes the changing nature of both the organization and its environment. Moreover, the model implies that a major role of management is to understand how the various components of the organization are interrelated and how such interrelationships can enhance the likelihood of organizational success. The three major dimensions of the model are: (1) the notion of goal optimization; (2) a systems perspective; and (3) an emphasis on human behavior in organizational settings.

Goal Optimization

The use of a goal optimization approach to organizational effectiveness allows for the explicit recognition that different organizations pursue different goals. As such, assessments concerning the relative success or failure of a particular organization should be made against organizational intentions, instead of against the investigator's value judgments. Moreover, the goal optimization approach acknowledges the fact that most organizations could not "maximize" on a particular goal (such as production) even if they wanted to. Instead, based on a recognition of the constraints on organizational behavior and performance, effective managers are seen as setting forth and pursuing optimized goals (that is, desired goals as constrained or modified by available resources). Optimization is thus a vehicle by which multiple and conflicting goals are balanced so that each goal receives sufficient attention and resources commensurate with its importance to the organization. It is suggested here that it is against this feasible goal set that effectiveness should be judged, instead of against the notion of a maximum goal set.

Systems Perspective

A second aspect of the multidimensional approach to an analysis of organizational effectiveness is the use of open systems theory. As noted by Etzioni (1975), Georgopoulos and Tannenbaum (1957), and others, the use of a systems perspective emphasizes the importance of organization-environment interactions. It focuses on relationships between components both inside and outside the organization as they jointly influence organizational success or failure. When these relationships are clearly recognized, it becomes easier for managers to take decisive actions to facilitate goal attainment because of their increased understanding of organizational dynamics.

Behavioral Emphasis

The final aspect of the approach suggested here is an emphasis on understanding the role of human behavior in affecting organizational performance. In other words, if we are to gain a clearer picture of determinants of effectiveness, it is necessary to examine the basic unit of analysis in such a determination; it is necessary to examine employee behavior. If the employees of an organization agree with the objectives of their employer, then we would expect their effort toward those objectives to be high. On the other hand, if organizational objectives are largely inconsistent with employee needs and goals, there is little reason to believe they would maximize their contribution. Hence, when we discuss organizational effectiveness, it is equally important to discuss the relationship between what employees want and what organizations want. When both sets of needs and goals are relatively homogeneous, the likelihood of increasing organization-wide performance is markedly improved.

MAJOR INFLUENCES ON EFFECTIVENESS

In any examination of a complex topic, it is useful to have a framework for analysis to guide in the understanding of the various aspects of the topic. The framework employed here iden- **177** tifies four sets of effectiveness-related variables: (1) organizational characteristics; (2) environmental characteristics; (3) employee characteristics; and (4) managerial policies and practices. Recent research from a variety of institutional settings suggests that all four of these areas play an important role in facilitating an achievement-oriented work environment.

Organizational Characteristics

Organizational structure and technology can influence certain facets of effectiveness in a variety of ways. In regard to structure, it has been found that improved productivity and efficiency often result from increases in functional specialization, organization size, centralization of decision making, and formalization. However, although productivity and efficiency tend to be positively related to these structure variables, job attitudes (particularly job satisfaction and commitment) tend to be inversely related to them. Such evidence suggests that managers have a responsibility to identify clearly their basic objectives and to recognize the effects that structural variation aimed at those objectives will have on attitudes and behavior. Where the outcomes of possible structural changes are conflicting (for example, where increased centralization leads to both improved performance and reduced job satisfaction), difficult decisions must be made concerning the desirability of such changes.

Technology can likewise have an effect on the subsequent degree of effectiveness, although the effect may not be a direct one. The available evidence indicates that technological variations interact with structure to influence organizational success. That is, effectiveness is apparently facilitated to no small degree by structuring an organization's resources (for example, mechanistic versus organic) in such a way that they are best suited to handle the prevailing technology. When structure and technology are consonant—that is, when they work together—fewer problems are encountered by employees in their goal-oriented efforts.

Environmental Characteristics

In addition to organizational characteristics, the external and internal environments have also been shown to influence effectiveness. Following the model discussed in Chapter 5 (Exhibit 5-4), the success of organization-environment relations appears to be largely dependent upon three key variables: (1) the degree of predictability of environmental states; (2) the accuracy of perception of environmental states; and (3) the degree of organizational rationality. These three factors influence the appropriateness of organizational response to environmental changes. The more appropriate the response the more successful the adaptation by the organization. This model has clear implications for the practice of management in pointing to a need to monitor environmental changes on a continuous basis (through market and economic research, legal advice, political activities, and so forth) and to adapt organizational design, technology, objectives, and behavior in response to such changes.

While the external environment represents the economic, market, and legal milieu where an organization attempts to secure resources and distribute its outputs, the internal environment (or climate) represents the cultural and social milieu where employee behavior is largely determined. As a result, in contrast to the external environment, discussions of climate typically focus on individual variables instead of on organization-wide variables. It was noted in Chapter 6 that the climate of an organization was perhaps best viewed as an intervening variable which moderates the influence of structure, technology, external environment, and managerial style on resulting individual effort and performance. A model of the role of climate in organizational effectiveness was presented in Exhibit 6-1. In general, available evidence indicates that the most suitable climate for facilitating goal-directed behavior is characterized by an achievement orientation and employee centeredness.

Employee Characteristics

The third major influence on effectiveness is the employees themselves. In fact, the members of an organization probably represent the most important influence on effectiveness because it is their behavior over the long term that either facilitates or inhibits organizational goal attainment. An awareness of the nature of individual differences among employees is essential because different employees respond in different ways to attempts by management to secure goal-directed effort. Knowledge of these differences allows managers to tailor their approaches to organizing and leading people at work, thereby improving the chances of cooperation and mutual support for organizational objectives.

A primary means of securing this needed support by employees is through integrating personal goals with organizational objectives. Where employees can enhance the likelihood of personal goal attainment by working toward organizational objectives, it is logical to assume that both attachment to the organization and job performance will be improved. On the other hand, where employees are placed in situations where their personal goals are in conflict with organizational objectives, employee effort can easily be dissipated, leading to a reduction in the total amount of energy available for effectiveness-related activities. In essence, **179** then, one key to organizational success is the recognition by managers of an exhange relationship between an organization and its members in which both parties help each other in return for assistance with their own objectives. The nature of this exchange relationship lies at the center of efforts to understand why people work and the relation between such work efforts and organizational effectiveness.

Managerial Policies and Practices

Finally, several specific mechanisms have been identified by which managers can improve the effectiveness of organizations. These include strategic goal setting, efficient resource acquisition and utilization, creating a performance environment, communication processes, leadership and decision making, and organizational adaptation and innovation.

Strategic goal setting. If effectiveness is concerned with management's capacity to secure and apply resources toward the attainment of organizational goals, the selection of such goals (both operative and operational) emerges as a critical factor. The notion of goal setting includes both the identification of common organizational purposes and the determination of how various departments, groups, and individuals can contribute toward such purposes. Where mutual support on goals exists among employees, the likelihood of high degrees of goal effort tends to increase.

Resource acquisition and utilization. Three related areas of concern have been identified with regard to managerial efforts in acquiring and utilizing resources. First, there is a need to integrate and coordinate the various subsystems of the organization (that is, productive, supportive, maintenance, adaptive, and managerial) so that each subsystem has the needed resources to carry out its principal tasks. Moreover, when such subsystems are properly coordinated (that is, balanced), more efficient energy is available for goal-directed activities.

A second area of concern relates to the establishment, implementation, and maintenance of policy guidelines. Policy guidelines can facilitate organizational effectiveness by insuring that the organization benefits from past decisions and actions and that it minimizes wasted energy and/or overlapping functions within departments. However, the utility of policy guidelines for effectiveness is predicated on the assumption that such guidelines are perceived by employees as being equitable and in the best interest of the organization. Where policy statements encourage doing things by the book, their usefulness for organizational effectiveness is obviously reduced.

Third, any systems approach to the study of organizations recognizes the existence of a series of feedback and control loops that serve a gyroscopic function in keeping the organization on target toward its goals. Although control systems can take many forms (financial, physical, and human), this book has focused primarily on the human aspects of control systems. Techniques such as human resource accounting seem to demonstrate potential for acknowleding more fully the centrality of human behavior as a factor in effectiveness. To the extent that such feedback and control systems can be successfully employed to monitor goal-directed activities, their usefulness for managers should not be minimized.

Performance environment. Many studies have demonstrated the importance of variations in the work environment in contributing to organizational success. It has long been recognized that behavior in organizations is largely a function of the interaction of the individual and his or her work environment (Lewin, 1938). Thus, it is incumbent upon managers to design the most facilitative work environment possible consistent with available resources. Management concern in this area includes directing attention toward: (1) employee selection and placement procedures; (2) employee training and development; (3) task design; and (4) performance appraisal and rewards. When used in concert, these activities can contribute substantially to improving the quality of the work environment, where organizational effectiveness is ultimately determined.

Communication processes. It is much easier to identify problems in organizational communication than to suggest solutions. For example, we recognize clearly the negative consequences of communication distortion, omission, overload, untimeliness, and nonacceptance (Guetzkow, 1965; Hall, 1972). A major step toward minimizing these problems consists of recognizing that communication in organizations is an evolutionary process, requiring time to develop into its current state. No company president decides that his firm will have open communications, for example. On the contrary, if open communication is his goal, it must be fostered and developed over time through the use of a variety of upward, downward, and horizontal communication strategies and techniques (see Exhibit 8-2). To the extent that information-gathering and information-sharing activities can be increased, uncertainty and anxiety can often be reduced and the quality of the subsequent decisions improved.

Leadership and decision making. Given the central role played by leadership and decision-making processes in organizational behavior, it is important to consider some of the ramifications of variations in such processes as they affect organizational success or failure. A major theme that emerges from the various **181**

studies on leadership focuses on the impact that participative decision making has on the quality and acceptance of decisions. It
has been argued that allowing employees greater involvement in
decisions affecting their jobs serves: (1) to clarify organizational
expectations for employees as well as the potential rewards for
successful performance; (2) to increase the psychological commitment employees have to carrying out decisions in which they had
a part; and (3) to increase the effects of social influence on behavior (Ebert & Mitchell, 1975). It has also been pointed out by several
investigators, however, that participation in decision making is not
always desirable (Vroom & Yetton, 1973). That is, when employees possess important information or when decision acceptance
is essential for implementation, participation can be useful. On
the other hand, when a rapid decision is imperative on a matter
only tangentially related to the employees, participatory techniques may actually be dysfunctional.

Improving the quality of leadership effectiveness can be facilitated in several ways. First, greater attention can be paid to the
initial selection and placement of managers. All too often, managers are selected on the basis of seniority or previous performance. In many cases, however, there is little relation between such
factors and leadership ability. Second, the available evidence suggests that managerial training can at times improve the quality
of leader behavior, although the results are not entirely consistent.
Third, reward systems for managers can be structured so that
they foster goal-oriented leader behavior. Fourth, reward systems
for subordinates can be designed so that they encourage goal-
directed efforts. That is, where personal and organizational goals
can be integrated so that efforts toward one facilitate the other,
performance and satisfaction can be increased. Finally, in those
cases in which attitudinal and behavioral changes seem unlikely,
structural changes may be necessary. For instance, when a manager has a high level of technical competence but is ineffective
in creating the appropriate work climate, it may be necessary to
change the nature of the work situation (that is, "to work around
him") so that vital technical activities are continued without sacrificing the more interpersonal aspects of the work environment.

Organizational adaptation and innovation. Throughout
our discussions on the nature of organizational effectiveness, emphasis has been placed on the need for managers to readily adapt
their organizations to changes in the environment. In fact, adaptation and innovation have been seen by many as the hallmark of
effectiveness itself (Bennis, 1962; Georgopoulos & Tannenbaum,
1957). The question for contemporary managers, however, is not
whether change is necessary but how best to design and imple-
182 ment such changes. As suggested by Katz and Kahn (1966) in

their notion of equifinality, there are often many ways to achieve the same goal. For example, several years ago laws aimed at reducing traffic injuries required auto manufacturers to install seat belts. When this action failed to have the desired consequences, further laws were passed requiring manufacturers to install lights and buzzers to remind drivers to use seat belts. Finally, laws were passed requiring manufacturers to install devices that made it mandatory to use seat belts before the car could be started. From the standpoint of equifinality, it would have perhaps been much simpler—and more effective—to simply pass one law nullifying accident insurance claims for drivers not wearing seat belts at the time of an accident. The point here is that managers (like legislators) need to examine carefully the approach they select for meeting a particular problem. This examination should most certainly include consideration of the cost-benefit ratios to be incurred in the various alternative solutions.

There are numerous approaches to implementing change in organization (Huse, 1975). The failure of many of these techniques may lie more in the inability of managers to diagnose the problem accurately and to select the appropriate technique than in the frailties of the techniques themselves. To the extent that managers can properly diagnose the problem and successfully select and implement a comprehensive program aimed at solving the problem, adaptation to an uncertain environment should be enhanced. Such success depends, however, on the qualities of the manager and on his or her willingness and openness to examine every aspect of a problem when it arises, instead of relying on unverified opinions, hunches, and so forth. Thus, the quality of the response appears to be equally important to the speed of response.

Based upon our examination of the nature of effectiveness in organizations, two general conclusions can be drawn that have important consequences for the practice of management. First, the notion of effectiveness is best understood in terms of a continuous *process* instead of an end state. Energizing, directing, and sustaining goal-directed effort by employees is an unceasing task for most managers. Given the ever-changing composition of the goals that are pursued by many organizations, managers have a continual responsibility to restructure available resources, alter technologies, modify climates, develop employees, and so forth, in an effort to use the talents at their disposal to their utmost to attain such goals. Hence, the manager emerges as the primary facilitator of organizational effectiveness through his or her actions and behavior.

Second, throughout our analysis, we have continually returned to the central role of *contingencies* in any discussion of effectiveness. That is, it is incumbent upon managers to recognize **183** the uniqueness of their own organizations—their goals, structures, technologies, people, environments, and so forth—and to respond in a manner consistent with that uniqueness. Such a conclusion cautions against attempts to prescribe "rules" or "principles" for achieving success. Given the diversity of organizations in our contemporary society, such rules are of limited value. Instead, responsibility falls to the organization to train its members so they can recognize the nature of a given situation and respond with appropriate means. By doing so, wasted energy is minimized, and the probability of efficiently utilizing an organization's resources for goal attainment is increased. To the extent that managers recognize both the need for continuous attention to goal-directed activities and the unique opportunities, aims, and problems of their own organizations, the possibility of attaining an effective level of operation moves closer to reality. To the extent that managers fail to recognize such needs and opportunities, the concept of organizational effectivness will remain an abstract notion discussed only in classrooms and textbooks.

REFERENCES

Acton Society Trust. *Size and morale*. London: AST, 1953.

Adams, J. S. Toward an understanding of inequity. *Journal of Abnormal and Social Psychology*, 1963, *67*, 422–36.

Aiken, M., & Hage, J. Organizational alienation: A comparative analysis. *American Sociological Review*, 1966, *31*, 497–507.

Allison, G. T. *Essence of decision*. Boston: Little, Brown and Company, 1971.

Argyle, M., Gardner, G., & Cioffi, I. Supervisory methods related to productivity, absenteeism, and labor turnover. *Human Relations*, 1958, *11*, 23–40.

Argyris, C. *Personality and organization*. New York: Harper and Bros., 1957.

Atkinson, J. W. *Motives in fantasy, action, and society*. New York: D. Van Nostrand Co., 1958.

Barnard, C. *The functions of the executive*. Cambridge, Mass.: Harvard University Press, 1938.

Barrett, J. H. *Individual goals and organizational objectives: A study of integration mechanisms*. Ann Arbor: University of Michigan, Institute for Social Research, 1970.

Bass, B. M., & Vaughn, J. A. *Training in industry: The management of learning*. Belmont, Calif.: Wadsworth Publishing Co., Inc., 1966.

Baumgartel, H., & Sobol, R. Background and organizational factors in absenteeism. *Personnel Psychology*, 1959, *12*, 431–43.

Bennis, W. G. Toward a "truly" scientific management: The concept of organizational health. *General Systems Yearbook*, 1962, *7*, 269–82.

Bertalanffy, L. von. The history and status of general systems theory. *Academy of Management Journal*, 1972, *15*, 407–26.

Blake, R. R., & Mouton, J. S. *The managerial grid*. Houston: Gulf Publishing Co., 1964.

Blau, P. M. *The dynamics of bureaucracy*. Chicago: University of Chicago Press, 1955.

Blau, P. M., Heydebrand, W. V., & Stauffer, R. E. The structure of small bureaucracies. *American Sociological Review*, 1966, *31*, 179–91.

Blau, P. M., & Schoenherr, R. A. *The structure of organizations.* New York: Basic Books, Inc., 1971.

Boland, W. R. Size, organization and environmental mediation: A study of colleges and universities. In J. V. Baldridge (Ed.), *Academic governance in the administration of higher education.* Berkeley, Calif.: McCutchan Publishing Corporation, 1971.

Bowers, D. G., & Seashore, S. E. Predicting organizational effectiveness with a four-factor theory of leadership. *Administrative Science Quarterly,* 1966, *11,* 238–63.

Brayfield, A. H., & Crockett, W. H. Employee attitudes and employee performance. *Psychological Bulletin,* 1955, *52,* 396–424.

Brief, A. P., & Aldag, R. J. Employee reactions to job characteristics: A constructive replication. *Journal of Applied Psychology,* 1975, *60,* 182–86.

Brown, W. B. The impact of a dynamic task environment: A study of architectural-engineering firms. *Academy of Management Journal,* 1969, *12,* 169–77.

Brummet, R. L., Flamholtz, E. G., & Pyle, W. C. Human resource measurement: A challenge for accountants. *The Accounting Review,* 1968, *43,* 217–24.

Buchanan, B. Building organizational commitment: The socialization of managers in work organizations. *Administrative Science Quarterly,* 1974, *19,* 533–46.

Burling, T., Lentz, E., & Wilson, R. N. *The give and take in hospitals.* New York: G. P. Putnam's Sons, 1956.

Burns, T., & Stalker, G. M. *The management of innovation.* London: Tavistock, 1961.

Campbell, J. P. *Research into the nature of organizational effectiveness: An endangered species?* Unpublished manuscript, University of Minnesota, 1973.

Campbell, J. P., & Beaty, E. E. Organizational climate: Its measurement and relationship to work group performance. Paper presented at the annual meeting of the American Psychological Association, Washington, D.C., 1971.

Campbell, J. P., Bownas, E. A., Peterson, N. G., & Dunnette, M. D. *The measurement of organizational effectiveness: A review of relevant research and opinion.* San Diego, Calif.: Naval Personnel Research and Development Center, 1974.

Campbell, J. P., Dunnette, M. D., Lawler, E. E., & Weick, K. E. *Managerial behavior, performance, and effectiveness.* New York: McGraw-Hill Book Company, 1970.

Caplow, T. *Principles of organization.* New York: Harcourt Brace & World, 1964.

Carlson, S. *Executive behavior: A study of the workload and the working methods of managing directors.* Stockholm: Stromberg, 1951.

Carpenter, H. H. Formal organizational structural factors and perceived job satisfaction of classroom teachers. *Administrative Science Quarterly,* 1971, *16,* 460–65.

Carroll, J. A note on departmental autonomy and innovation in medical schools. *Journal of Business,* 1967, *40,* 531–34.

Cartwright, D., & Zander, A. *Group dynamics.* New York: Harper & Row, 1968.

Chandler, A. *Strategy and structure,* Cambridge, Mass.: The M.I.T. Press, 1962.

Chapple, E. D., & Sayles, L. R. *The measure of management.* New York: Macmillan, Inc., 1961.

Cherrington, D. J. Satisfaction in competitive conditions. *Organizational Behavior and Human Performance,* 1973, *10,* 47–71.

Child, J. Strategies of control and organizational behavior. *Administrative Science Quarterly,* 1973, *18,* 1–17.

Child, J. Managerial and organizational factors associated with company performance—Part I. *Journal of Management Studies,* 1974, *11,* 175–89.

Child, J. Managerial and organizational factors associated with company performance—Part II. A contingency analysis. *Journal of Management Studies,* 1975, *12,* 12–27.

Cleland, S. *Influence of plant size on industrial relations.* Princeton, N.J.: Princeton University Press, 1955.

Comrey, A. L., High, W., & Wilson, R. C. Factors influencing organizational effectiveness: VI. A survey of aircraft workers. *Personnel Psychology,* 1955, *8,* 79–99.

Cummings, L. L., & Schwab, D. P. *Performance in organizations: Determinants and appraisal.* Glenview, Ill.: Scott, Foresman and Company, 1973.

Cyert, R. M., & March, J. G. *A behavioral theory of the firm.* Englewood Cliffs, N.J.: Prentice-Hall, Inc., 1963.

Dieterly, D., & Schneider, B. The effect of organizational environment on perceived power and climate: A laboratory study. *Organizational Behavior and Human Performance,* 1974, *11,* 316–37.

Dill, W. R. Environment as an influence on managerial autonomy, *Administrative Science Quarterly,* 1958, *2,* 409–43.

Downey, H. K., Hellriegel, D., & Slocum, J. W., Jr. Congruence between individual needs, organizational climate, job satisfaction and performance. *Academy of Management Journal,* 1975, *18,* 149–54.

Downs, A. *Inside bureaucracy.* Boston: Little, Brown and Company, 1967.

Dubin, R. *World of work.* Englewood Cliffs, N.J.: Prentice-Hall, Inc., 1958.

Dubin, R. Stability of human organizations. In M. Haire (Ed.), *Modern organization theory.* New York: John Wiley & Sons, Inc., 1959.

Dubin, R. Supervision and productivity: Empirical findings and theoretical considerations. In R. Dubin, G. Homans, F. Mann, & D. Miller (Eds.), *Leadership and productivity.* San Francisco: Chandler, 1965.

Dubin, R. *Theory building.* Glencoe, Ill.: Free Press, 1969.

Dubin, R. Organizational effectiveness: Some dilemmas of perspective. Paper presented at the Symposium on Organizational Effectiveness, Kent State University, April 4–5, 1975.

Duncan, R. B. The characteristics of organizational environments and perceived environmental uncertainty. *Administrative Science Quarterly,* 1972, *17,* 313–27.

Duncan, R. B. Multiple decision-making structures in adapting to environmental uncertainty: The impact on organizational effectiveness. *Human Relations,* 1973, *26,* 273–91.

Dunnette, M. D. (Ed.) *Handbook of industrial and organizational psychology.* Chicago: Rand McNally & Company, 1976.

Dunnette, M. D., Arvey, R., & Banas, P. Why do they leave? *Personnel,* 1973, *50,* 25–39.

Dunnette, M. D., Wernimont, P., & Abrahams, N. Further research on vocational interest differences among several types of engineers. *Personnel and Guidance Journal,* 1964, *42,* 484–93.

Ebert, R. J., & Mitchell, T. R. *Organizational decision processes: Concepts and analysis.* New York: Crane, Russak, & Company, Inc., 1975.

Emery, R. E., & Trist, E. The causal texture of organizational environments. *Human Relations,* 1965, *18,* 21–31.

England, G. W. Organizational goals and expected behavior in American managers. *Academy of Management Journal,* 1967, *10,* 108.

Etzioni, A. Two approaches to organizational analysis: A critique and a suggestion. *Administrative Science Quarterly,* 1960, *5,* 257–78.

Etzioni, A. *Modern organizations.* Englewood Cliffs, N.J.: Prentice-Hall, Inc., 1964.

Etzioni, A. *A comparative analysis of complex organizations* (Rev. ed.). New York: The Free Press, 1975.

Evans, M. G. The effects of supervisory behavior on the path goal relationship. *Organizational Behavior and Human Performance,* 1970, *55,* 277–98.

Evans, M. G. Extensions of a path goal theory of motivation. *Journal of Applied Psychology,* 1974, *59,* 172–78.

Fiedler, F. Engineer the job to fit the manager. *Harvard Business Review,* 1965, *43,* 115–22.

Fiedler, F. E., & Chemers, M. M. *Leadership and effective management.* Glenview, Ill.: Scott, Foresman and Company, 1974.

Filley, A. C., & House, R. J. *Managerial process and organizational behavior.* Glenview, Ill.: Scott, Foresman and Company, 1969.

Forehand, G., & Gilmer, B. Environmental variation in studies of organizational behavior. *Psychological Bulletin,* 1964, *22,* 361–82.

Frederickson, N. Some effects of organizational climates on administrative performance (ETS RM–66–21). Princeton, N.J.: Educational Testing Service, 1966.

French, J. R., Kay, E., & Meyer, H. H. Participation and the appraisal system. *Human Relations,* 1966, *19,* 3–19.

Friedlander, F., & Greenberg, S. Effect of job attitudes, training and organizational climates on performance of the hard-core unemployed. *Journal of Applied Psychology,* 1971, *55,* 287–95.

Friedlander, F., & Margulies, N. Multiple impacts of organizational climate and individual value systems upon job satisfaction. *Personnel Psychology,* 1969, *22,* 171–83.

Friedlander, F., & Pickle, H. Components of effectiveness in small organizations. *Administrative Science Quarterly,* 1968, *13,* 289–304.

Fullan, M. Industrial technology and worker integration in the organization. *American Sociological Review,* 1970, *35,* 1028–1039.

George, J., & Bishop, L. Relationship of organizational structure and teacher personality characteristics to organizational climate. *Administrative Science Quarterly,* 1971, *16,* 467–76.

Georgiou, P. The goal paradigm. *Administrative Science Quarterly,* 1973, *18,* 291–310.

Georgopoulos, B. S., *Hospital organization research: Review and sourcebook.* Philadelphia, Pa.: W. B. Saunders, Company, 1975.

Georgopoulos, B. S., & Tannenbaum, A. S. The study of organizational effectiveness. *American Sociological Review,* 1957, *22,* 534–40.

Ghiselli, E. E. Managerial talent. *American Psychologist,* 1963, *18,* 631–41.

Ghiselli, E. E. *The validity of occupational aptitude tests.* New York: John Wiley & Sons, Inc., 1966.

Ghorpade, J. *Assessment of organizational effectiveness.* Pacific Palisades, Calif.: Goodyear Publishing Company, Inc., 1971.

Gibson, J. L., Ivancevich, J. M., & Donnelly, J. H. *Organizations: Structure, process, behavior.* Dallas: Business Publications, Inc., 1973.

Goldstein, I. L. *Training: Program development and evaluation.* Monterey, Calif.: Brooks/Cole Publishing Company, 1975.

Golembiewski, R., Munqenvider, R., Blumbery, A., Carrigan, S., & Mead, W. Changing climate in a complex organization: Interactions between a learning design and an environment. *Academy of Management Journal,* 1971, *14,* 465–83.

Gouldner, A. W. *Patterns of industrial bureaucracy.* Glencoe, Ill.: Free Press, 1954.

Graen, G. Role-making processes within complex organizations. In M. D. Dunnette (Ed.), *Handbook of industrial and organizational psychology.* Chicago: Rand McNally & Company, 1976.

Graicunas, V. A. Relationship and organization. In L. Galick & L. Urwick (Eds.), *Papers on the science of administration.* New York: Institute of Public Administration, 1937.

Gross, B. M. What are your organization's objectives? A general systems approach to planning. *Human Relations,* 1965, *18,* 195–215.

Grusky, O. Administrative succession in formal organizations. *Social Forces,* 1960, *39,* 105–115.

Grusky, O. Corporate size, bureaucratization, and managerial succession. *American Journal of Sociology,* 1961, *67,* 261–69.

Guetzkow, H. Communications in organizations. In J. G. March (Ed.), *Handbook of Organizations.* Chicago: Rand McNally & Company, 1965, pp. 534–73.

Guion, R. M. A note on organizational climate. *Organizational Behavior and Human Performance,* 1973, *9,* 120–25.

Guion, R. M. Recruiting, selection, and job placement. In M. D. Dunnette (Ed.), *Handbook of industrial and organizational psychology.* Chicago: Rand McNally & Company, 1976.

Hackman, J. R., & Lawler, E. E., III. Employee reactions to job characteristics. *Journal of Applied Psychology,* 1971, *55,* 259–86.

Hage, J., & Aiken, M. Program change and organizational properties: A comparative analysis. *American Journal of Sociology,* 1967, *72,* 503–519.

Hage, J., & Aiken, M. Routine technology, social structure and organizational goals. *Administrative Science Quarterly,* 1969, *14,* 366–76.

Hall, D. T., & Lawler, E. E., III. Unused potential in research and development organizations. *Research Management,* 1969, *12,* 339–54.

Hall, D. T., & Schneider, B. Correlates of organizational identification as a function of career pattern and organizational type. *Administrative Science Quarterly,* 1972, *17,* 340–50.

Hall, F. S. Organization goals: The status of theory and research. In L. J. Livingstone (Ed.), *Managerial accounting: Behavioral foundations.* Columbus, Oh.: Grid, Inc., 1975.

Hall, F. S. Goal determination in public organizations. Working paper, University of Wisconsin, Parkside, 1976.

Hall, R. H. *Organizations: Structure and process.* Englewood Cliffs, N.J.: Prentice-Hall, Inc., 1972.

Halpin, A., & Croft, D. *The organizational climate of schools.* U.S. Office of Education, Department of Health, Education, & Welfare, Washington, D.C., 1962.

Hand, H., Richards, M., & Slocum, J. Organizational climate and the effectiveness of a human relations training program. *Academy of Management Journal,* 1973, *16,* 185–95.

Harvey, E. Technology and the structure of organizations. *American Sociological Review,* 1968, *33,* 247–59.

Hellriegel, D., & Slocum, J. W., Jr. Organizational climate: Measures, research, and contingencies. *Academy of Management Journal,* 1974, *17,* 225–80.

Hemphill, J. J. Personal variables and administrative styles. In *Behavioral Science and Educational Administration,* National Society for the Study of Education, 1964.

Herzberg, F., Mausner, B., & Snyderman, B. *The motivation to work.* New York: John Wiley & Sons, inc., 1959.

Hickson, D. J., Pugh, D. S., & Pheysey, D. C. Operations technology and organizational structure: An empirical reappraisal. *Administrative Science Quarterly,* 1969, *14,* 378–97.

Hinrichs, J. R. Personnel training. In M. D. Dunnette (Ed.), *Handbook of industrial and organizational psychology.* Chicago: Rand McNally & Company, 1976.

189

Hofstede, G. H. *The game of budget control.* Assen, Netherlands: Van Gorcum, 1967.

Holland, J. L. Vocational preferences. In M. D. Dunnette (Ed.), *Handbook of industrial and organizational psychology.* Chicago: Rand McNally & Company, 1976.

Homans, G. *Social behavior.* New York: Harcourt Brace & World, 1961.

House, R. J. A path goal theory of leader effectiveness. *Administrative Science Quarterly,* 1971, *16,* 321–38.

House, R. J., & Mitchell, T. R. Path-goal theory of leadership. *Journal of Contemporary Business,* 1974, Autumn, 81–97.

Hrebiniak, L. G. Job technology, supervision, and work-group structure. *Administrative Science Quarterly,* 1974, *19,* 395–410.

Hrebiniak, L. G., & Alutto, J. A. Personal and role-related factors in the development of organizational commitment. *Administrative Science Quarterly,* 1972, *18,* 555–72.

Hulin, C. L., & Blood, M. R. Job enlargement, individual differences, and worker responses. *Psychological Bulletin,* 1968, *69,* 41–55.

Hunt, J. G., & Larson, L. L. (Eds.), *Contingency approaches to leadership.* Carbondale, Ill.: Southern Illinois University Press, 1974.

Huse, E. *Organization development and change.* Minneapolis, Minn.: West Publishing Co., 1975.

Indik, B. P., & Seashore, S. E. *Effects of organization size on member attitudes and behavior.* Ann Arbor: University of Michigan, Survey Research Center, Institute for Social Research, 1961.

Ingham, G. *Size of industrial organization and worker behavior.* Cambridge, England: Cambridge University Press, 1970.

James, L. R., & Jones, A. P. Organizational climate: A review of theory and research. *Psychological Bulletin,* 1974, *81,* 1096–1112.

Johannesson, R. E. Job satisfaction and perceptually measured organizational climate: Redundancy and confusion. *Proceedings,* Eastern Academy of Management, 1971, pp. 27–37.

Johannesson, R. E. Some problems in the measurement of organizational climate. *Organizational Behavior and Human Performance,* 1973, *10,* 118–44.

Kaczka, E., & Kirk, R. Managerial climate, work groups, and organizational performance. *Administrative Science Quarterly,* 1968, *12,* 252–71.

Kahn, R., Wolfe, D., Quinn, R., Snoek, J., & Rosenthal, R. *Organizational stress: Studies in role conflict and ambiguity,* New York: John Wiley & Sons, Inc., 1964.

Kasarda, J. D. Effects of personnel turnover, employee qualifications, and professional staff ratios on administrative intensity and overhead. *The Sociological Quarterly,* 1973, *14,* 350–58.

Kast, F. E. Organizational and individual objectives. In J. W. McGuire (Ed.), *Contemporary management: Issues and viewpoints.* Englewood Cliffs, N. J.: Prentice-Hall, Inc., 1974, pp. 150–80.

Kast, F. E., & Rosenzweig, J. E. *Organization and management: A systems approach* (2nd ed.). New York: McGraw-Hill Book Company, 1974.

Katz, D., & Kahn, R. L. *The social psychology of organizations.* New York: John Wiley & Sons, Inc., 1966.

Katzell, M. E. Expectations and dropouts in schools of nursing. *Journal of Applied Psychology,* 1968, *52,* 154–57.

Katzell, M. E. *Productivity: The measure and the myth.* New York: Amacom, 1975.

Katzell, R. A., Barrett, R. S., & Parker, T. C. Job satisfaction, job performance, and situational characteristics. *Journal of Applied Psychology,* 1961, *45,* 65–72.

Kerr, W. A., Koppelmeier, G. J., & Sullivan, J. J. Absenteeism, turnover and morale in a metals fabrication factory. *Occupational Psychology,* 1951, *25,* 50–55.

Koch, J. L., & Steers, R. M. Job attachment, satisfaction, and turnover among public-sector employees. Working paper, University of Oregon, 1976.

Kornhauser, A. W. *Mental health of the industrial worker: A Detroit study.* New York: John Wiley & Sons, Inc., 1965.

Kriesberg, L. Careers, organization size, and succession. *American Journal of Sociology,* 1962, *68,* 355–59.

LaFollette, W. R., & Sims, H. P., Jr. Is satisfaction redundant with organizational climate? *Organizational Behavior and Human Performance,* 1975, *13,* 257–78.

Lawler, E. E., III. *Pay and organizational effectiveness: A psychological view.* New York: McGraw-Hill Book Company, 1971.

Lawler, E. E., III. *Motivation in work organizations.* Monterey, Calif.: Brooks/Cole Publishing Company, 1973.

Lawler, E. E., III., Hall, D. T., & Oldham, G. R. Organizational climate: Relationship to organizational structure, process, and performance. *Organizational Behavior and Human Performance,* 1974, *11,* 139–55.

Lawrence, P. R., & Lorsch, J. W. *Organization and environment.* Boston: Harvard University, Division of Research, Graduate School of Business Administration, 1967.

Lewin, K. *The conceptual representation and the measurement of psychological forces.* Durham, N. C.: Duke University Press, 1938.

Likert, R. *New patterns in management.* New York: McGraw-Hill Book Company, 1961.

Lindestad, H., & Norstadt, J. P. *Autonomous groups and payment by result.* Stockholm: Swedish Employers Confederation, 1973.

Litwin, G., & Stringer, R. *Motivation and organizational climate.* Cambridge, Mass.: Harvard University Press, 1968.

Locke, E. A. Toward a theory of task performance and incentives. *Organizational Behavior and Human Performance,* 1968, *3,* 157–89.

Locke, E. A. The nature and causes of job satisfaction. In M. D. Dunnette (Ed.), *Handbook of industrial and organizational psychology.* Chicago: Rand McNally & Company, 1976.

Locke, E. A., & Bryan, J. F. The directing function of goals in task performance. *Organizational Behavior and Human Performance,* 1969, *4,* 35–42.

Lynch, B. P. An empirical assessment of Perrow's technology construct. *Administrative Science Quarterly,* 1974, *19,* 338–56.

Macedonia, R. M. *Expectation-press and survival.* Unpublished doctoral dissertation, New York University, 1969.

Mahoney, T., & Frost, P. The role of technology in models of organizational effectiveness. *Organizational Behavior and Human Performance,* 1974, *11,* 122–38.

Mahoney, T. A., & Weitzel, W. Managerial models of organizational effectiveness. *Administrative Science Quarterly,* 1969, *14,* 357–65.

March, J. G., & Simon, H. A. *Organizations.* New York: John Wiley & Sons, Inc., 1958.

Marrow, A., Bowers, D., & Seashore, S. *Management by participation.* New York: Harper & Row, 1967.

Maslow, A. H. *Motivation and personality.* New York: Harper & Row, 1954.

McClelland, D. C., Atkinson, J. W., Clark, R. A., & Lowell, E. L. *The achievement motive.* New York: Appleton-Century-Crofts, 1953.

McCormick, E. J., & Tiffin, J. *Industrial psychology.* Englewood Cliffs, N.J.: Prentice-Hall, Inc., 1974.

191

Merton, R. K. *Social theory and social structure.* Glencoe, Ill.: Free Press, 1957.

Metzner, H., & Mann, F. Employee attitudes and absences. *Personnel Psychology,* 1953, *6,* 467–85.

Meyer, M. W. Expertness and span of control. *American Sociological Review,* 1968, *33,* 944–51.

Michels, R. *Political parties.* New York: The Free Press, 1949.

Milkovich, G. I., & Delaney, M. J. A note on cafeteria pay plans. *Industrial Relations, 1975, 14,* 112–16.

Miller, G. A. Professionals in bureaucracy: Alienation among industrial scientists and engineers. *American Sociological Review,* 1967, *32,* 755–68.

Mohr, L. B. Organizational technology and organizational structure. *Administrative Science Quarterly,* 1971, *16,* 444–59.

Mott, P. E. *The characteristics of effective organizations.* New York: Harper & Row, 1972.

Mowday, R. T., Porter, L. W., & Dubin, R. Unit performance, situational factors, and employee attitudes in spatially separated work units. *Organizational Behavior and Human Performance,* 1974, *12,* 231–48.

Murray, H. A. *Explorations in personality.* New York: Oxford University Press, Inc., 1938.

Negandhi, A. R., & Reimann, B. C. Task environment, decentralization and organizational effectiveness. *Human Relations,* 1973, *26,* 203–14.

Newman, W. H. *Constructive control: Design and use of control systems.* Englewood Cliffs, N.J.: Prentice-Hall, Inc., 1975.

Nord, W. Beyond the teaching machine: The neglected area of operant conditioning in the theory and practice of management. *Organizational Behavior and Human Performance,* 1969, *4,* 375–401.

Nunnally, J. *Psychometric theory.* New York: McGraw-Hill Book Company, 1967.

Opinion Research Corporation. America's growing anti-business mood. *Business Week,* June 17, 1972, No. 2233, p. 101.

Opsahl, R. L., & Dunnette, M. D. The role of financial compensation in industrial motivation. *Psychological Bulletin,* 1966, *66,* 94–118.

Osborn, R. N., & Hunt, J. G. Environment and organizational effectiveness. *Administrative Science Quarterly,* 1974, *19,* 231–46.

Parsons, T. A sociological approach to the theory of organizations. *Administrative Science Quarterly,* 1956, *1,* 63–85.

Payne, R. L., & Pheysey, D. G. Stern's Organizational Climate Index: A reconceptualization and application to business organizations. *Organizational Behavior and Human Performance,* 1971, *6,* 77–98.

Payne, R. L., & Pugh, D. Organizational structure and climate. In M. D. Dunnette (Ed.), *Handbook of industrial and organizational psychology.* Chicago: Rand McNally & Company, 1976.

Pennings, J. M. The relevance of the structural-contingency model for organizational effectiveness. *Administrative Science Quarterly,* 1975, *20,* 393–410.

Perrow, C. The analysis of goals in complex organizations. *American Sociological Review,* 1961, *26,* 854–66.

Perrow, C. A framework for the comparative analysis of organizations. *American Sociological Review,* 1967, *32,* 194–208.

Perrow, C. *Organizational analysis: A sociological view.* Belmont, Calif.: Wadsworth Publishing Co., Inc., 1970.

Porter, L. W., & Lawler, E. E., III. *Managerial attitudes and behavior.* Homewood, Ill.: Richard D. Irwin, Inc., 1968.

Porter, L. W., Lawler, E. E., III, & Hackman, J. R. *Behavior in organizations.* New York: McGraw-Hill Book Company, 1975.

Porter, L. W., & Roberts, K. H. Communication in organizations. In M. D. Dunnette (Ed.), *Handbook of industrial and organizational psychology.* Chicago: Rand McNally & Company, 1976.

Porter, L. W., & Smith, F. J. The etiology of organizational commitment. Unpublished paper, 1970.

Porter, L. W., & Steers, R. M. Organizational, work, and personal factors in employee turnover and absenteeism. *Psychological Bulletin,* 1973, *80,* 151–76.

Porter, L. W., Steers, R. M., Mowday, R. T., & Boulian, P. V. Organizational commitment, job satisfaction, and turnover among psychiatric technicians. *Journal of Applied Psychology,* 1974, *59,* 603–609.

Price, J. L. *Organizational effectiveness: An inventory of propositions.* Homewood, Ill.: Richard D. Irwin, Inc., 1968.

Price, J. L. The effects of turnover on the organization. Working paper, University of Iowa, 1974.

Pritchard, R., & Karasick, B. The effects of organizational climate on managerial job performance and job satisfaction. *Organizational Behavior and Human Performance,* 1973, *9,* 110–19.

Pugh, D. S. The measurement of organization structure. *Organizational Dynamics,* 1973, *1,* 19–34.

Radnor, M., & Neil, N. The progress of management science activities in large U.S. industrial corporations. Northwestern University, Program publication #4-71, Cooperative International Program of Studies of Operations Research and the Management Sciences, 1971.

Raven, B. H., & Rietsema, J. The effects of varied clarity of group path upon the individual and his relationship to his group. *Human Relations,* 1957, *10,* 29–45.

Read, W. Upward communication in industrial hierarchies. *Human Relations,* 1962, *15,* 3–15.

Reimann, B. C. Dimensions of structure in effective organizations: Some empirical evidence. *Academy of Management Journal,* 1974, *17,* 693–708.

Reimann, B. C. Organizational effectiveness and management's public values: A canonical analysis. *Academy of Management Journal,* 1975, *18,* 224–41.

Revans, R. W. Human relations, management and size. In E. M. Hugh-Jones (Ed.), *Human relations and modern management.* Amsterdam: North Holland Publishing, 1958, pp. 177–220.

Rhode, J. G., & Lawler, E. E., III. Auditing change: Human resource accounting. In M. D. Dunnette (Ed.), *Work and nonwork in the year 2001.* Monterey, Calif.: Brooks/Cole Publishing Company, 1973.

Ronan, W. W., & Prien, E. P. An analysis of organizational behavior and organizational performance. *Organizational Behavior and Human Performance,* 1973, *9,* 78–99.

Ross, I. C., & Zander, A. Need satisfaction and employee turnover. *Personnel Psychology,* 1957, *10,* 327–38.

Sapolsky, H. Organizational structure and innovation. *Journal of Business,* 1967, *40,* 487–510.

Schein, E. A. *Organizational psychology.* Englewood Cliffs, N.J.: Prentice-Hall, Inc., 1970.

Schneider, B., & Bartlett, C. Individual differences and organizational climate I: The research plan and questionnaire development. *Personnel Psychology,* 1968, *21,* 323–34.

Schneider, B., & Hall, D. T. Toward specifying the concept of work climate: A study of Roman Catholic Diocesan priests. *Journal of Applied Psychology,* 1972, *56,* 447–56.

Seashore, S. E., & Yuchtman, E. Factorial analysis of organizational performance. *Administrative Science Quarterly,* 1967, *12,* 377–95.

Selznick, P. *TVA and the grass roots*. Berkeley, Calif.: University of California Press, 1949.

Sheldon, M. E. Investments and involvements as mechanisms producing commitment to the organization. *Administrative Science Quarterly,* 1971, *16,* 143–50.

Shull, F. A., Jr., Delbecq, A. L., & Cummings, L. L. *Organizational decision making.* New York: McGraw-Hill Book Company, 1970.

Shure, G. H., Rogers, M. S., Larson, I., & Tassone, J. Group planning and task effectiveness. *Sociometry,* 1962, *25,* 263–82.

Sills, D. *The volunteers: Means and ends in a national organization.* New York: The Free Press, 1957.

Simon, H. A. *Models of men: Social and rational.* New York: John Wiley & Sons, Inc., 1957.

Simon, H. A. *The new science of management decision.* New York: Harper & Row, 1960.

Simon, H. A. On the concept of organizational goal. *Administrative Science Quarterly,* 1964, *9,* 1–22.

Spencer, G. M., & Reynolds, H. J. Validity information exchange. *Personnel Psychology,* 1961, *14,* 456–58.

Starbuck, W. H. Organizations and their environments. In M. D. Dunnette (Ed.), *Handbook of industrial and organizational psychology.* Chicago: Rand McNally & Company, 1976.

Steers, R. M. The concept of organizational goals: A research review. Working paper, University of California, Irvine, 1971.

Steers, R. M. Effects of need achievement on the job performance—job attitude relationship. *Journal of Applied Psychology,* 1975, *60,* 678–82. (a)

Steers, R. M. Personality, situation, and participation in decision-making. *Proceedings of the Midwest Regional Meeting of the American Institute of Decision Sciences,* Indianapolis, 1975. (b)

Steers, R. M. Problems in the measurement of organizational effectiveness. *Administrative Science Quarterly,* 1975, *20,* 546–58. (c)

Steers, R. M. Task-goal attributes, n achievement, and supervisory performance. *Organizational Behavior and Human Performance,* 1975, *13,* 392–403. (d)

Steers, R. M. Antecedents and outcomes of organizational commitment. University of Oregon, Office of Naval Research, Technical Report #2, 1976. (a)

Steers, R. M. Factors affecting job attitudes in a goal-setting environment. *Academy of Management Journal,* 1976, *19,* 6–16. (b)

Steers, R. M. Individual differences in participative decision-making. *Human Relations,* in press.

Steers, R. M., & Porter, L. W. The role of task-goal attributes in employee performance. *Psychological Bulletin,* 1974, *81,* 434–52.

Steers, R. M., & Porter, L. W. *Motivation and work behavior.* New York: McGraw-Hill Book Company, 1975.

Stogdill, R. *Handbook of leadership.* New York: The Free Press, 1974.

Stone, E. F., & Porter, L. W. Job characteristics and job attitudes: A multivariate study. *Journal of Applied Psychology,* 1975, *60,* 57–64.

Talacchi, S. Organization site, individual attitudes and behavior: An empirical study. *Administrative Science Quarterly,* 1960, *5,* 398–420.

Tannenbaum, R., & Schmidt, W. H. How to choose a leadership pattern. *Harvard Business Review,* 1958, *36,* 95–101.

Taylor, F. W. *Principles of scientific management.* New York: Harper & Row, 1911.

Taylor, J. C., & Bowers, D. *Survey of organizations: A machine scored standardized instrument.* Ann Arbor: University of Michigan, Institute for Social Research, 1972.

Terreberry, S. The evolution of organizational environments. *Administrative Science Quarterly,* 1968, *12,* 590–613.

Thompson, J. D. *Organizations in action.* New York: McGraw-Hill Book Company, 1967.

Thompson, J. D., & McEwen, W. J. Organizational goals and environment. *American Sociological Review,* 1958, *23,* 23–30.

Thorndike, R. L. *Personnel selection: Test and measurement techniques.* New York: John Wiley & Sons, Inc., 1949.

Thune, S. *An investigation into the effect of long-range planning in selected industries.* Unpublished MBA thesis, Bernard M. Baruch School of Business, City University of New York, 1967.

Turner, A. N., & Lawrence, P. R. *Industrial jobs and the worker: An investigation of response to task attributes.* Boston: Harvard University Press, Division of Research, 1965.

Vroom, V. H. *Work and motivation.* New York: John Wiley & Sons, Inc., 1964.

Vroom, V. H. A new look at managerial decision making. *Organizational Dynamics,* 1973, *1,* 66–80.

Vroom, V. H., & Yetton, P. *Leadership and decision-making.* Pittsburgh, Pa.: University of Pittsburgh Press, 1973.

Walker, C. R., & Guest, R. *The man on the assembly line.* Cambridge, Mass.: Harvard University Press, 1952.

Wanous, J. P. Effects of a realistic job preview on job acceptance, job attitudes, and job survival. *Journal of Applied Psychology,* 1973, *58,* 327–32.

Watson, J. R. *Communication effectiveness in a university executive management program: A field experiment.* Unpublished doctoral dissertation, University of Illinois, 1973.

Webb, R. J. Organizational effectiveness and the voluntary organization. *Academy of Management Journal,* 1974, *17,* 663–77.

Webber, R. A. *Management: Basic elements of managing organizations.* Homewood, Ill.: Richard D. Irwin, Inc., 1975.

Weick, K. E., Jr. Reduction of cognitive dissonance through task enhancement and effort expenditure. *Journal of Abnormal and Social Psychology,* 1964, *68,* 533–39.

Weick, K. E., Jr. *The social psychology of organizing.* Reading, Mass.: Addison-Wesley Publishing Co., Inc., 1969.

Weiss, E. C. Relation of personnel statistics to organization structure. *Personnel Psychology,* 1957, *10,* 27–42.

Weitz, J. Job expectancy and survival. *Journal of Applied Psychology,* 1956, *40,* 245–47.

Whyte, W. H., Jr. *The organization man.* New York: Simon & Schuster, Inc., 1956.

Woodward, J. *Management and technology.* London: Her Majesty's Stationery Office, 1958.

Woodward, J. *Industrial organization: Theory and practice.* London: Oxford University Press, 1965.

Worthy, J. C. Organizational structure and employee morale. *American Sociological Review,* 1950, *15,* 169–79.

Yolles, S. F., Carone, P. A., & Krinsky, L. W. *Absenteeism in industry.* Springfield, Ill.: Charles C Thomas, 1975.

Youngberg, C. F. *An experimental study of job satisfaction and turnover in relation to job expectancies and self expectancies.* Unpublished doctoral dissertation, New York University, 1963.

Yuchtman, E., & Seashore, S. E. A system resource approach to organizational effectiveness. *American Sociological Review,* 1967, *32,* 891–903.

195

Yukl, G. Toward a behavioral theory of leadership. *Organizational Behavior and Human Performance,* 1971, *6,* 414–40.

Zald, M. Comparative analysis and measurement of organizational goals: The case of correctional institutions for delinquents. *Sociological Quarterly,* 1963, *4,* 206–30.

Zaltman, G., Duncan, R., & Holbek, J. *Innovations and organizations.* New York: John Wiley & Sons, Inc., 1973.

Zwerman, W. L. *New perspectives on organization theory.* Westport, Conn.: Greenwood Press, 1970.

NAME INDEX

SUBJECT INDEX

203